Richard J. Spota became a police officer at age 22 and has had a long and illustrious career in law enforcement. He received the highest police award for saving the life of six people in a fire. He took on organized crime and survived two assassination attempts. And he is now a retired chief of police. He is a husband, father, and grandfather. *With God on My Side* is his first book.

First and foremost, this book is dedicated to our Blessed Mother, Dear Jesus, God the Father, and God the Holy Ghost for all the times this sinner asked for your help. For all the times I asked you, our Blessed Mother, to please ask your Divine Son to intercede on my behalf. You have always answered my prayers. You have allowed me to be credited with your answers to my requests. In the early years, when I was frustrated with organized crime and police corruption, I would ask you if you considered such crimes a sin. But the truth was like the story of *Footprints in the Sand*. In the end, there was one set of footprints and they were yours because you carried me all the way.

Richard J. Spota

WITH GOD ON MY SIDE

AUSTIN MACAULEY PUBLISHERS™

LONDON • CAMBRIDGE • NEW YORK • SHARJAH

Ordering Information:
Quantity sales: special discounts are available on quantity purchases by corporations, associations, and others. For details, contact the publisher at the address below.

Publisher's Cataloging-in-Publication data
Spota, Richard J.
With God on My Side

ISBN 9781641828666 (Paperback)
ISBN 9781641828673 (Hardback)
ISBN 9781645366256 (ePub e-book)

Library of Congress Control Number: 2019913080

www.austinmacauley.com/us

First Published (2019)
Austin Macauley Publishers LLC
40 Wall Street, 28th Floor
New York, NY 10005
USA

mail-usa@austinmacauley.com
+1 (646) 5125767

Chapter One

I was born at Royal Hospital in the South Bronx, New York, and baptized at St. Martin of Tours Roman Catholic Church. The son of Joseph O. and Rita M. Dineen Spota; my father was of Italian descent and my mother was an Irish Catholic. When I was born, my father was 52 and my mother was 31. My parents were married at the Church of St. Patrick in Bedford, New York, on December 11, 1937. My mother's sister, Loretta Farrell, and her brother-in-law, Joseph Farrell, lived in the area at that time in Mount Kisco, New York. My uncle, Joe Farrell, would say that the congregation probably thought that Joseph O. Spota and Rita M. Dineen were two Irishmen when their marriage vows were read. Of course, that was not the case. At the time of their marriage, the Italian-Americans were considered to be on the lowest social scale of immigrants to this country. The Irish were only considered to be a notch up on the social scale. Although I can't remember them ever saying anything that reflected adversely on any ethnic group, I know they had their share of heartache because of their ethnic differences. They met at the Democratic Club in the Bronx, New York. My father was one of seven children born to his parents on Mott Street in the Little Italy section of New York. He went to school at night to become a building contractor. His company, Spota & Marrano, built large commercial buildings and apartment houses. Although my father had survived the stock market crash of 1929, he had lost a considerable amount of money. He would continue to invest in the stock market for the remainder of his life.

The house where my parents lived when I was born was 777 Grote Street, Bronx, New York, and the house next door was built by my father's company. That house and the one next door were made of brick and are two of the only houses still standing in that area today. A 60-family brick apartment house at 4054 Carpenter Avenue in the Bronx, New York, was the last apartment house to be built by my father's company. He retained ownership of this house for investment purposes until the 1950s. Despite being a successful self-made businessman and contributor to the Democratic Party in the Bronx, he was told within the party, dining the 1930s and early 40s that he would not be elected to office within the party because of his Italian heritage. I heard mother mention this on several occasions.

My father's first wife had died, leaving him with their five children to raise. My brother Joseph (Spots) was 20 when I was born. My sister Carmella was 24. My brother George was 27 and Jerry, the oldest, at 29 years of age. They all lived at 777 Grote Street in the Bronx, New York, when I was born. I can remember in my early years that it was nice having older brothers and a sister. My mother was born to John and Anne McLaughlin Dineen. Her father was born in St. Louis, Missouri, before coming to the New York area. He was a tall, dark, good-looking man, who was a paid fireman. Her mother was a small woman who everyone loved. They had two children, my mother and her sister, Aunt Loretta. My mother's grandparents were born in County Cork, Ireland.

I can vaguely remember living at the Grote Street home until I was five years old. Sister (Carmella) would take me to the Bronx Zoo which was at the end of our street. She would also take me in my stroller to Arthur Avenue to buy me pizza. About 1944, when I was five, my father bought an old house at 20 Manhattan Avenue in Crestwood (northeast Yonkers, New York) for us to live in. I can remember him doing a lot of work on the house himself. My Aunt Loretta and Uncle Joe lived up the street from with us at the time with their son, my cousin Skippy (Richard Farrell). Next door to our house was a school, P.S. 15. I can remember sleigh riding from the high banks at the end of the bail field in the winter. My cousin Skippy taught me how to play baseball at the P.S. 15 ball field. On the fourth of July, they would have games and contests at the ball field. I would enter the sprint races and this skinny little kid would do well, surprising everyone including myself.

My brother George graduated from Fordham University in the Bronx, New York, and Hahnemann Medical School in Philadelphia. After medical school, George went into the army as a captain during World War ll. He had married a nurse from Potsdam, New York. She lived with us for a while during the war. I remember my dad receiving a letter that stated George had saved several lives during a battle. He received the Bronze Star. I remember the day that my mom and Eleanor took me to the Crestwood train station to meet George as he came home from the war. They all hugged and kissed. George picked up his little brother in the air. I remember my dad being happy that the war was over, and George was home alive and well. He could have stayed in the army to be promoted to major in the Medical Corps, but he chose to go into private practice. My dad helped him buy a house on Westchester Avenue in Crestwood, where George set up his medical office and home. He would practice medicine at Lawrence Hospital in Bronxville, New York, and at St. Joseph and Yonkers General Hospitals.

My brother Joseph (Spots) finished his tour of duty in the army after the war and married Martha, a girl from Chattanooga, Tennessee, who he met during the war. My dad gave them an apartment in his apartment house on Carpenter Avenue, Bronx, New York. Spots would start a career at the Mount Vernon Dental Lab in

Mount Vernon, New York. My sister Carmella married Louis Matranga after the war. I remember Louie marrying Carmella in his army uniform and their wedding reception at this big place off the Bronx River Parkway in nearby Tuckahoe, New York. They also took an apartment in Dad's apartment house in the Bronx. My brother Jerry handled my father's business interests. He married Lena, and they moved into Dad's apartment house. I remember it being great to visit Dad's apartment house because I could see Spots and Martha, Jerry and Lena, Carmella and Louie, along with one of Dad's brothers, Uncle Sal and Aunt Doris (who was Jewish and one of my favorites) and their son, and my cousin, Bill. We were also able to visit various cousins and everyone else Dad had given an apartment to. About the time I was in the second or third grade in Annunciation Elementary School on Westchester Avenue, Crestwood, Dad started to build a new house for us at 41 Juana Street in the northern end of Crestwood. This was a wooded area that was not completely developed. I remember observing Dad and his workers doing their various areas of expertise while building the house. Some of his people were of Italian descent. Some Irish, but some were of Hispanic descent although I did not know the specific areas they were from, and some were black. I remember my father and his people all working well together, all showing respect for each ether. Dad helped with the actual work.

Annunciation School was in a big house until a school was finally built across the street. Father Timothy Dugan ran the parish, of which the church was in a basement type structure for many years. Father Dugan was an older, no-nonsense priest, who had started the parish by himself, from a red barn about a block and a half away. He taught a class for altar boys in the rectory which I attended. I'll always remember serving Mass for him. If anyone came in after Mass had started, he stopped saying Mass and told the late arrival to leave. One Sunday, after serving the eight o'clock Mass with him, I waited for the next altar boy for the 9:15 a.m. Mass before leaving, as we had been taught to do in case no one showed up. This Sunday, for some reason, no one (altar boy) showed up for the 9:15 a.m. Mass, the eleven or the twelve o'clock Masses. So it was my job to serve all of them. After the twelve o'clock Mass was over, Father Dugan in a stern voice told me to come into the sacristy. I was saying to myself as I walked into the sacristy, "What did I do wrong? Did I drop any marbles or what during one of the masses?"

When I got into the sacristy, Father Dugan handed a set of rosary beads with dust from the catacombs inside of the crucifix to me and said, "This is for you." I thanked him and remember leaving, just happy to be in one piece. I can remember thinking about becoming a priest when I grew up. This ended when I discovered girls. The Dominican nuns at Annunciation School could be stern themselves. Of course, anything they did to us was well-deserved. Sister Mary Ann, Sister Margret Louise, Sister Rose Patricia, and Sister Barbara, these unselfish, hard-working, dedicated servants of God made us better students and prepared us to be better people. It would be a three or four-block walk from where we were now living on Juana Street to school. George's house would be another two-block walk south of Annunciation School. Mom made sure that I called George, "Doctor George," if I saw him when I was with my classmates.

Around the time I was in the fifth grade, I hoped to get a bike. Dad wasn't one to buy anything, but he said if I had a 100% average at the end of the school year, he would get me one. Needless to say, I fell several points short on my final average, but one of the nuns sent a note home that stated they did not give perfect scores. Dad relented and bought the bike for me. I then got a newspaper delivery route for after-school hours. In the summertime, I would mow lawns in the neighborhood to earn money. When I got a little older, I would walk across the Bronx River Parkway to Leewood Country Club to caddy. Single bags were good money; and if you were fortunate enough to get doubles (2 bags), you could earn more.

When November and the cold weather came, I would go home from school at lunch time and check the pond in the woods at the end of our street to see if it was frozen. I would then report back to my classmates in the afternoon. I think that I spent all of my available time after school, during the winter, playing hockey. I would play until it was dark, and I had to go home. I really loved hockey and still do today. I remember Dad building a smaller house on the lots behind our home on George Street. He sold the house on Juana Street when the new house was finished. The smaller house cost less to keep and maintain.

There was only Dad, Mom, and myself living at home. The standing rule was that once a week the lawn would be mowed, in spring and summer, before I could go anywhere. The wooded area around where we lived had many people starting to build houses for themselves. Many New York City firemen and policemen started to build. My father was retired, and he spent almost every day helping people with the architectural plans for their houses and then the actual construction, from foundation to completed house.

He was happy to help these eventual neighbors to complete their homes. He never took anything for this help. The people appreciated his expertise and labor. I can remember him sitting at his desk with the big blueprints with the white lines, drawing the completed house.

I believe it was around the fifth or sixth grade when Father Dugan had raised enough money to build the new Annunciation School opposite the house that was used for the school. When it was completed, we moved into our new school, complete with a big gym with a basketball court. When the school was to be dedicated, Francis Cardinal Spellman came up from St. Patrick's for the ceremony. All of the altar boys were there to assist with the blessing of the school, and then a program was held in the gym hall. Mr. Amend, a father of several students, who lived opposite the rectory was M.C. He told of Father Dugan coming to Crestwood years before to start a parish out of a red barn on the property of St. Eleanor's home, a few blocks away. He told of his building, the church, buying a house for the nuns, the priest's rectory, a house for the school, and now the school. Father Dugan sat and listened. He never spoke of his accomplishments. He did what he had done for the love of God. We all knew this was a very special man. After Mr. Amend finished, he introduced Cardinal Spellman. Cardinal Spellman acknowledged the tremendous job that Father Dugan had done. He then said that when he got back to St. Patrick's Cathedral, Father Dugan would be wearing a new garment, that of Rt. Rev. Monsignor! The hall erupted into loud applause; women were clapping and crying at the same time. I clapped harder than I ever had in my life. On the stage, you could see tears in Father Dugan's eyes as people hugged him. God, this was a great day!

We had a ball field behind the church property. It was alright to play baseball there, but there were too many rocks and too hard a surface for football. So we would ride our bikes down to the south part of Crestwood to play football on the grass fields of the Bronx River Parkway near the Asbury Methodist Church. This skinny kid would love to get the ball and run with it or to intercept a pass and run with it. We would play as a team from P.S. I5, and our sixth grade would play against the seventh grade, and the seventh grade against the eighth grade. Our class graduated from Annunciation School in June 1953. Some of the boys went to Archbishop Stepinac in White Plains, Iona Prep in New Rochelle, Regis in New York City, and Fordham Prep in New York. I went to Iona Prep. Albert Krug, my altar boy partner and friend, went to Stepinac. At the time, his uncle, Monsignor Krug, was the principal there. My cousin Skip Farrell was at Iona, so I at least knew someone there. There were no school buses to New Rochelle, so you got to ride when you could. Mom helped out, driving many of us, or if we got out late, we hitched a ride home. The Irish Christian Brothers were the strictest of all teachers. There were times when you got hit by a piece of wood (off a back of a chair) thrown at you. One brother had a thick rubber strap. If he observed you talking during class, he motioned for you to go outside of the classroom, then had you hold out your hands and then you felt the strap. The initial sting was replaced with a burning sensation and swelling that lasted for the day. I can remember taking one such welt one day and then later practicing with the Junior Varsity Football Team, fumbling the ball and getting a boot from the coach. Did we deserve it when we got hit? Yes, except for a rare error and then it made up for one we missed. The first year of football I had both of my ankles sprained at the same time and I wasn't able to accomplish very much. The school did not sponsor a hockey team because of cost factors, insurance, etc. We would play club type hockey anywhere we could—the lakes opposite New Rochelle High School, reservoirs, rivers, ponds, etc.

The following summer I ran and worked out a lot in preparation for the football season. I felt I had prepared properly. My favorite part of football practice after school each day was running the 100-yard dash. There was one player who had a football scholarship mainly because of his speed. I don't remember him or anyone else beating me in the 100-yard dash. My mother had worked as a salesperson at Macy's to help pay for my tuition in the beginning and then in real estate. My father was 66 years old and retired at the time. I started the season playing fullback, tall and 157 pounds. I probably should have been a halfback or a flanker. I remember in a scrimmage running, the ball came back on a kickoff return. I ran from about our ten to about midfield when someone had a hold of my leg, and I tried to spin away. Then, I got decked by the pack of defenders. I yelled out in pain. It was my knee. I guess I was too stupid to quit, so they wrapped my right knee up in a brace. The coach switched me to middle linebacker. Our home field was behind the school. One game I had an interception and a fumble recovery. I jumped up to try to bat down a pass; and when I landed, my right leg gave away. The coach asked me if I was okay. Of course I said, "Yes." Another game was against our catholic school rival at Archbishop Stepinac. I played the whole game on defense, but we lost by one point. When I would get home from daily practice, I'd be tired, cold, or wet, etc. There were students who participated in athletics who could get good grades too. I was not one of them. But I thought I had this gift of speed to play sports. What else could it be for?

When I was 17 and had my driver's license, I wanted to get a car for transportation. Dad told me that if I wanted a car, I would have to earn the money for it. I worked at a hardware store and saved about $160.00. I had seen a 1949 Ford on a used car lot. The dealer said it was $150.00. I gave Dad the money, and he took me to the car lot, and we bought the car. I worked on it to make it look and run better. About this time, a friend of mine and I decided to join the Navy. The Navy said we could join for a Kiddie Cruise, which would be approximately three and a half years of active duty, and the remainder of the six years would be served on reserve duty. There were education benefits. I thought everyone should serve their country and that I might as well get it over with. My friend and I left on September 20, 1956 for the Navy and basic training at Bainbridge, Maryland. After having our heads shaved and uniforms issued to us, we were assigned to our barracks. Reveille was usually at 5 a.m.; and after showering and shaving, we were inspected. Then, it was marching with our rifles and off to the mess hall. After eleven weeks of training, we graduated on December 11. You could either put in for a school or go out to sea.

I opted for school. I was selected for the U.S. Navy Hospital Corps School in San Diego, California. I was given leave to come home and then report to school on December 24, 1956. It was about this time that I learned that my father had cancer of the larynx and that it had metastasized. This was said to be a result of his cigarette smoking. At that time, cigarettes were freely advertised everywhere. After visiting my parents, I had to leave on Christmas Eve to fly to San Diego, California. After the long flight, I reported in and was assigned to my barracks. School started on January 7, 1957. My courses were Minor Surgery, First Aid, Anatomy and Physiology, Material Medicine, Toxicology, Pharmacy, Metrology, Basic Bacteriology and Laboratory Technique, Radiological Safety, and Hygiene and Sanitation. I passed my exams and graduated from school on May 3, 1957. After graduation, I was assigned to the dispensary in San Diego. When I learned that my father was dying, I was sent to the U.S. Naval Hospital St. Albans, New York. My father had weighed over 200 pounds and had always been healthy until the cancer. He weighed less than 100 pounds when he died on September 18, 1957, at age 70. I remember racing home when I got the message. At his death, in addition to family and friends were almost all of the people that he had helped to build their homes when he was retired. George would remind me that Dad always said, "The only thing you came into this world with is your name." I was 18 years old when my father died.

I then finished my tour of duty in the Navy. After having finished my obligation to my rank in the Navy, I was assigned to Master-at-Arms duty. The Shore Patrol handled the outside security on Naval Bases and the Master-at-Arms handled the inside security. I enjoyed this work. I was honorably discharged from the Navy after completing my active duty of three years and four months on January 22, 1960.

I was 20 years of age and would be 21 on February 25, 1960. I wanted to enter law enforcement. I would take the next examination for police officer given in Westchester County. Shortly after my discharge from the Navy, I became an investigator for Pinkerton National Detective Agency doing undercover and regular investigations. This was in the career direction that I wanted to go in. I could work, take the exam for police officer, then continue to work until appointed to the police force. My first assignment as an undercover investigator was at an auto agency in Westchester County for a couple of months. After each day's work, I would submit a report on what had transpired during the day. The investigation was successful, and the proper action taken at its climax.

I then began regular investigative work. A senior investigator there, Jack Tierney, had been with the ABC (Alcoholic Beverage Control) years before. Jack had expertise in all areas of investigation and was kind enough to share his knowledge with several of us. We did many investigations with him guiding us. Many of the investigations would involve theft of property. After many months of these investigations, I was assigned to work an undercover case out of Westchester County at a steel plant in the Bronx, New York. This case lasted for several months. It was good for staying in shape. The client suspected several areas of wrongdoing but did not know how they were occurring. Contraband was being brought into the plant and things were being removed from the plant, but the plant owners and supervisors did not know how it was done. While on the night shift, I observed a large steel plate that covered a truck opening in the rear of the steel yard. There was a locked gate in this area. At night, when they thought no one was observing, several workers would slide the plate several feet under the gate and put items in the hole that was under the plate. They would then pull the plate back to its original position. When dinner or a coffee break came, they would go outside of the rear gate, slide the plate inward, and remove the items. They reversed this procedure to bring contraband into the plant. On a night that there was a raid, a green substance was put on the items under the plate from the outside. When the items were brought in, the raid commenced, and a special light was used by the regular investigators to shine on and illuminate the hands of those involved. The investigation was deemed to be successful after the guilty parties were removed from the plant. I did some other investigations for the Manhattan office before returning to the Westchester office. Again, I did regular investigations in the area along with a few out of the area.

About this time, the election for President of the United States was at hand. Why couldn't an Irish Catholic with outstanding credentials be elected President? This was the first time I would vote. Of course, my mother and Aunt Loretta wanted Kennedy to be elected. I would vote as an independent. I voted for this intelligent, energetic, Irish Catholic Senator from Massachusetts. Mom had said that she worked for his father in one of his theaters many years ago. I watched the election results late into the night because it was so close. When Kennedy was projected as the winner, I really thought he would be an outstanding leader for our country. Maybe someday we would have an Italian Catholic president. A big barrier had been broken.

During this period, the exam came up for police officer for the towns and villages of Westchester County. There are 33 towns and villages in Westchester. Upon passing the exam and placing high enough on the list, you could be appointed to any of the towns or villages. Two other investigators that I worked with, Nat Carpinelli and Joe Perillo, took a class with me in preparation for the exam. After taking the exam, we waited for the results, which came out in the spring of 1961. I had done well enough to be considered for appointment. I went for an interview in the Village of North Tarrytown, New York. Tuckahoe was the closest village to where I lived in Crestwood, but I felt it would be better to go somewhere I did not know anyone so that I would be totally effective in the performance of my duties. At the time of my interview in North Tarrytown, their police department was in the top ten salary-wise and had one of the best schedules (work hours).

In addition, they would fund college classes in Police Science and Criminal Justice. Shortly after the interview, I was offered the position and I accepted. At a board of trustees meeting in North Tarrytown, I was appointed to the position of patrolman effective June 18, 1961. I was now 22 years old. Joe Perillo accepted a position with the Village of Tuckahoe Police Department, and Nat Carpinelli decided to start his own detective agency, Capital Investigations, which went on to be successful.

Chapter Two

I began my career as a police officer on June 18, 1961. North Tarrytown had a population of approximately 8000 with another 5000 persons coming into the village daily to work at General Motors, the largest employer in Westchester County at the time. The GM plant was located at the west end of Beckman Avenue on the Hudson River. North Tarrytown was a very diversified community that was almost a microcosm of New York City. I would enjoy working in such a community. I obtained a map so that I could learn the location of all the streets. Bordered on the west by the Hudson River and on the east by the huge Rockefeller property, the northern pan of the village had two nice residential areas with Phelps Memorial Hospital at the northern border. The south end was much more modest with numerous commercial establishments. The village was said to have more bars and clubs per person than any other area of the county or state.

I would work rotating shifts 8 a.m. to 4 p.m., 4 p.m. to midnight, midnight to 8 am. There were always a lot of calls on the 4 to 12 and 12 to 8 shifts to break up fights and remove inebriated and unwanted persons from the bars. The day shift would be taken up with issuing summonses, directing traffic (a large portion attributed to GM) and answering calls for service. The first two hours of the 4 to 12 shift would be to direct traffic related to GM. I joined the Department Pistol Team, and we would shoot against the other police departments in the Hudson Valley Police League in addition to special tournaments. I would practice at the department range in the basement of Police Headquarters at 28 Beekman Avenue and at the Westchester County Police Rifle and Revolver Outdoor Range in Ardsley, New York. Upon the completion of my three-month probationary period, I was recommended for permanent appointment by Police Chief Francis Hogan. Chief Hogan was an older chief, who was a good man and he treated everyone fairly. At this time, it was not unusual to be on the police department before going to the police academy. The academy itself was in its early years. The academy, formerly known as the New York State Municipal Recruit Training School, was held in the basement of the County Jail with some classes at Westchester Community College. I started the school on October 16, 1961, and graduated on November l, 1961. I did not know how much longer I would be able to play hockey in the two leagues I was playing in, given my around the clock work schedule. Of course, I would put my law enforcement profession before any sport. I would continue to attend every police related school available to me.

After the police academy, it was back to patrol, car, and foot. While walking my beat "downtown," the lower end of the village, people would occasionally ask for a dollar for food. If the person appeared to need food and not wine or liquor, I would tell the person to come to the diner with me when I ate and pay for his food. I enjoyed learning how to use the department's radar unit, which was mainly used on Route 9 (Broadway). I continued to shoot on the pistol team and started to shoot well. When I arrived home from the day shift on June 9, 1962, I was told that my brother Joseph (Spots) had had a heart attack. I went to the hospital that night with George and Jerry to see him. He appeared to be doing well. When I was leaving, he thanked me for coming. When I arrived home from the day shift the next day, Mom told me that Spots had died. I couldn't believe it. George explained to me that the clot did not dissolve, causing Spots to die. Spots was the closest to me in terms of age. He would write to me when I was away in the Navy and send me five dollars. He was 43 years old. His son, my nephew Joseph, was only eleven years old at the time. After the funeral, Spots' wife, Martha, would take Joseph and return to Chattanooga Tennessee to live with her parents and raise my little blond nephew. I would miss them. Carmella had two girls, Clo and Eleanor. Jerry and Lena had Jerrylyn. My brothers enjoyed calling me Uncle Richard since I was an uncle at so early an age.

Back on patrol in North Tarrytown, New York, one of the things I observed, especially during the day and 4 to 12 shifts was an abundance of runners and other people that appeared to be involved in illegal gambling activity. Many of them would come out of the GM plant and go into local bars and stores. Others would go into certain establishments without ever buying anything. In 1963, there appeared to be some type of activity in an older apartment house at Cortlandt Street, North Tarrytown. Men from out of the village were seen going in and out of the building. The building was diagonally opposite Alias Market, which was located on the southeast corner of Cortlandt and College Avenue. I reported what I had seen there to some of my superiors. They told me to make notes of what I was observing. I used the Union Hose Firehouse second floor to survey the area. The Firehouse was across the street from Alias Market. By looking south on Cortlandt Street from the firehouse, you could observe the building on Cortlandt Street and the parking lot adjacent to it. The building on Cortlandt Street was owned by the Alias Family. Some of the people in the surveillance met with John Alias before going into the building on Cortlandt Street. A rear entrance to the building was used by these people.

2 Raids Cripple $4.5 Million Bets Ring; Police Nab 3 Men in North Tarrytown

On November 13, 1963, 1 was told that there would be a raid on Cortlandt Street and Clinton Street, which was approximately two blocks southwest of Cortlandt Street, the following morning.

On the morning of November 14, 1963, I was told where and when to go for the raid. The North Tarrytown Police Officers involved under Chief Hogan, Lt. Jandrucko and others along with investigators of the Westchester County District Attorney's office under Senior Assistant District Attorney Thomas Facelle conducted the raid on the two buildings. As the raiding party went up the backstairs to the second floor of 25 Clinton Street, I observed a male jump out a second floor window and run west on Clinton Street. I chased him and apprehended the male about two blocks away. He was identified as Alex Craig, age 20 years, who was said to be a sheet writer (a person who takes bets over the phone). Arrested in the apartment was Pasqual "Duffy" Bollini, 45, also reported to be a sheet writer and James Lawrence, 25 years old, charged with maintaining a place for bookmaking, a misdemeanor. Cullio and Bayonne were charged with feloniously operating a policy and bookmaking business. Cullio was released on $5000 bail and at the time of the raid was under indictment from a December 1962 gambling arrest in Port Chester. Bayonne was released on $2500 bail. He had a gambling conviction in June of this year and was named in a SIC (State Investigation Commission) inquiry recently. District Attorney Leopard Rubenfeld, in a press conference at the DA's office, stated that over $10,000 in bets was seized in the raid at the two locations. He stated that this was a $4,500,000 a year bookmaking and policy operation that extended throughout the metropolitan area. He further stated that the syndicate was headed by Westchester gambling czar, Peter Vitchelli of North Tarrytown. This story made the headline on the front page of the local Daily News of November 15, 1963. Peter Vitchelli was the brother of two of our policemen. They had always stated that they had nothing to do with their brother, and I had no reason to believe otherwise at this time. The officers involved in the raid felt good that in a small way we did something to combat organized crime in our area.

When I was subpoenaed to testify in the Grand Jury about the raid, I took a seat in the area for those who would testify. While sitting there, John Alias came out of the Grand Jury room. He walked over to me and said, "We don't want people like you in North Tarrytown." On another occasion, when he saw me, he said, "An Italian hurting Italians is a disgrace." He was involved in local politics and had either run for or had been elected a village trustee before I started on the police department. From this raid forward, my life would never be the same again. Within

18

days after the raid, I was walking my beat downtown when I observed one of the runners connected to the syndicate that we had raided. As he passed by me, he said, "You guys really knocked us out of business."

I said to myself "If we knocked you out of business why are you making your rounds."

Eight days after the raid, I was on the day shift, directing traffic on Broadway (Route 9) St. Paul's Hill area, when a motorist stopped his car, rolled down his window, and in an excited voice stated that the President had been shot. When I checked with police headquarters, I was told that President John F. Kennedy had been killed on the 22nd of November 1963. I was as sad, depressed, and upset as almost all Americans were. Our outstanding President was dead. What would happen to his brother Bobby (RFK), the Attorney General? To young persons in law enforcement, Bobby Kennedy was a hero, taking on organized crime as no other Attorney General had. I thought back to January 1961 when I had taped President Kennedy's Inauguration. I watched along with most of this country the sad days that followed.

In the end of 1963 and the beginning of 1964, some of the officers I worked with were changing their attitude toward me. On the 4 to 12 shift after directing traffic from GM on Beekman Avenue and walking your beat, you would sometimes go with an officer who was driving a patrol car for the last two hours of the shift to help answer calls. One such officer told me in an angry tone of voice that I was fucking up the job (P.D.). When I asked what he was referring to, he said pulling Blacks out of fires, paying for your meals, and locking up bookmakers. On the midnight shift, I was walking downtown when I made an arrest for disorderly conduct. I called headquarters from a call box with my prisoner at my side. My Sergeant, Hugh Robertson, was an older person who treated everyone well. He called the squad car several times to tell them to meet me with my prisoner and transport us to headquarters for booking. When they wouldn't respond, he said, "I don't know what you are going to do." I couldn't let the prisoner go because he might injure someone or do something worse. It wouldn't be fair to the prisoner to keep him handcuffed all night in the street. So, I commandeered a passing motorist and had him drive us to Headquarters. The prisoner was booked, and I walked back to my beat downtown.

On March 9, 1964, at approximately 8:50 p.m., while I was driving a patrol car, I received a radio call from my desk sergeant that there was a fire on Cortlandt Street. This was a two-story apartment and rooming house containing approximately six families and numerous rooms that were rented. I rushed to the scene, arriving before the responding firemen and found a mass of flame and dense smoke emitting from the building. As I entered the first floor, I found five or six inhabitants who were groping in the smoke-filled hallway in a futile attempt to find the exit. I led them out to the front door and returned to the first floor and up the stairs to the second floor, where I found some people in the hallway and got them to the stairs, so they could escape to the first floor and out of the building. I stayed on the second floor where it was extremely difficult to breathe due to the smoke and heat. I was forced to crawl along the hallway floor until I got to the right front apartment on the southeast part of the building. The apartment was a mass of flame and enveloped in smoke. I found a man lying on the floor in the apartment with his clothing on fire. I rolled the man over several times and smothered the remaining flames from his clothing with my police overcoat, then pulled him into the hallway. I shouted to the firemen who were entering the building to bring a stretcher. The victim was subsequently carried out of the building and conveyed to the hospital by a fire emergency unit. At this point, I was groggy and near collapse due to the exhaustion and smoke poisoning. The firemen assisted me from the building and administered oxygen to me. I received medical treatment for second-degree burns to the right leg. The firemen attacked the fire from the outside and inside of the building. These dedicated volunteer firemen made a great stop and saved the rest of the building from being totally burned to the ground. Approximately 12 hours later, the rescued victim, Equilla Davis, age 50, died of serious burns and smoke poisoning.

On March 24, 1964, I received a commendation from the North Tarrytown Board of Trustees for the aforementioned action. Chief Hogan submitted a report to the Macy Westchester Newspaper Awards Committee for consideration. A short time after the fire, I received a letter from the family of the late Equilla Davis. His family lived in the south and explained to me in the letter that they were a black family of very modest means but that they wanted to thank me for what I had done. This meant a lot to me and lifted my spirits that were a bit down since the victim had died.

On April 29, 1964, I received the First Place Exception Merit Risk of Life Award from the Westchester Newspapers. This is the highest police award given and is voted on by a committee of police chiefs. My mother was presented a check of $100 from the newspaper editor since I could not accept it. My mom had hung my uniform clothes outside of our house on the night of fire because of the smell. I also received an honor from Mayor John E. Flynn and Councilman John Lee of my hometown of Yonkers, New York.

TELEPHONE
ME 1-0800

FRANCIS J. HOGAN
Chief of Police

Police Department
Village of North Tarrytown, N. Y.

April 7, 1964

TO: Honorable John E. Hoy, Vice-Chairman, Police Honor Awards
SUBJECT: Recommendation of Patrolman Richard Spota for Commendation

As Chief of Police for The Village of North Tarrytown, N.Y.,
I hereby submit with pride a recommendation for commendation to the
Macy Westchester, "Police Honor Awards Committee," an extraordinary
act of valor by patrolman Richard Spota, whose actions where truly
above and beyond the call of duty and exhibiting a complete disregard
for his own life so that he might save the life of another in a fire
and smoke filled dwelling.

At approximately 8:50 P.M. on March 9, 1964, while patrolman
Spota was assigned to patrolling our village in a patrol car, he
received a radio call from his desk sergeant reporting a fire at
107 Cortlandt Street, in said village, which incidentally is a two
story dwelling containing approximately six families. The officer
immediately rushed to the scene; arriving before responding firemen
he found the building a mass of flame and emitting dense smoke.
Before water could be played on the flames he entered the first
floor of dwelling and led 5 or 6 inhabitants to safety who had
been groping in the smoke filled hallway in an obvious futile
attempt to find the exit.

The officer encountered extreme difficulty in breathing due
to the repelling smoke, nevertheless, with a tenacious determination
to save life he continued his search of the rest of the apartment
on the second floor for any trapped persons. While being forced
to crawl along the floor, groping his way around he entered the
right front apartment which was a mass of flame and enveloped in
smoke, herein the officer observed a man later identified as
Equila Lavis, age 50 years, lying on the floor completely helpless
and obviously unconscious, with his entire clothing on fire. It
was in this instance that officer Spota exhibited alert thinking,
persistence and courageousness, inspite of the flames, toxic smoke,
extremely poor visibility, and to say little of the officers already
over exposure to smoke inhalation; he immediately rolled the victim
over several times and smothered the remaining flames from victim's
clothing with his police overcoat, then pulled the victim out into
the hallway and shouted to fireman who where now entering the building
to bring a stretcher, whereupon victim was subsequently carried out
of building and conveyed to the hospital by a fire emergency unit.

TELEPHONE
ME 1-0800

FRANCIS J. HOGAN
Chief of Police

Police Department
Village of North Tarrytown, N. Y.

At this point Officer Spota was extremely groggy and near collapse due to exhaustion and smoke poisoning, requiring assistance from building by firemen. The officer was immediately administered oxygen at scene by The North Tarrytown Fire Patrol emergency squad and subsequently received medical treatment for 2nd degree burns of the right leg, incurred during this heroic rescue.

Approximately 12 hours later the rescued victim Equila Davis, succumbed to serious burns and smoke poisoning. However, the officers efforts where not in vain. His alert thinking and courageousness not only enhanced our police image but also reassures our citizens of a policeman's unwavering faithfulness and willingness to accomplish our primary purpose of protecting life even when faced with insurmountable odds. It is indeed gratifying to have a police officer under my command so fearless and conscientious; he has set a high standard of courage and bravery under the most difficult conditions.

Therefore, I sincerely feel that the "Police Honor Awards Panel," after evaluating Officer Spota's superior acts of bravery will award him with recognition commensurate with his intrepid performance on the night of March 9th, 1964.

The North Tarrytown Board of Trustees have already cited the officer and a copy of said commendation is enclosed herewith, together with a front page article by our local Tarrytown Daily Newspaper.

Respectfully Submitted,

Enc.

FRANCIS J. HOGAN
Chief of Police

While on vacation, from April 27, 1964, through May 1, 1964, I attended the criminal investigation school sponsored by the Federal Bureau of Investigation, the New York State Association of Chiefs of Police and the New York State Sheriffs Association that was held in Rye, New York.

After vacation, it was back on patrol again. I enjoyed shooting on the pistol team in the Hudson Valley Police Revolver League. I was raising my average on the team.

While off duty one night, I stopped on a store on Central Avenue in Yonkers, New York. While in the store, a person came in and told me that he saw a group out on the street striping license plates from parked cars. I went outside and to my surprise observed that the license plate was missing from my car. I noticed a car driving off. I got in my car to give pursuit. A Yonkers policeman, who had been tipped on plates being stolen, came along and joined me. About two blocks away, we succeeded in cutting off the fleeing car. We had noticed a bunch of license plates being thrown from the car. One of them turned out to be mine. The quartet was taken into custody by the Yonkers policeman and was to appear in court.

In January 1965, a mutual friend introduced me to a beautiful blond who was home from the holiday break from SUNY at Cortland, New York. She was in her senior year and was an elementary education major. She lived in North Tarrytown with her family. We dated before she returned to school for her final semester. At the time, she was 21, and I was 25. Her name was Patricia Kofka.

While on patrol, on 10:50 p.m. one evening, in 1965, there was a spectacular fire which gutted the second floor of an apartment on Depeyster Street in the south end of the village. When fireman Glen Ambesbury and I arrived, Mrs. Parker was on rear porch, shouting for someone to save her husband. We went up the backstairs to the second floor apartment and tried to enter through the kitchen but were driven out by the flames. We maneuvered ourselves to a position on the side of the house and smashed a window. The smoked poured out in the volume. With the pressure relieved, we were able to see Gilbert Parker wandering in a dazed condition. We got him to approach the window. We grabbed him and lowered him to the ground where Fire Patrol took over.

JOHN E. FLYNN
MAYOR

OFFICE OF THE MAYOR
CITY HALL
YONKERS 2, N. Y.

June 5th, 1964

Patrolman Richard Spota
4 George Street,
Yonkers, New York

Dear Patrolman Spota:-

May I express the sincere congratulations of the citizens
of Yonkers for the honor paid to you in receiving the first place
citation for exceptional merit.

Having read the story of your bravery in action on March 9th
preventing the loss of many lives, it certainly is gratifying to know
that public servants continue to live up to the fine standards and
tradition of their Police Department. You have not only brought
honor upon yourself and your family, but to the City of Yonkers also.

May I express our sincere thanks for your wonderful contribution in the saving of human lives.

Sincerely yours,

John E. Flynn
Mayor

JEF:CS

I received the Top Gun Award for the 1965–66 pistol team season.

I was notified that I would have the minimum amount of time necessary to take the promotion exam for police sergeant on May 21, 1966. I had been taking the September to December 1965, and the January through May, 1966, Police Promotion course given in Mount Vernon, New York. On May 21, 1966, I took my first Police Promotion Exam for sergeant along with many other police officers throughout Westchester County.

On July 3, 1966, Patricia Ann Kofka and I were married at Holy Cross Church in North Tarrytown, New York. A friend of mine, Father Menna, married us at the 5 p.m. mass. At 107 degrees, it was said to be one of the hottest days in the history of New York. After our reception, which was attended by our families, friends, and many of the members of the police department, we went to Mexico on our honeymoon. We had taken an apartment on Beacon Hill Drive in Dobbs Ferry, New York. Pat would drive to Ossining, New York where she would teach at the Brookside Elementary School after having taught on Long Island for the first year.

In the last week of August 1966, I was notified by the New York State Department of Civil Service in Albany that I had passed the Police Sergeant's exam with a grade of 83.9. It was noted that I would not receive the 2.5 credit that is added on to your score if you are a veteran. The reason given was that although I had over three years active duly in the Navy, no war had occurred during that time period.

Early in 1967, Lt. Anthony Del Ventura, PTL. Carmen De Falco, and I were assigned to work in New York City with the N.Y.P.D Narcotics Squad for three weeks. The drug abuse problem in our area was starting to get bad and we had to learn all we could about drugs and how to handle the situations that would arise in the world of narcotics. Working in plain clothes to blend into the areas of New York City with detectives from the Manhattan Narcotics Division of the New York City Police Department, we spent a week in Harlem (where your life is on the line), several days in Spanish Harlem, about a week in the east and west village and a few days in Queens. The training we received was invaluable. We worked with some of the detectives who made the French Connection Case. In this strange and dangerous world, the first consideration of the junkies is the "fix." Pushers and junkies alike constantly are on the alert for plainclothesmen. Addiction and crime related to addiction spiral in an endless vicious cycle. In Harlem, we learned how to spot pushers and junkies and find where they hang out prior to "scoring" (obtaining heroin or making a buy). The junkies would look for a place in hallways and alleyways to shoot up as soon as they could. Almost every junkie had a set of works (a cooker, spoon, or bottle cap with a wire handle), hypodermic needle and syringe or eyedropper. With this equipment, the addict can cook his heroin into liquid form, draw it into his syringe, and shoot up. We learned to go for the pusher's hands first when making an arrest because the pusher will throw the heroin out a window or swallow it if it is in a balloon. When we made buys using an informant or an undercover officer, we would test it with a field test kit before sending the person, making the buy back for a second buy. If the pusher was suspicious of the undercover, he might have sold him a false substance. If the undercover went back for the second buy under these circumstances, he could be killed. The heroin reaching the street would be cut (diluted many times with milk, sugar, lactose, or virtually anything available). One apartment we raided was on the fourth floor of the apartment building. The pushers dropped the heroin out the window when we broke down the door. A detective was placed in an alley observing the window and saw a cord attached to the package of heroin as it was dropped. The cord was attached under the windowsill. If we had not seen the heroin, they would have retrieved it. When we could convince the judge issuing the search warrant that we need speed and surprise and that the evidence would be destroyed without same, a no-knock search warrant would be issued. When we were raiding the place where cocaine was being used by the pushers, we were taught to be very fast and careful, or we could be shot by the person or persons involved. It was always better to have at least two buys (sales) on a pusher before raiding his/her residence and/or vehicle. The person would be charged with the sales in addition to any drugs we seized with the search warrant. When conducting a raid, it was important to find out by the undercover officer or informant if the pusher had a weapon and where the drugs were usually hidden. False sections of walls, ceilings, floors, and almost any other place you could think of were used to hide the drugs. It was a sad sight to observe junkies at the crack of dawn congregating together in areas of the city, waiting to cop (buy drugs). By observing who met with them, you could trace the supply back to the main supplier. All of the detectives had informants supplying information to them. Usually, they had been arrested for drug violations and were supplying the information to gel a reduced sentence in court. Others were paid for their information. It was almost impossible to infiltrate a major drug group without this information. Depending on the size and scope of the operation, an informant would be used to introduce an undercover policeman or Woman to the pusher. The undercover would make as many buys as possible from the pusher involved before indictments and arrests were made. We had to walk a tightrope of giving the undercover as much protection as possible without burning him or her. A mistake could cost the undercover his or her life. We surveilled an elementary school on the east side of the city. We observed a pusher-selling heroin to fourth and fifth graders. This was very depressing. There had to be a better way. Education in all grades of all schools would be a better way. Of course, the pushers would have to be arrested. It was not that easy because there were no undercovers that young to infiltrate the schools. We would also observe much older adults (seniors) buying drugs. Working the east and west village, we found the area to have mostly pot (marijuana), LSD, and pills. Of course, on any given day or night during a raid, we would seize almost any drugs. One female undercover we worked with dressed like a hippie and gave the appearance of a female that was about 17. I admired her for her guts and determination. She produced many good arrests. When we worked in Queens, we found the situation to be similar to Westchester County in that pot and pills were primarily used at this time.

I felt that the three weeks were very informative in addition to making many good arrests. When we returned, we would educate the parents on what to look for in actual evidence as well as symptoms of drug abuse. We would make up a drug board to display to parents and educators. Seminars on drug abuse should be started in all of our schools. Getting a person or persons who have been involved in drug abuse to talk with their peers would be helpful. On the other hand, many of the detectives we had worked with were later indicted and convicted of drug related corruption charges. This epidemic had no social or economic barriers. There would be no profession that it would not touch. We had a lot of work to do and not any time to waste.

In the spring of 1967, when I was off duty from my uniform patrol shifts, I conducted surveillances of suspected drug activity. I would obtain search warrants for the suspects and conduct raids. This would take place on Beekman Avenue, a main street in the village where persons involved in drugs would gather, at Rockwood Hall area, a wooded area overlooking the Hudson River in the northern end of the village and on Cortlandt Street and other areas of the south end or downtown section of the village. The training in New York City helped in these investigations. I had the persons involved in drugs swallow same to avoid arrests. They would be taken to Phelps Memorial Hospital and have their stomachs pumped and then later be booked at Police Headquarters when they were well.

While off duty from May 8 through 12, 1967, I completed the F.B.I. sponsored Fingerprint School in Valhalla, New York. Also, while off duty this year, I completed the eight-week Juvenile Delinquency Treatment and Control course sponsored by the Westchester County Young Services Division on July 3, 1967.

I had obtained information on a person who was selling drugs to high school students. This would not be an easy investigation because the persons involved were 15 to 18 years of age. When the school year started at Sleepy Hollow High School in September 1967, I was able to identify a main supplier of drugs from the students. There were no undercover police officers young enough to assign to the investigation. Through informants I had developed, I was able to make "buys" of drugs from this pusher.

The investigation went into the fourth week of October 1967. When I had enough information and controlled buys, I was able to obtain a search warrant. My information and surveillances showed that the pusher was making sales at the high school during school hours. Armed with a search warrant early on the morning of

October 24, 1967, I surveilled the pusher as he entered the school. I was aware that the controlled buys were only good for the purpose of obtaining the search warrant and that I would have to get the pusher dirty (with drugs on his person). I was aware of a possible lawsuit if this did not turn out right, but I believed this risk had to be taken to stop these sales to students. I entered the school just after the start of the second period with my superiors, Lt. Del Ventura and Chief Jandrucko. This was timed so as not to arouse student attention. The school principal, Dr. Richardson, gave full cooperation. Dr. Richardson accompanied us to the second floor hallway. The principal went into the classroom and asked for Jose Noran to step out in the hallway. Noran was told who we were. He was shown the search warrant and searched. In his pants pockets were six yellow pay-type envelopes, referred to as "nickel bags" by pushers. Each nickel bag contained one-quarter ounce of marijuana and sold for $5 a bag. Noran was stunted and shrugged. He was charged with first-degree criminal possession of a dangerous drug, a felony. Noran was taken to police headquarters where he was booked, fingerprinted, and his mug shot (photo) was taken. He was arraigned before Judge John B. Whalen and released on $1,000 bail. I had identified between 25–30 students who were buying from Noran.

3 STUDENTS NABBED WITH DRUGS

A 'Main Supplier' Caught At SHHS

The next step was to notify those students and their parents to come in for a conference. At all drug seminars that we gave, I always stated that all those who used pot would not go on to heroin, but that everyone that I knew that used heroin had started with pot. An investigation such as this could not succeed without the cooperation of school officials and the police. The local daily news carried this story as their headline the following day with pictures. I'm sure they realized the severity of the drug problem. Governor Nelson Rockefeller, a resident of North Tarrytown, would enact though drug laws during his tenure as governor.

In November 1967, Chief Jandrucko and I received the Fraternal Order of Eagles Good Neighbor Award for the investigation and arrest of Jose N. The awards are presented whenever events warrant by the national Eagles organization through the local aerie, in this case the Tarrytown Aerie I042 in North Tarrytown through their officers, John Remenar, president and Glenn Amesbury, chairman of the awards program. I appreciated the award.

On December I5, 1967, I received a commendation that was very special to me from a person that was a hero of mine although I did not know him personally. The commendation read *"United States Senate, Washington D.C. Dear Patrolman Spota, I recently learned that you received the Good Neighbor Award from the Fraternal Order of Eagles of Tarrytown for the apprehension of a major drug distributor at Sleepy Hollow High School. I want to congratulate you on the award and express my respect and admiration for your fine police work. I know that the people of North Tarrytown are grateful for your outstanding dedication. With best wishes for the future, Sincerely, Robert F. Kennedy."*

I remember touching the signature and saying to myself, "He really did sign it." I had, of course, admired President Kennedy a great deal. But Bobby Kennedy as Attorney General was outstanding. Being only a police officer, I had someone to look up to who would take on organized crime. What a breath of fresh air from the run of the mile political leaders, someone who couldn't he bought. During one of his campaigns, his caravan stopped at Patriot's Park in North Tarrytown. I was off duty, but I drove to the village that day, staying in the background to listen to him and just observe anyone in the area. He had many of his family members with him. To a young person in law enforcement, it was very special to have national figure who would take on organized crime. His commendation had touched me and really motivated me.

ROBERT F. KENNEDY
NEW YORK

111 EAST 45TH STREET
NEW YORK 10017

United States Senate
WASHINGTON, D.C. 20510

December 15, 1967

Patrolman Richard Spota
24 Beacon Hill Drive
Dobbs Ferry, New York

Dear Patrolman Spota:

I recently learned that you and
Chief Jandrucko received Good Neighbor Awards
from the Fraternal Order of Eagles of Tarrytown for the apprehension of a major drug
distributor at Sleepy Hollow High School.

I want to congratulate you on the
award and express my respect and admiration
for your fine police work. I know that the
people of North Tarrytown are grateful for
your outstanding dedication.

With best wishes for the future,

Sincerely,

Robert F. Kennedy

Chapter Three

Starting in January 1968, I had the responsibility of organizing the detective bureau, setting up files and various systems that are necessary for its operation. I had information of a policy operation (numbers) on River Street in January 1968. Anchor Motors was the firm that transported the new cars that were made at the General Motors plant, which was located next to Anchor Motors. I put two suspects under surveillance and continued to gather information. I used my personal car for the surveillance because the unmarked police vehicle would have been detected by the suspects. After gathering enough information, a search warrant was obtained. On January 26, 1968, I along with Patrolman Vince Butknovich searched Alexa Caldone, age 54, of Yonkers on River Street, a short distance south of Anchor Motors. After finding gambling records in his possession, he was arrested and taken to Police Headquarters by Lt. Anthony Del Ventura. Approximately ten minutes later PTL. Butknovich and I arrested George Caldone, 46 years, of Tarrytown at Pat's 85 Club, after finding gambling records on him. George Caldone worked the night shift at Anchor Motors and his brother, Alexa, worked the day shift there. The Policy Ring was reportedly handling at least $100,000 a year.

I was one of the arresting officers of Eugene Mills, 29 years of age of the Bronx, New York at the General Motors plant in North Tarrytown. Mills was arrested at the plant for assaulting and threatening a person with a gun inside of the plant. At the time of the arrest, the GM plant employed over 5,000 people. Many of these employees lived in the New York City area. It was like having a precinct in the city within the village.

I had information in January 1968 of a drug operation on Cortlandt Street in a second floor apartment of the three-story building. Surveillance was required on weekends and weeknights. Drugs were believed to be supplied to pushers in other areas of Westchester County from this apartment. It was not possible to simply send an undercover officer into such an operation without the officer knowing anyone in the building. I developed an informant from the southern part of the county who was able to go into the building and make contact with the person selling drugs. To make a purchase or "buy" from a pusher using an informant I would give money to the informant, search him before entering the building, observe him, and meet him when he left the building, take the drugs from him, search him again, then bring the drugs to the county lab for examination and evaluation. We continued to surveil the operation, observing, and following the persons suspected of selling and others buying and reselling the drugs. On Friday night, March 29, 1968, we had obtained search warrants for the suspects and premises. We observed the operation for approximately three hours to ascertain that they were operating normally. After that, the key elements were speed and surprise. A no-knock warrant was issued by the judge so that the evidence would not be destroyed, flushed down toilets, or thrown out of the windows. An officer would be assigned to stay on the ground level beneath windows of the second floor apartment. The raid went off like clockwork. We seized a large quantity of marijuana and drug-related items. Miguel Guzzi, 24, who lived in the apartment was charged with criminally selling a narcotic drug and criminal possession of a narcotic drug, both felonies, and maintaining a criminal nuisance and loitering for the purpose of using drugs. William Isidro, 26, Jose Rios of Cortlandt Terrace; and Jose Alvarez of Yonkers were charged with criminal possession of a dangerous drug and all including a sixth person were charged with loitering for the use of drugs. A large quantity of marijuana was packaged in "nickel bags," packets of marijuana selling for $5 each. Another item found was a copy of the Daily News from the previous October which had a picture on the front page of the Chief, Lt. Del Ventura and myself after a drug raid. It is believed these pictures were used to aid in identification of the officers investigating narcotics sales.

We set up a program to take our Narcotics Identification Board into the schools before groups of parents and before civic groups. We would identity the drugs, show how they are used, and the symptoms to observe in users. A question and answer session would follow.

I continued to be involved in many narcotics investigations, making arrests for the sale of dangerous drugs whenever possible. Undercover investigators of the Westchester County Sheriff's Department, Narcotics Unit would make the purchase of drugs from the pushers. At 5:45 a.m. one morning, Lt. Del Ventura and I crashed through the triple-locked door of an apartment on Cortlandt Street with members of the sheriff's department. We seized a felony quantity of heroin and other drugs. Eduardo Elez, 22 years of age and Nancy Hughes, 19 years of age, of White Plains were both charged with possession. Elez was charged with three counts of felonious sale and three of felonious possession.

Routine investigations would result in arrests for burglary and possession of stolen property. Other investigations for auto theft would result in grand larceny and possession of stolen property charges. I attended the F.B.I. sponsored Photography School held in Valhalla from April 29 through May 3, 1968.

I conducted an investigation and surveillance of the Eternal Light Holy Candle Shop at 66 Beekman Avenue with members of the district attorney's investigation unit. The shop specialized in grave lights. After three months of extensive investigation, we raided the shop on May 7, 1968. Arrested and charged with promoting, gambling, and possession of gambling records were Al Letti, 57 years and Chrissy Letti, 55, who resided in North Tarrytown. District Attorney Carl Vergari stated that extensive gambling records were seized. The headquarters of the million dollar gambling operation was the Eternal Light Holy Candle Shop. Connected to the operation and arrested by D.A.'s Investigators and Tarrytown Police were Fank Rizzo, 48 years of age, outside of Cortlandt Street, Tarrytown, charged with possession of gambling records and promoting gambling second degree; Samuel Kaplan, 60 years, of Tarrytown, arrested in a restaurant on Main Street, Tarrytown, and charged with possession of gambling records; and Jorge Pozos of Tarrytown, arrested at his Lucky Seven Grocery Store and charged with possession of gambling records. Connected with the raid was one by the Bronx County District Attorney's office and the New York City Police Department at an apartment on Van Cortlandt Park Avenue West, the Bronx where "extensive" gambling records were seized. No arrests were made there because the apartment was empty at the time. D.A. Vergari stated that the gambling operation included bets on policy numbers, the Cuban lottery, horses, and sports.

In the evening of May 24, 1968, I participated in a coordinated raid by five police agencies: the sheriff's department, the D.A.'s office, the White Plains Police Department, the Tarrytown Police Department, and the North Tarrytown Police Department. At 9:00 p.m., we arrested Rosario Soza, 36 years of age, on two counts of promoting gambling second degree and one count of possession of gambling records. The agencies involved in the raid arrested three men in Tarrytown for promoting gambling and possession charges and Carlos Sanchez, 31 years, and Anne Sanchez, 42, in White Plains for possessing and promoting gambling. The group was reported to have been a $2 million a year gambling operation.

On May 29, 1968, I graduated from the New York City Police Academy's Community Relations Training Symposium which was held from May 19 to May 29, 1968. I learned a great deal on police community relations at this school.

On May 31, 1968, PTL. Vince Butkovich and I arrested Don Travia, 25 years, of the Bronx on charges of selling fireworks. He was accused of selling fireworks to local youths at 10:30 a.m. on Beekman Avenue. Several dozen cherry bombs and 1 1/2 inch firecrackers were seized. This followed an investigation of several weeks.

Although I had been assigned to detective duty in January 1968, I was still receiving Patrolman First Grade pay. A police officer may laterally be assigned and transferred to detective or plain-clothes duty by police personnel, but an increase in pay grade must be approved by the Board of Trustees. As of June 1, 1968, the board voted to increase my salary to $500 above First Grade Patrolman after voting to establish a detective bureau.

I attended and received a diploma from the United States Department of Justice, Bureau of Narcotics, and Dangerous Drugs School held at Westchester Community College from June 16 to June 20, 1968.

During the summer of 1968, I conducted a surveillance of a suspected gambling operation at Johnny's Stationery Store. Investigators of the district attorney's office also conducted an investigation and surveillance. They were able to determine where the bets were being laid off (that is where the larger bets were being sent). On August 8, 1968, at approximately 3:15 p.m., we conducted a raid of Johnny's Stationery Store, armed with a search warrant. We seized 876 policy slips worth in excess of $400. John Hines, 40 years, who resided in Ossining, New York, was charged with possession of gambling records, first degree, and promoting gambling in the first degree, both felonies and maintaining a place for gambling, criminal nuisance. District Attorney Carl Vergari stated that it was a $2,500 a week operation and was believed to be a "part of the Pete Vitchelli operation." At the same time, members of the state police raided a store in Nyack and arrested Joseph Poche of the Bronx, who they charged with possession of gambling records, a misdemeanor. Mr. Vergari said that some gambling slips were found in Nyack, but the bulk of the records were destroyed. He said, the slips were written on water, soluble paper, and traces of the paper were found in a wastepaper basket filled with water next to a desk. I was satisfied that we had seized all the records that we could (felony amount) but disappointed that the state police did not get the bulk of the records across the Hudson River in Nyack, New York. Hines was indicted by the grand jury for first-degree possession of gambling records, first-degree promotion of gambling and maintaining a criminal nuisance.

I entered Westchester Community College in September 1968, majoring in police science. If I was working at daytime, I could attend class at night and when working on nights I could attend class during the day.

Late in the summer of 1968, I started an investigation and surveillance of the P&J Luncheonette. The luncheonette was located at the northwest corner of Beekman Avenue and Theresa Street. The front of the luncheonette on Beekman Avenue had a glass front, as did the side facing Theresa Street. The Central Shoe Repair Store, which was located diagonally southwest of the P&J Luncheonette was connected to the luncheonette. I secured a room nearby to conduct a surveillance of the P&J Luncheonette. Many out-of-town persons who went into the luncheonette then left without having anything to eat or drink. Since I didn't know many of the people going into the luncheonette, I used a camera to take motion pictures. Sitting down with the D.A. and some of his staff, we observed the moving pictures that I had taken. The D.A.'s staff was able to identify some of the persons, however, in using the home-style camera, I shot the window bar and other things on some of the shots. D.A. Carl Vergari stated to his staff, "Get him some decent camera equipment." Senior Investigator John McKeon and his staff of investigators came with the camera equipment and his expertise of organized crime investigations. Every day, I learned a lot from John McKeon. Standing behind the camera that he had on a tripod, he would identify known persons going into the luncheonette. Chewing on this rubber cigar holder, he would explain many details of the investigations to me. Philip Polsino, who was always at the luncheonette, was meeting people as they came in and then he would go into a rear room, sometimes by himself and at other times not alone. Polsino's son, Gerald, and another person, James Green, also worked there. Anthony Polsino, Philip Polsino's brother, would go into the luncheonette on occasion, spending only a short period of time and then he would leave. Anthony Polsino was a made member of the Genovese Crime Family, the family that had been started by Vito Genovese. After over a month of surveillance, search warrants were obtained.

Police Raid Gaming Den

Twenty runners (persons who collect bets) were employed by Polsino and were observed on a daily basis, going into the luncheonette. They represented almost all areas of Westchester County. Anthony Polsino had been observed at the Central Shoe Repair. I had a statement from a person who Polsino had offered to sell the shoe repair equipment to, stating that he (Anthony Polsino) did not need it. On October 7, 1968, armed with the search warrant, Senior Investigator John McKeon, Investigators of the D.A.'s Office, D.A. Carl Vergari, Chief Jandrucko, and I raided the P&J Luncheonette and the Central Shoe Repair Store. We were able to seize the records in the rear of the luncheonette before they could be put into a sink by the defendants. Some gambling records were on submarine paper, which dissolves in water. Policy records seized indicated a weekly play of $2,400 and bookmaking records seized indicated a weekly play of $2,000. Philip Polsino, of New York, was charged with first and second-degree promotion of gambling, two counts of possession of gambling records, and tampering with a telephone; and James Green, 24, of 179 Beekman Avenue was charged with second-degree possession of gambling records. D.A. Vergari stated that 20 runners were employed by the alleged ring and identified Philip Polsino as the comptroller. Anthony Polsino drove up during the raid and sped away when he observed what was going on. D.A. Vergari said that the grand jury would investigate the $500,000 a year operation.

In November 1968, Assistant D.A. Lawrence Martin Jr. began the process of a grand jury probe into the gambling investigation in North Tarrytown and related areas. It is a Class E Felony to disclose any testimony or information of persons testifying before a grand jury, so I will not comment on those proceedings. Almost all of the 20 runners were subpoenaed to appear before the grand jury. I was working with the D.A.'s investigators and Asst. D.A. Larry Martin in serving the subpoenas on the persons mentioned and bringing them forth with to the D.A.'s office to testify before the grand jury. I was testifying regularly during this probe. On the evening of November 16, 1968, when I arrived home, my wife was asleep. She left a note, reminding me to walk Fritz, our schnauzer, before I went to sleep. I put Fritz's leash on and walked to the sidewalk outside of our garden-type apartment building. We were walking down the sidewalk on Beacon Hill Drive when we got to a private driveway that runs behind our building. I heard the sound of gravel being kicked up by a car to my right and saw a vehicle coming at me. As it was going to hit me, I pulled back, lifting Fritz with my left arm and taking my gun out with my right hand. As the car came up on the lawn area that I was now on, behind the building, the driver realized he would go into the brick building if he continued. He put the car in reverse and went back, off the lawn, as I pointed my gun toward him. He then drove off. When I reentered the house, I made a report of the mini accident. The following week, I continued to testify before the grand jury.

On Tuesday, November 19, 1968, I testified before the grand jury during the day and attended classes in police science at Westchester Community College at night. I would arrive home at approximately 10 p.m. I was driving on Ashford Avenue, Dobbs Ferry, when I slowed down to make a right turn onto Beacon Hill Drive, which goes up a hill. A shot rang out, and my passenger window, which was closed, disintegrated. I jammed the car into the park, which caused it to rock back and forth, and ducked my head down. There was a wooded area to my right and a large park to my left. I didn't know where the shot came from. There was blood on my forehead, because I had smashed my head on the car's air conditioning unit as I went down. There was also blood on my hand where I had cut myself moving around on broken glass. I eventually drove up the hill with my head down. When I walked into our apartment, my wife asked me what happened. I asked, "Why?"

She said, "Because you have blood on your forehead." I notified the authorities. Assistant D.A. Larry Martin came over and had me go to the police surgeon to get cleaned up. As I lay on the table, he gave me a lot of encouragement. Well, it was back to testifying in the days ahead, with one difference, I had an armed guard wherever I went and at my house 24 hours a day. Pat will always remember going to Mass with me at Sacred Heart Church on Thanksgiving weekend. We stayed up in the balcony of the church with a plain-clothed police officer carrying a sawed-off shotgun. The grand jury continued its probe with Assistant D.A. Larry Martin presenting evidence along with Assistant D.A. Bill McKenna of the Rackets Bureau and Chief Assistant D.A. Tom Facelle. When the grand jury finished, they had indicted Philip Polsino of Mt. Vernon, his brother Anthony Polsino of Mt. Pleasant, Gerald Polsino of Mt. Vernon, and James Green. Two North Tarrytown men, one a village official, were indicted for criminal contempt. The grand jury indicted Joseph Bianco, of New York for a "deliberate attempt to run me down" on November 16, 1968. The grand jury awarded me a commendation for courage, honesty, tenacity, dedication, and initiative in finding and presenting evidence in the gambling investigation.

Officer Probing Bets

Bushwhacker's Bullet
Just Misses Det. Spota

| U.S. Jets Down Near Da Nang | *Detective Says He Was 'Sitting Duck'* | | Gunshot Smashes Car Window |

DET. RICHARD SPOTA

Around-Clock
Guard Placed
On Detective

November 27, 1968

Chief of Police
North Tarrytown Police Department
North Tarrytown, New York

Dear Chief:

We, the members of the November B Grand Jury
of Westchester County, herewith commend Detective Richard
Spota of the North Tarrytown Police Department for his
courage, honesty, tenacity, dedication and initiative in
finding and presenting evidence in the gambling investigation
in North Tarrytown, New York.

/s/ Sherwood C. Chatfield
_____
Foreman of the Grand Jury

/s/ Fred A. Hanken
_____
Clerk of the Grand Jury

cc: Grand Jurors' Association
    Sheriff's Office
    Officer's File Jacket

I was offered a position with a prestigious agency where I could work on organized crime. I thought about this for a period of time. It would be great to work with people who all had the same goals, a breath of fresh air. Someone who I respected told me that it would be very difficult to go back to work in North Tarrytown, I was on the Sergeant's list there, but more importantly, thinking of Bobby Kennedy. If not me, who? If not now, when?

District Attorney Carl Vergari in this probe and all others unequivocally did everything in their power to put the leaders of organized crime away. I was one of three police officers of the tri-village area honored as 1968 Police Officer of the Year by the Exchange Club of the Tarrytown, at their dinner held at the Pickwick Post Restaurant. District Attorney Carl A. Vergari was the guest speaker and made the presentations to us along with some very kind words.

There were the routine investigations and arrests starting in 1969. Narcotics and organized crime investigations continued. On April 9, 1969, at 10:30 a.m., a sheriff's criminal investigator and I arrested Ramon Quiroa, 29 years of age, of the Bronx, while he worked the day shift at the GM Plant. We had an arrest warrant, charging Quiora with two counts of promoting gambling in addition to the possession of policy slips for the American and Puerto Rican numbers games that we found on this person. Quiora, a welder in the former fisher body division, operated a $50,000 a year policy (numbers) business at the plant.

I had the opportunity to speak with Peter Maas, author of the recently published *"The Valachi Papers."* He agreed to speak before the monthly meeting of the Westchester County Detectives Association of which I was Secretary at our April 23 dinner meeting in White Plains, New York. We had more than 60 members present at the meeting. He stated that he was the only reporter allowed by the federal government to interview Joe Valachi, a soldier in Vito Genovese's "family" in his maximum-security cell. Mr. Mass painted a vivid, often violent picture of the psychological and interrogation pressures which forced a man sworn on pain of death to secrecy "to show us the face of the enemy." In 1962, Valachi was in the federal penitentiary in Atlanta "subject to a series of unique pressures." He believed the narcotics charge of which he had been convicted was a frame. For another, he had been placed in Vito Genovese's cell, along with one of the boss's henchmen. This was awkward since Vito apparently believed Valachi had informed the Bureau of Narcotics of certain activities and had issued a contract against him. Valachi tried to get two letters out, asking for help but was unsuccessful. Because of his potential value, Valachi was moved to the Westchester County Penitentiary and kept there under an assumed name. An F.B.I. agent assigned to the case was able to get Valachi to talk. He was transferred to Fort Monmouth, New Jersey, and then to Washington, D.C., dressed as a soldier. He identified more than 700 members, and he helped solve many previously unsolved crimes. In a question and answer session, Mr. Maas stated that he believed that the *Cosa Nostra* does have a strong hold in Westchester—a lot of numbers, infiltration into legitimate businesses and service industries, such as garbage collection and loansharking. Mr. Maas stated that organized crime is the biggest business in America. Mr. Maas maintained that organized crime probably can't be wiped out, but it can be contained by highly motivated law enforcement agencies, backed by a public that cares.

Thursday, May 8, 1969. A stolen car had been observed earlier this week near a bank in Dobbs Ferry, New York. We had been alerted to watch for it. At 10:15 a.m., PTL. Stanley Lapicki of the Tarrytown Police observed a suspicious looking car near the A&P on Broadway and Wildey Street, Tarrytown, not far from the First National City Bank on Broadway in Tarrytown. He observed that the license plates were the same as that reported by Dobbs Ferry Police on a car stolen from the Bronx. He tailed the vehicle but lost it. He notified Tarrytown Police Headquarters who in turn notified North Tarrytown Police. Lt. Anthony Del Ventura was with me in an unmarked police car. We observed the vehicle while on New Broadway, North Tarrytown. I followed the vehicle as it drove by the First National Bank of North Tarrytown on Beekman Avenue. Lt. Del Ventura had radioed police headquarters with the information and instructions. PTL. Mario DeFelice was in a marked police vehicle at the time. I followed the stolen car through Webber Park, a residential section of North Tarrytown. As the stolen vehicle got on Route 9 (Broadway), a roadblock was attempted, but the three suspects in the stolen vehicle sped up Broadway (Rt. 9) north at a high rate of speed. We pursued the late model stolen vehicle which was holding the road better than our 1964 Chevrolet at 100 miles per hour. I had to press the gas pedal to the floor to keep up with them, sometimes having to go into the southbound lane. All other departments had been alerted. Four miles from our starting point, at Scarborough Road and Route 9, the stolen vehicle appeared to attempt a right turn, but the suspects left the vehicle almost sideways in the middle of the road. I tried to slow down as much as I could to avoid crashing into the vehicle. I could not slow down enough, but I managed to spin the rear of our car so that it just missed the stolen car. The three suspects alighted and ran past the Scarborough Presbyterian Church and fled into a wooded area behind the church, I drove through to the rear woods, and we pursued them on foot. As we saw one of them stop and turn with a gun in his hand, we fired several shots and told them to throw their weapons down. Two did and we had them face down in the woods. The third suspect went east. At this point, PTL. Mario DiFelice entered the wooded area from the north and we had him handcuff the two suspects on the ground as we covered them. By this time, police from Mount Pleasant, Briarcliff Manor, Ossining Town, Ossining Village, the State Police, Tarrytown, and North Tarrytown were on the scene. The third suspect had fled through the wooded area to a home at 653 Scarborough Road. He came out of the house, attired in different clothing but was challenged and arrested by PTL. Leon White of the Ossining Police Department and PTA Sam Paonessa of The Briarcliff Manor Police Department. The two persons we arrested—Edward Reese, 31 years, of New Haven, Connecticut, and William Bertch, 26 years, Milford, Connecticut—along with the third suspect, Ralph Mossuli, 31 years, of East Haven, Connecticut were taken back to the North Tarrytown Police Headquarters and charged with possession of a loaded gun, possession of a stolen car, and possession of a stolen license plate. Mossuli was additionally charged with burglary in the third degree for entering the house in Scarborough. Mossuli was out on bail of $250,000 for an armed robbery of the Harnden National Bank in Connecticut. Reed was out on bail in connection with a holdup of the Long Branch of the first New Haven National Bank in April 1967. When I put Bertch in a jail cell, he said thanks to me.

I asked, "For what?"

He said, "For not killing me. If the F.B.I. had gotten there first, they would have killed me."

I responded, "If I knew the type of weapons you had, I might have too." The 357 Magnum revolver was far superior to my snub-nosed Detective Special. A second revolver, a .38 caliber Smith & Wesson, fully loaded was found by Mount Pleasant Police on the east side of the base of Arch Hili (Rt.9) about a quarter of a mile north of Phelps Memorial Hospital. Also found were two full-face rubber masks, a wooden ski mask, three men's fedora hats, gloves, and canvas bags. They all wore a change of clothes under their regular clothes. When the F.B.I. arrived, they knew of the long criminal history of the defendants. Later that night, Sgt. Aubrey Mason located two stolen cars with Connecticut license plates in Windy Park, Tarrytown, New York.

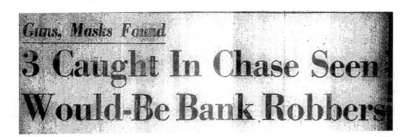

Guns, Masks Found
3 Caught In Chase Seen
Would-Be Bank Robbers

Spota Run-Down Suspect Caught In
Gambling Ring R

Other officers who took part in the investigation were Lt. Sam Rubin, Ossining P.D., Mount Pleasant Police Chief, Paul Oliva, Lt. David Wylock, Sgt. James Crisfield, and Det. Victor Cioffiede Tarrytown Det. Lt. Robert Lipsky, Det. Barney Parra Sgt. Adolphus Fair and Patrolman Douglas Dullin, Briarcliff Police Chief Joseph Melienry, LL Arthur Johnson, and Patrolman John DeCrenza.

On May 25, 1969, in the northern end of the village Rockwood Hall area, Lt. Del Ventura and I arrested Steven A. Kirschner, 19, of the Bronx, for second-degree criminal possession of a dangerous drug, a class D felony. He had 24 grams of marijuana in his possession. He was indicted by the grand jury for the charge.

During the summer of 1969, I conducted an investigation of several suspected drug pushers. Because of their age and other factors, I could not get an undercover officer to make buys from them. I used an informant to make buys from them. I obtained arrest warrants for the suspects from Judge John B. Whalen. On August 20, 1969, 1, along with Patrolman Vincent Butkovich and Patrolman John Doran, arrested Edward O'Leary, 18 years old, Joseph Colter, 18 years, both of North Tarrytown; and Richard M. for two counts each of possession and selling dangerous drugs. The drug involved was heroin. They would be indicted on all charges by the grand jury on September 8, 1969. The September 1969 grand jury voted a special commendation to me for the resourceful performance of my duties which resulted in the apprehension of the three drug violators, and the intelligent manner in which I testified.

On Tuesday, August 26, 1969, District Attorney Carl Vergari announced the raid and arrests of eight persons including the top man in Eastchester, New York. He stated that this was the nerve center and bank for the operation that involved agents in virtually every community in Westchester and New Jersey, Connecticut, New York City, Long Island, and Rockland County. Those arrested included one of the top men, Michael Cellini, 42, of Yonkers, and Joseph Bianco, 62, of Yonkers, who is out on bail and awaiting charges that he tried to run me down in Dobbs Ferry on November 16, 1968. More than $10,000 cash was seized along with tens of thousands of dollars in bets. He said that the records were so extensive it would take several weeks to reconstruct the operation and make an estimate of its size. A "wire room" on Sawmill River Road, Yonkers, New York, was also raided.

On Thursday, August 28, 1969, I received the First Place Citation of Exceptional Merit of the Police Honor Awards Program of the Westchester Rockland Newspapers along with Lt. Del Ventura for the May 8 capture of the three bank robbers.

On September 5, 1969 I had just worked the 4 p.m. to 12 midnight shift and had gone home when I received a call that the Bridge View Tavern had been held up. The Bridge View was located opposite the GM Plant and in addition to being a restaurant and bar, they cashed checks for the GM employees. When I arrived at the Bridge View, Det. Carmen DeFalco, who was now working with me in the Detectives Bureau, was at the scene, as was the Chief, Patrolman Mockler, and others. The holdup occurred at 12:30 a.m. when Thomas Norlen, the proprietor of the Bridge View, came to the tavern, joining Thomas O'Rourke, one of the bartenders. At the tavern were six black men, all in their 20s. One, a General Motors employee who Mr. Norlen was familiar with asked to have his check cashed. After having his check cashed, the man and a friend left, leaving four strangers at the bar. Mr. Norlen walked behind the bar to see if he had enough change for business that night. He turned to find a man with a gun behind him. Simultaneously, the other three men stood up and pointed guns. Mr. Norlen was told to put his hands on the bar. Mr. O'Rourke was told to empty his pockets and then hand over his wallet, watch, car keys, and everything else. Mr. Norlen turned to the man watching him and told him to take his wallet, indicating his front jacket pocket.

The man replied, "Give me the wallet in the other pocket." Mr. Norlen did not know how he knew about it, reaching around to get it, the man found a revolver in Mr. Norlen's pants pocket. He shouted, "This S.O.B. has a gun!"

Mr. Norlen suddenly felt the world blow up in his ear, and he fell to the floor. The man had hit him in the head with the gun and the gun discharged, sending a bullet through the ceiling. Mr. Norlen was conscious, but with blood pouring out of his head, he thought he was shot and played dead. When the four men left, he called police headquarters. Mr. Norlen was taken to Phelps Memorial Hospital and received seven sutures to close the head wound. The men had taken $20,000. In addition to the usual methods of investigation, I contacted Patrolman Frank Morano of the Mount Vernon Police Department soon after the holdup. We brought Mr. Norlen and Mr. O'Rourke to Mt. Vernon Police Headquarters where Patrolman Morano sketched out three pictures of the suspects. We kept following leads.

District Attorney's Office
Court House
White Plains
New York

September 8, 1969

Chief of Police
North Tarrytown Police Department
North Tarrytown, New York

Dear Chief:

        The September, 1969 Term of the Westchester County
Grand Jury has voted a special commendation to Det. Richard
Spota for the resourceful performance of his duties which re-
sulted in the apprehension of three drug violators,   in the Town of North
Tarrytown, and the intelligent manner in which he testified.

                                        A.M. Freije
                                Foreman of the Grand Jury

JJP:ftd

cc: Grand Jury Association
      Westchester County Sheriff
      Officers File Jacket
      Mayor, Board of Trustees and
      Police Commissioner of No. Tarrytown

Ernest Kindgren who is on va-   genhan, a member of the   Sarno.

WINNER of a first-place Citation of Exceptional Merit,
North Tarrytown Detective Richard Spota, center, is congratulated by his chief, John
Jandrucko. The detective was
cited for his part in the chase
and capture of three men casing a bank. A fellow officer,
Lt. Anthony DelVentura, was
honored for his participation
in the same case. At right is
Det. Spota's wife, Patricia,
who holds a check for $100
presented in conjuction with
the award.—Staff Photo by
Jerry Sarno.

Investigati
On Garba
To Contin

WHITE PLAINS—
Westchester Dist. Atty.
A. Vergari said yesterday
his office will continue its
tigation into the garbage h
business in Westchester.
"We have maintained :
tinuing investigation of :
tions of wrongdoing in the
ing industry in Westcheste
will continue to do so," he
The prosecutor added: "
present time we are inve
ing the unusual circums
surrounding bidding on th
rent refuse hauling contr
Mount Vernon.
Mr. Vergari's statement
lowed disclosures in the
chester Rockland News[
showing Mafia control c
firm that presently has th
bage hauling contract
Mount Vernon. That contra
pires Nov. 24 and the firm
last week to bid on a new
ing contract.
An investigation two year
by the Westchester prosec
office led to the indictmen
garbage firm official fc
legedly coercing a comp
However, the charge wa
missed in County Court
spring, Mr. Vergari said
fice is appealing that court
sion."

FIRST PLACE Citation of
Exceptional Merit is displayed
by North Tarrytown Police L
Anthony DelVentura, second
from left, awarded him for his
participation in the chase and
capture of three men believed
to be casing a bank. His wife,
Rose, holds check for $100 in
conjunction with the award,
presented by a Westchester
Rockland Newspapers. At left
is Sheriff Daniel F. McMahon,
vice chairman of the awards
selection committee, and at
right is Tuckahoe Police Chief
John C. Bova, a member of
the awards committee.—Staff
Photo by Jerry Sarno.

Today's Chuc
It takes two kinds of p
to make the world go
write the glories of au
and the rest of us to
them.
On Homecom

Of Irvington Force, Ptl. Dulin Also Honored   FRIDAY, August 29 1969

Kindgren, Jones, DelVentura, Spota Top I

Ventura, Spota Top Police Award List

In the middle of October, I received some information regarding possible suspects. I took Thomas Norlen and Thomas O'Rourke to the Bronx County Courthouse where some possible suspects were to appear. Both suspects entered the courtroom separately, sitting in different locations, pretending not to know each other. One suspect identified as Melvin Green, the man who held a gun on Mr. O'Rourke, sat near us. The other, identified as Harold Ross, sat across the room and did a double take when he saw Mr. Norlen. This was the man who had emptied the cash register. I was alone that day and although you can make an arrest in a case like this without a warrant, I thought innocent bystanders in the courtroom could get injured. I returned with Mr. Norlen and Mr. O'Rourke and got arrest warrants from Judge John B. Whalen. I returned to the courthouse the following week with Det. Carmen DeFalco. We had Mr. O'Rourke and Mr. Norlen go to the courthouse to observe a third suspect that day, but the courtroom was very crowded, and they missed him. Det. DeFalco and I arrested Melvin Greeny, 22 years, of Manhattan and Harold Rossman of Vernon, New York when they went into the hallway of the Bronx County Courthouse. Detectives of the Bronx D.A.'s staff assisted us, and no one was injured in the crowded courthouse. We took them to the precinct just north of Yankee Stadium for booking and then returned to our headquarters with them. On Thursday, November 13, 1969, a felony hearing was requested by the defendant's attorney. Mr. O'Rourke testified and identified Melvin Greeny. Assistant D.A. Orazio Bellantoni had Thomas Norlen take the stand. He asked Mr. Norlen if he could describe the man who held the gun on him. He said he could. Mr. Bellantoni asked, "Would you recognize him if you saw him again?"

Mr. Norlen said, "Yes."

Mr. Bellantoni asked, "Is he in the courtroom today?"

Mr. Norlen replied, "Yes, he's back in the third row on the end." The suspect—identified as Percy Barclay, also known as Samuel Greeny of Manhattan, New York—was asked to stand up by Mr. Bellantoni. He asked Mr. Norlen if that was the man and Mr. Norlen replied, "Yes, definitely." He was arrested by Det. DeFalco and myself as the third man in the holdup. The victims did not see him in the Bronx County Courthouse, because he ducked in and out of the courtroom. He believed that he was not identified by the victims, so he took a chance and came to the hearing. Mr. Norlen then identified Harold Rossman as the man who emptied the cash registers. The case was sent to the grand jury and the three defendants were indicted by the grand jury on two counts of first degree robbery, and one count each of second degree assault, petit larceny, second and third degree grand larceny, and possession of a weapon, and possession of a dangerous instrument and appliance.

I submitted PTL. Frank Morallo's name and a description of the work he had done on the sketches to the Westchester County Detectives Association for consideration for a special commendation, which he received. The time he spent on the sketches and their accuracy was tremendous. In November of 1969, I conducted an investigation and surveillance of a large-scale policy (numbers) operation at the GM Plant. I had found an area where I could observe the GM parking lot below. The D.A.'s office joined in the investigation with Senior Investigator John McKean and Investigator Ronald Jordan participating. A search warrant would be obtained by me. The main difference between a search warrant and an arrest warrant in an investigation is that with a search warrant you have to get a person named in the warrant with the items named (gambling records) and with an arrest warrant an undercover officer would have placed the bets with the suspect and you just had to arrest him. The search warrant is good for ten days.

After obtaining the search warrant, we observed the operation and noticed several things that weren't right. A marked police car, on certain days, would drive through the lot before the suspect would drive into the lot and pick up all of the day's work (policy bets). Everyone was not on the same page, so to speak, maybe not the team either. Many days went by on the search warrant without us taking action because we had to be sure we had the suspect in possession of the gambling records. With only a day or two to go on the search warrant, I had another problem. Pat was about to give birth to our first child.

On the evening of December 18, 1969, she told me it was time, so we left our apartment in Dobbs Ferry for Phelps Memorial Hospital in North Tarrytown. Pat was having a difficult time and morning came without the baby being delivered. Later in the morning, I asked one of the doctors how long it would be and he stated, "At least 45 minutes." I knew that we had to execute the search warrant that morning. I joined the D.'s investigators and Detective DeFalco, and we set up our surveillance. The suspect drove into the lot and parked near the escalator for the plant. The work was given to him, and we set into motion our plan. As the suspect was driving up the ramp out of the lot, he was stopped by the Chief, Basil Garzia, Sr. Inv. John McKean, and Inv. Ron Jordan. The suspect threw the policy slips to the railroad tracks, 60 feet below the ramp. Detective Carmen DeFalco and I observed this and ran down and recovered them. Anthony Torino, 43 years, of Yonkers, New York, was arrested and charged with promoting gambling first degree, a felony and possession of gambling records first degree, a felony.

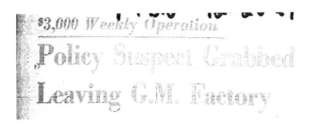

$3,000 Weekly Operation
Policy Suspect Grabbed
Leaving G.M. Factory

The suspect was taken to headquarters for booking. I then left for the hospital. Pat had not given birth yet. At 12:44 p.m., she gave birth to our son, Todd. A son. God, was I happy! The doctors had to give her extra medication, and she was still not awake. The doctor told me to try to wake her up. After a while, she awakened. Her father came up to the hospital because her mother realized it had been too long. I returned to headquarters to help with the count of the gambling records.

Jack McKean, who had returned to the D.A.'s office, called me, and asked, "What did you have?"

I told him it was a felony.

He replied, "No. A boy or a girl?"

I said, "A boy. Everyone is okay." He was happy too. I always had my priorities in life, God, my family, and my profession, but I had them in reverse order. My profession first and God and family second or third. I left to go back to the hospital to see my wife and new son. I thought of us leaving to go to the hospital the night before and finding a flat on the car and taking the older vehicle to the hospital, the long night, Pat delivering a son and putting an organized crime figure in jail in between. I said a prayer and thanked Our Blessed Mother for everything turning out alright. Would I get my son Todd a hockey stick, a football, or a baseball glove first?

On January 16, 1970, at approximately 6:20 p.m., Detective DeFalco and I, along with investigators of the Westchester County Sheriff's Department, arrested Stanley D. Farris, 24 years, on two counts of a sale of a dangerous drug, possession of a hypodermic instrument. The drug sold was heroin. He also had a cutting agent for cutting heroin in his possession. He was arrested on a sealed indictment from the grand jury for selling to an undercover officer. He cooperated and then agreed to enter a drug program.

Detective DeFalco and I gave a drug seminar for the youth of the community during the month of January 1970.

I was contacted by Daniel Sagarin, the Assistant United States Attorney for the U.S. Department of Justice in Connecticut and asked to testify in Connecticut in reference to the arrests of the bank robbers, Ralph Mossuli, Edward Reese, and William Bertch that we had arrested on May 8, 1969. The U.S. Attorney told me that Ralph Mossuli, supposedly the toughest of the group, had agreed to testify. He added that William Bertch, who had thanked me for not killing him, was missing and assumed dead, possibly because the group thought he was the weakest link and might cooperate with the authorities. He told me that the courtroom would represent a who's who of bank robbers, letting Mossuli know flat that they were aware of him cooperating. When I testified, I glance out around the courtroom and was amazed at seeing the room filled with bank robbers. The following commendation was sent to my chief of police on January 27, 1970.

"Dear Chief, as you are probably aware Detective Richard Spota testified on behalf of the United States Government in a case resulting from an attempted bank robbery and high speed chase of three individuals. These three individuals, Ralph Mossuli, Edward Reese, and William Bertch were part of a notorious bank robbery ring which operated in the State of Connecticut as well as in surrounding states. Of the three individuals, Mr. Mossuli has since become a cooperative witness in this and several other cases, Mr. Bertch is missing and presumed dead, and Mr. Reese has been convicted on the federal charges arising out of this arrest. In addition, he is presently on trial in another bank robbery case. With this background, I should like to especially commend the actions of Detective Richard Spota which were instrumental in apprehending Mr. Reese. Moreover, Detective Spota's candid and forthright testimony was a credit to your entire police department and in my opinion, a significant factor leading to Mr. Reese's conviction.

Perhaps, more importantly, the efforts of Detective Spota and your department showed how important local and federal cooperation is in apprehending dangerous individuals. We thank you for making Detective Spota available to us.

Sincerely, Stewart H. Jones, United States Attorney, By J. Daniel Sagarin, Assistant United States Attorney."

On March 5, 1970, John F. Malone, assistant director in charge of the New York office of the F.B.I. and State Police Superintendent, William E. Kirwin Jr. announced the arrest of eleven men including four top New York State Police Officers on charges of bribery and interstate gambling involving reputed gambling enterprises in metropolitan New York as well as Westchester and Rockland counties. The gambling combine, a 650 million dollar a year operation was engaged in illegal horse and sports betting activity, Mr. Malone stated. The Governor Nelson A. Rockefeller was kept fully advised of the investigation. The key figures arrested were a reputed capo in the Genovese Crime Family and owner of three Westchester garbage hauling firms, who allegedly supplied the ring with money to finance its operation, and the head of the operation, of North Tarrytown, New York. Both of them were under federal charges in another case of bribing Internal Revenue Service agents. The four state troopers arrested were a reputed Lieutenant of Tappan, who had been with the State Police since 1958, a Sr. Investigator of Yonkers, New York, one of the top men in the BCI, a Sr. Investigator from Dobbs Ferry who had been in the BCI since 1957, and an 18-year veteran formerly of Troop K in Westchester County. Superintendent William Kirwin Jr. said bitterly of his four troopers, "They acted in the role of protector." In turn, all four enjoyed free vacations to Puerto Rico, autos, tickets to sporting events, free meals, and cash. He further stated that Sr. Inv. Joseph F. Colligan proved the hero of the investigation, infiltrating the ring and accepting $1,000 a month from Novare. A wire room was located in the Ramapo area which was estimated to handle $30,000 daily in bets. However, he added that only a fifth of the combined operation was in Rockland, the remainder being in Westchester. The F.B.I. was involved because interstate gambling was involved. The F.B.I. stated that one of the investigators received a Cadillac for turning over license plate numbers of police trying to investigate the operation. The state police should be commended for rooting out the corruption. I had admired the state police before this investigation, and I admired them more at this time.

United States Department of Justice

UNITED STATES ATTORNEY
DISTRICT OF CONNECTICUT
NEW HAVEN 06500

January 27, 1970

Mr. John Jandrucko
Chief of Police
Police Department
North Tarrytown, New York

Dear Chief Jandrucko:

As you are probably aware recently Detective Richard
Spota testified on behalf of the United States Government in a
case resulting from an attempted bank robbery and high-speed chase
of three individuals. These three individuals
were part of a notorious bank
robbery ring which operated in the State of Connecticut as well
as in surrounding states. Of the three individuals Mr. Maselli
has since become a cooperative witness in this and several other
cases, Mr. Albrecht is missing and assumed dead and Mr. Reed has
been convicted on the federal charges arising out of this arrest.
In addition he is presently on trial in another bank robbery case.

With this background I should like to especially commend the actions of Detective Richard Spota which were instrumental in apprehending Mr. Reed. Moreover Detective Spota's
candid and forthright testimony was a credit to your entire
police department and in my opinion was a significant factor
leading to Mr. Reed's conviction.

Perhaps more importantly the efforts of Detective Spota
and your department showed how important local and federal cooperation is in apprehending dangerous individuals.

We thank you for making Detective Spota available
to us.

Sincerely yours,

Stewart H. Jones
United States Attorney

By J. Daniel Sagarin
Assistant United States Attorney

JDS/mp

51

In the spring of 1970, I had an investigation and surveillance of a suspected heroin dealer. It is not always possible to have an undercover officer make buys from a pusher. There are many reasons for this. However, I was able to get a search warrant from Judge John B. Whalen. At 9:45 p.m., Patrolman Ted Wydskida, Patrolman John Doran, and I stopped and searched William Dossel, 23, of Tarrytown, New York, on Francis Street. We searched the person and the vehicle and came up with 181 bags of heroin. We arrested Wayne Gill as he was about to buy heroin. He was charged with loitering for the purpose of using drugs. Dossel was charged with felony possession of heroin and held on $10,000 bail.

In June 1970, the three men we had arrested for the armed robbery of the Bridge View Tavern on September 5, 1969, Percy Barkley a.k.a. Samuel Green, of Manhattan, Melvin Greeny and Harold Rossman had been convicted of all charges and were sentenced to up to 15 years imprisonment by County Court Judge George Burchell.

One week after the aforementioned sentencing, on Friday, June 19, 1970, at 10:25 a.m., I heard the desk officer Patrolman DiFelice say that the Bridge View Tavern was being held up. I thought they were pulling my leg at first. I ran out of the door to headquarters and jumped into the police car. Patrolman Fred Galella jumped in as I was making a U-turn and heading toward GM. This was the GM morning break at the plant. The traffic was almost at a standstill. I drove up on the sidewalk at one point and got to the Bridge View Tavern, taking up a position on the south side of Hudson Street with Patrolman Galella. Patrolman Butkovich drove to Hudson Street. The chief and Patrolman Lawlor also arrived. Thomas Norlen, the proprietor, had returned from the bank with money for the day's business. He observed through the window, his bartender with his hands in the air. Realizing a holdup was in progress, he had called headquarters from a police call box on Beekman Avenue near Hudson Street opposite GM. Two men had been sitting at the bar for approximately half an hour. This was check cashing and payday. One of the men went into the kitchen and held a gun to the chef, Mrs. Julia Slagle. Also in the kitchen were Mrs. Norlen and her niece, Mrs. Ellen Rochelle, who was visiting and had her baby with her. The women were marched out into the main barroom by the gunmen. A shot was fired into the ceiling and it was announced to the approximately twenty customers, "This is a holdup. Everybody down on the floor." They mistook one of the customers for the owner and demanded the key for the money. Mrs. Norlen, fearing the man would be injured, said that she had the key and went to the safe, opened it, and handed over the money. One of the men stuffed bills into an attaché case. The other stuffed money under his shirt. The man with the attaché case asked Mrs. Norlen, "Where's the rest of the money?"

She stated, "It's still at the bank. Her husband hasn't gotten it." At that point they heard the sirens of police cars. Mrs. Norlen told him not to go out the front.

Go out the back. They had a car pointed in the wrong direction on Hudson Street (one-way street) for a getaway so out the back door they went. Mrs. Norlen slammed the rear door shut. But the back door was in fact a way to get to the rooming house upstairs and not to the street. She had trapped them, and they ran up to the second floor. One of the robbers was spotted above where Patrolman Fred Galella and I were positioned by the detective's car. At that point, Mrs. Norlen came running out a side door between us and the robbers, screaming that the baby was outside in the carriage in the rear. I yelled for her to drop down and roll toward the wall, getting her out of the line of fire. I told the one robber above us, "Hold it, drop the gun or I'll shoot!" He obeyed and came downstairs and was grabbed by Patrolman Butkovich and others. The other man came to me window and hollered, "I give up!" I told Fred Galella to cover me, as I ran upstairs and got him with the attaché case. I had him against a wall, asking him where the third person was. There was a rooming house, rental rooms behind me, and I was worried that I'd be shot in the back.

He said, "You got us. There's no one else." The attaché case opened with the money dropping out. Chief Jandruoko came up the stairs at this point. We took him in. The baby in the carriage was downstairs, outside of the back door, and was okay. Patrolman DiFelice at headquarters had notified Tarrytown P.D., they responded and would have prevented an escape south, and Mt. Pleasant P.D. came into the village to block off Bedford Road and Broadway for an escape. Great backups from both departments. Among the arrested were Ronald Bozeman, and Burnell Harris, both from the Bronx. After it was over, I thanked Fred Galella for watching my back. Tom Norlen said, "That's it. No more. Two is too much."

I said, "I think I have to get a better weapon than my snub nose Detective Special, so I can at least be on even footing with these people."

We continued to make arrests for the sale of dangerous drugs and for organized crime (gambling). In the summer of 1970, I had been on the sergeant's list for four years. I had hoped to get promoted to detective sergeant, a move that would only increase my salary $500 and with no cost of replacing me, because I would remain in the detective bureau. However, the list which was good for four years was allowed to run out. A friend of mine, Father Menna, who had married Pat and me in 1966, had a parish in Massachusetts. His family was from and lived in North Tarrytown, so that we would meet when he came home. I would ask him if God considered organized crime a sin. Why would he allow these people to run so much of this world?

On September 1, 1970, a call had been received from Sgt. Vanier of the DeKalb County Police Department, Decatur, Georgia that one Harold Tallon, male, black, was wanted by that police department for armed robbery. Tallon, along with two others, had held up five police officers, tied them up, pistol whipped two of them and took two revolvers. The subject was considered armed and dangerous. The subject had made a remark that he would not be taken alive. He might be visiting an aunt and possibly attending a funeral in the area. On September 2, we received a warrant from Sgt. Vamer on Tallon. Investigation revealed that a subject similar in name and date of birth was applying for a job at General Motors. GM Chief of Security, Tom Leo, provided us with information. In the afternoon of September 5, 1970, five of us went to the GM Plant. Tallon was to be interviewed by the personnel department at 3:00 p.m.

2 Grabbed In Tavern Holdup

All GM personnel were sent out of the area of the interview room. Chief Jandrucko and Sgt. Garzia were in plain clothes outside of the office. Patrolman Thomas Smith was in the room, acting as a laborer being interviewed. Detective DeFalco and I acted as interviewing personnel. At approximately 3 p.m., Thomas came to the desk to announce his name and was brought to the interview room. Tallon was seized by us after a brief struggle and brought to headquarters for booking (arrest procedures). Georgia authorities were notified and now have gone through extradition proceedings to bring him back to Georgia. The Georgia authorities commended us.

On September 2, 1970, I received the second place Westchester Rockland Newspapers Police Honor Award for the capture of the two persons holding up the Bridge View Tavern (the second robbery of the tavern). Patrolman Fred Galella, Vincent Butkovich, Mario DiFelice, and Joseph Lawlor also received the award.

We had been working for months on the sale of dangerous drugs in the area. The investigations would overlap so that we would be working with Detective Barney Parra and the Tarrytown Police Department and with the undercover officers of the Westchester County Sheriff's Department under Sheriff Daniel F. McMahon. All three departments met early in the morning of September 10, 1970, armed with arrest warrants as a result of sealed indictments for sales from the grand jury and search warrants for the pusher's person, home, and vehicles; Detective DeFalco and I, along with Sgt. Variano, Patrolman Andres, Patrolman Hayward, Patrolman Butkovich, Patrolman Galella, Patrolman Porteous, and Tarrytown.

Detectives Lipsky, Parra, and men from their department met to conduct a raid. We raided six apartments in the area and arrested six pushers for sale and possession of dangerous drugs. One apartment on Valley Street resulted in the seizure of 56 bags of heroin. An apartment on Clinton Street that I raided had enough drugs, narcotic instruments, and guns/rifles to warrant a van to remove the evidence. In all, 95 bags of heroin were seized in the morning raids. Many of the officers stayed on with us through the night when we again set up raids. This time, the target was the GM Plant. GM officials had cooperated with us, throughout the investigation. At the GM Plant, we arrested five pushers for sales and possession of dangerous drugs. Charles Duoise, 30, of New York City, was charged with three counts of sale and three counts of possession of heroin. He had three bags of heroin in his possession at the time of the raid. Carlos Marez, 28, of the Bronx, was charged with two counts of sale and two counts of possession of cocaine. Antonio Penier, 24, of the Bronx, was arrested on two counts of sale and possession of marijuana.

6 G.M. Employes

9-11-1970

Raids Nab 11 As Pushers

95 Bags Of Heroin Seized By Agents

Praises Heaped On Local Police

12th Grabbed At G.M. In Drugs Crackdown

We would make another two arrests before this was concluded. The sales of some of those arrested were not only to GM employees, but to persons who lived in the area of the GM Plant. Excellent police work by all of those involved.

Back to working on organized crime (gambling investigations). One evening, my mom called me. She said that a man had just phoned her and stated, "If your son sees the light, nothing will happen to you." I told her that I would take care of it, not to worry. Brave men, threatening a widow who lives alone.

My brother, George, would receive telephone calls in office, stating that his sister-in-law was laid out at a certain funeral parlor. He would be concerned because that funeral parlor was where our father and other relatives had been laid out. I'd tell him I was working on a case, and he would understand. The next day, after the call to Mom, I came into work. I drove to where a collector (runner) was making his rounds. At about 6'1" he was bigger than me. I picked him up and slammed him into the wall. I told him to go back and tell Pete (the head of gambling in Westchester and Rockland) that if they ever bother my family again, I would kill every f***ing one of them. A very short period of time went by that day before two uniformed officers told the chief that there was a complaint against me by this upstanding citizen. He called me in and told me what had been reported. I told him what happened and why. I didn't hear any more of the complaint after that day.

I attended the Federal Bureau of Narcotics and Dangerous Drugs School held at the New York City Police Academy from October 25 to October 29, 1970.

On December 11, 1970, Lt. John Pankovic, Detective Carmen DeFalco, and I arrested three members of the United Auto Workers, Local 664 on charges of coercion after they allegedly threatened to blow up the local union headquarters at 193 Beekman Avenue when they were denied its use for a private meeting. The UAW president, Raymond Calore, stated that the rank and file group that wanted to use the, hall was a "Caucus group." He said that such a group has no right to use the hall on its own. This must be done through the union representative, who would then conduct the meeting. The UAW president issued the following statement, "UAW Local 664, through its officers and representatives, have filed charges in, civil court against three members of the Rank and File Committee. The charges filed by Local 664 include coercion and intimidation, including threats of violence. In a free and democratic society and in a free and democratic union, there is room for differences of opinion, freedom of expression, and freedom of political choice. We will not tolerate any violation of these freedoms, and we will not permit violation or threats to become a way of life in our society or in our union. The officers do not like the position our union was forced to take. However, under the circumstances, we have an obligation to all our members to eliminate the elements of fear and violence from our lives and our union activities." Mr. Calore added that members of the Rank and File Committee made threats last week after they were told they could not use the union hall for the purpose of a mass meeting in support of a man who had been discharged by the company. He added that rallies and mass meetings in support of a discharged employee are improper. "We have a grievance procedure under our contract, which must be followed."

At the regular meeting of the Westchester County Detective Association at the end of 1970, I was elected first Vice President of the Association for 1971.

The Tarrytown and North Tarrytown Detective Bureaus, along with the Westchester County Sheriff's Department concluded a three and a half month investigation into a gambling ring that was operating in the Tarrytown-North

Tarrytown area. When we were able to infiltrate the operation with undercover officers, they were able to place bets. On Friday, January 8, 1971, at approximately 1:30 p.m., we arrested nine persons in what Sheriff Daniel F. McMahon stated was a significant and major strike at on important gambling operation in our country. He estimated that the annual take was in the multi-millions. Arrested by the three departments were Henry Bellini, 37 years, arrested at the Knotty Pine Tavern, North Tarrytown charged with 18 counts of promoting gambling, second degree, one count of possession of gambling records, second degree, and one count of possession of a dangerous weapon, a .38 caliber revolver and ammunition, Robert Gill, Tarrytown, nine counts of second degree promoting of gambling, Donny Sachelli, 57 years, of Yonkers, New York, six counts of promoting gambling, second degree, Edith Faust of Ossining, four counts of promoting gambling, second degree, Dominick Satelli, 47, of Ossining, New York, two counts of second degree promoting of gambling and one count of second degree possession of gambling records. Satelli was arrested at the GM Plant. Caesar Forte, 50, of North Tarrytown, one count of promoting gambling, second degree and one count of possession of gambling records, second degree. Forte was arrested by us at the GM Plant and taken to his residence in North Tarrytown where a search warrant was executed, Charles Johnson, 59, of 20 Ross Street, White Plains was charged with one count of second degree possession of gambling records and one count of loitering for the purpose of gambling. Joseph Perry, 62, of Tarrytown, New York, was charged with one count of second degree possession of gambling records and one count of loitering for the purpose of promoting gambling. George Collins, 51, of North Tarrytown, was charged with one count of second degree possession of gambling records and one count of loitering for the purpose of promoting gambling.

We continued to make arrests for the sale and possession of dangerous drugs. Again, whenever possible, purchases were made from the pushers. Various apartments were raided and drugs, heroin, methadone, marijuana, seconal, syringes, needles, and other related drug paraphernalia were seized.

In April 1971, I traded in my snub nose Detective Special for a Smith & Wesson 9-mm model, 39 automatic. It holds eight rounds in the clip and one in the chamber. It is very accurate and dependable. Police officers should have weapons that are at least as good as those of the criminals.

Our lease was up on our three and a half room apartment in Dobbs Ferry. With three of us, we would need more space. We moved to a five-room apartment in the Van Tassel Apartments, North Tarrytown. It was off Pocantico Street and was a fifth floor walk-up. My brother George said that we would never have a heart attack with all that walking.

On April 15, 1971 I assisted the State Police and Investigators of the D.A.'s office in a gambling, and loan sharking raid in Westchester County, Rockland

County, Orange and Bronx Counties. Seventeen people were arrested in what was described as a ten million dollar a year operation. In North Tarrytown, we raided and arrested Vincent Anthony Leblanc, 43 years of age. He was charged with possession of gambling records and two illegal weapons, a .25 caliber automatic and a .38 caliber revolver. The state police, D.A.'s Investigators, the chief, and I found more than $4,000 in small bills in shopping bags that were folded in an orderly pile. Change was removed in a bucket. Policy slips were found as was a drawer filled to overflowing with money. Bets were received at this location from a wire room across the Hudson River in Rockland County.

In the evening of April 15, 1971, we had a gambling raid at the GM Plant. We used our own undercover personnel to place bets in an investigation that lasted several weeks. Warrants were issued by Judge John B. Whalen. Robert Epstein, 42 years of age, of New York City, was arrested.

The section of the Van Tassel Apartments that we had moved to was G. It was opposite the Morse School and playground. Walking up from the ground floor, there were two apartments on each floor. Living on the fourth floor to the left underneath our fifth floor apartment was Rita Hernandez and her son, Richard (Ricky) Hernandez. Ricky graduated from Sleepy Hollow High School in North Tarrytown in June 1971. He was a member of the wrestling team before graduating. Many times, when I would be coming home or leaving our building I would see Ricky playing basketball at Morse School. He would be wearing his jeans and a red bandanna. He worked at the Malloy Battery Company in North Tarrytown. Ricky and his mother were close. They were really nice people. On the morning of August 10, 1971, his mother attempted to awaken him to go to work. He was moaning and vomiting. Rita Hernandez called police headquarters for help. Ricky was rushed to Phelps Memorial Hospital. He was pronounced dead at 7:55 a.m. His lungs were flooded, and he suffocated. I'll never forget how he looked in the emergency room of the hospital. His mother was devastated. He was her only child. I would find out from the medical examiner that he died from an overdose of methadone. Ricky was a fine young man. He was not a regular drug user or addict. His system could not tolerate the methadone. I was depressed. I kept saying to myself, "We've put away so many drug pushers. We're giving so many seminars on the dangers of drugs. How did this get by me?" Ricky had been home the previous night and kissed his mother before going to bed.

He had some friends over. I started to interview them. I promised his mother I would find the person responsible for Ricky's death. Usually when I was investigating a serious crime, people would hesitate to cooperate, but not in this case. I would meet with D.A. Carl Vergari's staff on the case. I was totally and completely consumed with finding the person or persons responsible for Ricky's death. Every time I walked up to our fifth floor apartment, I would look at the door to Ricky's apartment. After weeks of investigating, I knew that the methadone in liquid form was sold to Ricky for $20. Had Ricky been a hard-core drug user, he would have lived. But because he was not, his system could not handle the 120 milligrams. I had gathered the evidence of who sold the drug to him, where it was sold, why it was sold, and for how much. I had witnesses who were willing to testify for me. In meeting with the D.A.'s staff during the entire investigation, I had told them that I wanted a charge of homicide in addition to the sale and possession of a dangerous drug. I was told this had never been done before.

All I could think of were the words of Bobby Kennedy, *"Some men see things as they are and say why. I dream of things that never were and say, why not."* Chief Assistant D.A. Thomas Facelle told me they wanted me to get a confession. I had arrested the pusher several times for drug charges and for attempted grand larceny and criminal possession of a forged instrument at the First National Bank. I said to myself, "He will never give me a confession." I was driving down the New York State Thruway on my way to the Ridge Hill Rehabilitation Center off the Thruway in Yonkers, New York, to try to get a statement from Lawrence Briggs, 23 years of age, for selling the methadone to Ricky. As I was driving down the thruway, I did what I always did when I didn't know how to achieve something. I said a Hail Mary. I asked Our Blessed Mother to ask her son to help me. Too many kids were dying of drug overdoses. Then I said, "I know I'm asking for the impossible, but I need your help." When I arrived at the center, I was taken to a room where I could interview the suspect. He reacted about how I had expected him to. But he said that if I showed him the medical examiner's report that he might give me a statement.

He wanted to see what drug was listed as the cause of death. He didn't say that, but that is what he wanted to know. I had just received the medical examiner's report, and I had it in the case file with me. The M.E. had mistakenly issued a wrong cause of death. He had stated on his report that the cause of death was intravenous narcotism. That would have meant that Ricky had died from an overdose of heroin. The M.E. was going to issue a new report. I took the report out of the case file and gave it to Briggs to read. After reading it, he seemed relieved.

He gave me a statement that he had given Ricky a five-ounce container of orange juice. That's what methadone came in. He signed the statement. As I left and started to drive back up the thruway, I looked up and said, "Forgive me, Dear Jesus, for thinking that anything is impossible with you." God had really humbled me that day. I could also visualize down the line at a hearing, the defendant's attorney accusing me of having a false M.E. report. What would I do? I'd tell it exactly as it happened. I got back to the D.A.'s office. A date was set to testify before the grand jury. Rita Hernandez would have to testify, along with myself and witnesses. One witness was a minor named Michael. He was a student at Sleepy Hollow High School, a clean-cut friend of Ricky's who would testify for me.

On the morning of the grand jury, Sr. Asst. D.A. James Demetriou of the Grand Jury Bureau told me that we would present evidence for a sale and possession of a dangerous drug but not for the homicide. I told him I wanted to go for the homicide. He talked with D.A. Carl Vergari who said it would be up to the grand jury. After the grand jury proceeding, I waited with Rita Hernandez, Michael Giuisti, and other witnesses. When I was told that indictment was for manslaughter second degree, felony sale, and possession of a dangerous drug, I told Rita Hernandez. She hugged me and cried. I told her that long after we are gone from this world they will always remember Ricky. We all went out for lunch. I remember telling Michael Giuisti how proud I was of him. I kidded him that he still could only have a soda with lunch, because of his age.

Late in the evening of Friday, September 3, 1971, Chief Jandrucko drove down to the Ridge Hill Rehabilitation Center off the Thruway in Yonkers. We arrested Lawrence Briggs for manslaughter second degree, felony possession, and sale of a dangerous drug in the drug overdose of Ricky Hernandez. We brought him back to police headquarters. He was arraigned before Judge John B. Whalen and bail was set at $25,000. In the event that bail was posted, we had a detainer to return him to the Ridge Hill Center. District Attorney Carl Vergari released a statement that, "The grand jury indictment is believed to be the first of its kind, stemming from a drug overdose case." The second-degree manslaughter charge is made in killings caused by "reckless conduct" without the specific intent to take a life. The charge carries a maximum of 15 years in prison on conviction. Briggs was accused of giving Richard Hernandez, 18, a quantity of methadone in liquid form on August 9. The "gift" was to make up for cheating Hernandez on a sale of the drug the day before, the D.A. stated. Briggs had been enrolled in a methadone treatment program for heroin addiction.

In November 1971, I went to the Manhattan Federal Courtroom of Federal Judge Irving Cooper, where the trial often defendants arrested on March 5, 1970, for running a 650 million dollar, 21-year gambling operation in Westchester and Rockland counties was taking place. The reputed Capo of the Genovese Crime Family, Nicholas Ronetti, was represented by Attorney Roy M. Cohn. His top gambling man, Peter Vitchelli, had pled guilty and was sentenced to three years in Federal Prison. The four state policemen indicted in the case were there along with six other defendants and their attorneys. Court had started when I entered the courtroom, so I sat down.

Apparently, I had been noticed and the defendants' attorneys were asking the judge to have me removed from the courtroom. Ronetti's wife asked him which one was Det. Spota, and he looked at me and nodded. So much for anonymity. If I was going to testify, I would have to leave the courtroom, but I was not, so I could stay.

I was there to meet with the prosecutor, Daniel Hollman, Chief of the U.S. Organized Crime Task Force and State Police Lt. Joseph Colligan who had infiltrated the operation. Lt. Colligan was on the stand, testifying. I met with them in private during recess. The U.S. Attorney told me that I made his day by upsetting the defense attorneys. All of the key figures either plead guilty or were found guilty after trial. The Supreme Court would refuse the appeals of the group. Did this mean that we didn't have to worry about police protecting organized crime? Of course not. But I would hate to think of how much more powerful they would be if this case were not broken.

On November 18, 1971, at the November meeting of the Westchester County Detectives Association, I was elected President of the Association for 1972. We had approximately 350 members from over 40 police departments in Westchester County. I had become a member of the Association in 1968 and had been Secretary and Vice President that year. The Association is a close-knit group that exchanges information and assistance to fellow members. The dedication, professionalism, and expertise of the membership is unequaled. There were so many members that had helped me on numerous investigations. I felt very humble and proud to be elected their president.

On Saturday, November 20, 1971, at 7:12 a.m., Mrs. Gertrude Giusti called police headquarters, requesting assistance for her son, Michael. The North Tarrytown Ambulance Corps and police responded. Michael was unconscious when he arrived at the emergency room of Phelps Memorial Hospital. He was pronounced dead at 8:15 a.m. When I observed him at the hospital, I recognized the same things that I had seen in Ricky Hernandez. It would be awhile before the medical examiner made a report on the cause of death, but I believed I knew what it would be. Michael was 16 on October 12 of that year. I went to talk with his parents, Michael and Gertrude Giusti, at their home. I kept saying to myself, "No, not again, not Michael." His parents asked me if someone had done this to him because he testified in the Ricky Hernandez case.

I said, "No, I don't think so." I promised them I would find out who was responsible and that I would arrest the person. After getting as much information as possible, I left their house. To say I was depressed would have been an understatement. We had continued to arrest the drug pushers. We had continued to give drug seminars to every group that would listen to us. I kept thinking back to having lunch with Michael in September. Like Ricky, he was a good, decent young man who was not a hardcore drug user and that is why he was dead. If he had been a user, his system would have tolerated the methadone that I suspected in his death. I remember telling him that I wouldn't lie and say that everyone who smoked pot would end up using heroin but that every person that I knew that was on heroin started on pot. Why would he have drunk the orange juice with methadone? To experiment? I really felt like a failure.

61

I wanted to solve the case and then I just didn't know. I had told his parents that I would get the person responsible though I had very little information. But I did know one thing. A seller whose drugs caused a death could now be charged with a homicide. Det. Carmen DeFalco and I knew what would be needed to secure a homicide indictment, because we had Ricky Hernandez's case as the blueprint. We would receive calls daily from detectives who were working on their overdoses who would ask how the indictment had been obtained. No matter how busy we were, we always made time to supply that information. We continued to interview people who we believed had information on Michael's death. During the Christmas holiday season when I would go home to get a little sleep, I would walk up past the door of Rita Hernandez's apartment and think of how I would feel if Todd, who was two on December 19, had died. I knew how badly she felt. By now, Det. De Falco and I knew who had sold the methadone to Michael. The medical Examiner's report had, of course, stated the cause of death to be methadone. We continued to meet with D.A. Carl Vergari's staff. We would get advice from Chief Asst. D.A. Thomas Facelle on where we were and what additional evidence would be needed. Again, unlike organized crime investigations when people would tend not to cooperate, we did have people cooperating in this case. By the end of January 1972, we had gathered almost enough evidence.

On February 1, 1972, Det. DeFalco and I had obtained a warrant of arrest from Judge John B. Whalen. On February 2, 1972, we arrested Lawrence Briggs of North Tarrytown, just after noon-time. He was charged with criminal sale, second degree, and possession of a dangerous drug, fourth degree. He was held on $30,000 bail. The following Tuesday, Lawrence Briggs was indicted on charges of criminally negligent homicide; criminal sale of a dangerous drug, second degree; and criminal possession of a dangerous drug, fourth degree. Briggs allegedly sold a bottle containing 100 milligrams of methadone for $7.00 to Michael Giusti at 6:30 p.m. on November 9, 1971.

Youth Faces Manslaughter Charge In Methadone Overdose Death Here

The defendant was, at that time, a patient of the methadone maintenance treatment program at Grasslands Hospital. This was now the fourth case resulting in a homicide indictment of a seller whose drugs caused a death. The first was in the Ricky Hernandez case, September 3, 1971. In that landmark case, Lawrence Right had plead guilty to criminally negligent homicide and misdemeanor drug possession charges. On December 9, 1971, Lawrence Right was sentenced to three years in state prison.

During 1971, there had been some 15 unsolved burglaries in the Philipse Manor and Sleepy Hollow Manor sections of the community. Det. DeFalco and I had checked a police teletype from the New Castle Police on December 31, 1971. The suspect, William Watkins, 21, a.k.a. Elmo and Jefferson Watkins. He had been in possession of a man's ring and other jewelry in addition to other items. Positive identification of a man's ring was made by the owner whose house had been burglarized in our community. Other residents identified Caribbean coins taken from their home. Enough evidence was obtained to connect Watkins with four additional burglaries committed here in 1971. The suspect's mode of operation would earn him the nickname of the "Train Burglar." We found out that there was a reason the police would not observe Watkins entering the community. He would take a train to a residential area and choose a house to burglarize. He then rang the doorbell and, if someone answered, he would explain that he was selling magazines to further his education. If no one was at home, he burglarized the house and returned to the train station where he got on the next train. Watkins was now being held at the Westchester County Jail. We placed detainers on him at the jail and continued to investigate him in connection with other burglaries in the area.

After becoming President of the Westchester County Detectives Association in 1972, I realized that we had to take action in reference to the county's methadone program. There were nine methadone clinics in Westchester County. There were nine deaths in 1971 that were the result of methadone overdoses. Ricky Hernandez and Michael Giusti were two of them. It was a giant step forward that we could now charge a seller whose drugs had caused a death with homicide, but as hard as we worked on drug cases, with our close proximity to the New York City drug suppliers, we still had a major problem. That problem was the heroin addicts that were on the methadone program and were being given take-home doses. This created a flourishing methadone black market. The addicts who took methadone had built up a tolerance to the drug. No matter how many drug classes and seminars we continued to give, we could not take a chance that a youngster who tried marijuana would try and experiment with methadone.

County Detectives 'Unanimously' Support 7-Day Methadone Program

This was a death sentence. The County Methadone Clinics in some cases were allowing addicts to come in four days a week and then give them take-home doses for the remaining three days. This is where the methadone was being sold by the addicts. The proposal that I put forth to the membership was to have seven-day programs of methadone with no take-home doses. The membership of 350 detectives and investigators strongly supported the proposal. Dr. Edward Gordon,

Director of the Westchester Methadone Project, did not feel that there should be no take-home doses. There would be considerable amount of additional funding needed for this. Both he and County Executive Edwin Michaelian agreed that not affording a responsible patient the chance to come into the clinic fewer days a week after a several month period would destroy the rehabilitative process. We could understand their position, but we disagreed because of the deaths that had occurred and the deaths that we were certain would occur. Our only interest was to save lives. We had to go to the public with our proposal. We went to the Westchester Rockland Newspapers and on the radio. Radio station WFAS and several other stations allowed me to put the proposal of the Westchester County Detectives Association on the air and explain why we were doing this. The Westchester Rockland Newspaper also carried our plea. They did an investigation of the methadone program and revealed a flourishing methadone black market in Westchester County. County Executive Edwin Michaelian agreed to attend our next meeting to discuss the problem. He seemed very sincere at the meeting and let us explain why we were trying to change the system. Shortly after this meeting, he announced that eight of the nine clinics were on a seven-day-a-week basis and that the ninth at Grasslands would start a seven-day-a-week schedule on April 15. A lot of credit must go to the parents of youngsters who had died trying methadone. They had written letters to the public officials, telling them of their loss and backing our proposal.

On March 22, 1972, Det. DeFalco, Det. Parra from Tarrytown P.D. and I were investigating the theft of equipment and souvenirs from the Sleepy Hollow High School Store. I had received some information that the stolen property might be in the auditorium of the school. I had climbed up a ladder in the wings of the auditorium above the stage area. I observed something red-colored at the highest point. As students from the Drama Club waited to start their dress rehearsal of "Murder in a Nunnery," Det. Parra and I were clambering around the ceiling fixtures in the darkened backstage area. We found bundles of jackets, book bags, and many other items. We started throwing them down onto the stage prop bed where Det. DeFalco retrieved them. We looked like we were doing aerial acrobatics on the railings and platforms. We recovered more items than what was reported missing. Two students, one 15 years old and one 16 years old, were charged with the theft and released to their parents, one because of age to appear in Family Court and the other, North Tarrytown Court.

On Monday, March 27, 1972, at the meeting of the North Tarrytown Board of Trustees, I was promoted to the rank of provisional Detective Sergeant. The sergeant's list that I was on ran out in the summer of 1970. It was first mentioned that the next Sergeant's exam would be held in September 1972, but it was later learned that the exam would not be given until the spring of 1973. When there is not a promotional list, provisional appointments may be made. I would have to finish in the top three on the next examination to keep the rank of detective sergeant. I would change some of my college classes in order to attend other classes for promotional study. I believed that you should be at the top of the promotional list. That means that people who may score higher than you should not be bypassed to get to you on the list. I knew, with my work schedule and the amount of overtime I put in that this would not be an easy task. The trustee that proposed the promotion was Demetrios Jim Caraley, a professor at Columbia University. He is one of the rare persons who ran for public office with the sole intent of making the community a better place to live in. He had no hidden agenda. He had made another proposal for a provisional sergeant at this meeting that met with resistance and was voted down. Apparently, there was a discussion of five or six of the officers leaving or asking for transfers to other departments during a six-month period. The board spoke with the public and members of the department who felt that seniority should outweigh achievement in making provisional promotions.

We had a three-week investigation and surveillance of the Golden Key Club on Clinton Street. The club was an illegal afterhours drinking and gambling operation. We used undercover officers to enter the club and observe the activity. Det. DeFalco and I had obtained a search warrant and arrest warrants. On Saturday, April 8, 1972, at approximately 3:30 a.m., 16 officers from our department raided the Golden Key Club. We arrested 13 people on a variety of charges. John Hayes, 44 years, of Ossining, New York, the proprietor of the club was charged with promoting gambling three counts, three counts of maintaining a criminal nuisance (the club), and three counts of violation of the Alcoholic Beverage Control law (operating the club without a liquor license).

Mini Vegas Hits Losing Streak; 13 Nabbed On Game Charges

Tarrytown Police Nab N.T. Man On Gambling Counts

Roosvelt Simms, 29, of 46 Hudson St., North Tarrytown was arrested at midnight Friday on charges of possession of gambling records, two counts, and promoting gambling, two counts. Tarrytown

Edward Greenly, 25, was charged with two counts of promoting gambling. He was running the crap table in the rear room. Edith Woods, 33, of Ossining, was charged with two counts of violation of the ABC law. Sylvester Gordon, 24 years, of Greenburg, was charged with possession of a dangerous drug, sixth degree, and loitering for the purpose of gambling. Eleven other people from Westchester County, New York City and Long Island were charged with loitering for the purpose of gambling. We confiscated the foam rubber padded crap table and thirty bottles of liquor as evidence.

On March 17 and March 31, 1972, the proprietor of Brunt & Brooks Pharmacy reported that someone had stolen a bottle of sodium secobarbital pills. The bottles had contained 1000 of these pills that are known as "red devils" on the street. They sell for 50¢ to $1.00 each when sold by drug pushers. It was noted that both of the thefts occurred when deliveries were made to the store. It was arranged that the proprietor would notify police headquarters when this person made his next delivery to the store.

On May 29, 1972, the store proprietor called headquarters and reported to Sgt. Floyd Variano, the suspect was making a delivery. He notified PTL. Gus Andres and myself. We found the suspect in possession of a bottle of 1000 secobarbital taken from the pharmacy that day. After being advised of his rights, the suspect Andrew Foley, 21 years, of Corona, New York, admitted to taking another bottle on March 17, 1972. He was charged with criminal possession of a dangerous drug with intent to sell and two counts of petit larceny.

Pat and I were attending mass at our parish, Holy Cross Church on Cortlandt Street, North Tarrytown. Our pastor Msgr. Cyril Potocek was saying the mass. I can remember years ago; when I was an altar boy, we couldn't wait for the homily to be over. Now, I always looked forward to hearing Msgr. Potocek's homily each week. His homily was always interesting and informative with a short time span. At this Mass, he explained what was meant when it was said, "With God on your side, who can your enemies be?" He stated that if you are living a good Christian life and God is with you, who can these people who oppose you be? I felt this had a special meaning for me, that if I was doing what was right and God was with me, who could be those who opposed me?

On Monday, January 8, 1973, at approximately 1:30 p.m., James Guy, 27 years of age, of Greenburgh, New York, was shot in the chest at the General Motors parking lot. He was taken to Phelps Memorial Hospital where he died at approximately 2:10 p.m. At lunchtime, in White Plains, New York Linwood Arlington of White Plains was approached by Leo "Gyp" Tedesco, 32 years of age, of White Plains, N.Y. Tedesco questioned Arlington about some money he had borrowed. Arlington promised Tedesco that he would get the money as soon as he could. Arlington left White Plains in a white Cadillac and drove to the G.M. Plant. Arlington was accompanied by his cousin, his uncle, and James Guy.

Tedesco followed them. Arlington, his cousin, and Guy waited in the Cadillac while the uncle went into the G.M. Plant to finalize his retirement papers. Tedesco came over to where they were parked and again asked about the $20. Standing outside of the car with Arlington, Tedesco told him that he better have the money in 20 minutes. Guy, in an attempt to stop the bickering between the two men, got out of the car. He said to Tedesco, "Why don't you take it easy? The man said he would give you the money, didn't he?" With this Tedesco took out a handgun and fired at Guy, hitting him in the chest.

Guy slumped to the ground. Tedesco started waving the gun at Arlington. Tedesco told Arlington and his cousin, "Don't try to follow me." Tedesco jumped into the '63 black Cadillac he was driving and drove out of the parking lot. While making his escape, he hit a parked car in Tarrytown but continued to make his escape. Arlington and his cousin placed Guy into the white Cadillac and tried to get him to the hospital, but he struck a vehicle in the lot and another outside the plant on Beekman Ave. An ambulance was called and took Guy to the hospital. Edward Williamson, of Mount Vernon, had lent the black Cadillac to Tedesco. He later received a call from Tedesco, who said that he was in trouble. Tedesco told Williamson, the car had broken down in the Bronx, N.Y. Tedesco asked Williamson to come down and get the car. Det. DeFalco and I, along with investigators from the Westchester County Sheriff's Department, searched for Tedesco until about 3:00 a.m. the following day. Leo "Gyp" Tedesco had been arrested 25 times. He had received fines and sentences on the many charges from $25 to a two and a half to five year sentence at Sing Sing.

We spent the next three plus weeks in White Plains, Greenburgh, the Bronx, N.Y. and Harlem, searching for Tedesco. Day and night we followed leads and information on his possible whereabouts. We surveilled people who were expected to meet with him. In several places, we had just missed him by minutes. He continued on the run, knowing we were close to him. We had been very close to apprehending him in Harlem. While Det. DeFalco and I were out of town surveilling a place where Tedesco might go, his attorney contacted police headquarters. He arranged to surrender Tedesco to Chief Jandrucko in Hartsdale, N.Y. in the beginning of February. He was arraigned on the murder charge and was undergoing psychiatric observation at the request of his attorney. We had many off-duty police officers assisting us in the investigation and received assistance from the White Plains, Greenburgh, and New York City Police Departments. The investigators of the Westchester County Sheriff's Department had stayed with us during the surveillances. With us watching all of his known haunts and the media attention, it left him with two options—either surrender or be apprehended.

I was reelected President of the Westchester County Detectives Association for 1973. Membership in the Westchester County Detectives Association is open to federal and state law enforcement officers stationed in Westchester County, as well as detectives who worked in the County. We had an annual citizens' award dinner to honor citizens for their assistance. That year I had the honor of presenting the award to a 15-year-old Elmsford boy, who was also cited by the U.S. Postal Service for his part in the capture of Robert F. Diaz of New York City. The boy saw Diaz going at a mailbox with a crowbar. He noted the license number of the man's car.

Tarrytown Police spotted the car the next day and arrested Diaz with mail including $4000 worth of checks in his possession. Four North Tarrytown women Connie Zarelli, Maria Sereghy, Isabelle Weinberg, and Patricia Speno were cited for their part in educating people in North Tarrytown about drugs through an organization they started several years ago called Citizens Against Drug Abuse. As a result of their efforts, young people and adults alike have become aware of the effects of drugs and the laws governing drug use. They have made people aware that they can come to the police when they have a drug problem. They have let young people know that they can meet with the detectives for help with their drug problem.

Pat and I were expecting our second child in February 1973. When she did not have the baby at the end of February, the doctors told her to come to the hospital on March 1, 1973, and they would induce labor. We arrived at Phelps Memorial Hospital on the morning of March 1. While Pat was with the nurses, I was surprised to meet a friend of mine, Det. Hank Kaufmann of the Briarcliff Manor P.D. Hank's wife was at the hospital to give birth too. Hank and I were sitting in the waiting room with Dr. Brady, the anesthesiologist.

He was interested in the drug overdose case and particularly methadone and how the homicide arrests were achieved. We were in discussion about that subject when a nurse told Dr. Brady that both of our wives were ready. Dr. Brady said, "They can wait. We're in a serious discussion." Of course, he left to attend them. Pat gave birth to a beautiful baby girl, Melissa. I notified Pat's mom and dad and my mom that everybody was alright. When we brought Melissa home, Todd, who was now three years old, was waiting. He sat in his little chair and we let him hold his new baby sister.

An investigation of a heroin operation that started almost a year ago came to a conclusion in May 1973. The investigation was started by the North Tarrytown and Tarrytown Detective Bureaus, following a series of complaints from tenants on Valley Street, College Avenue, and River Plaza. Sales were made at College Arms, College Avenue. The Dobbs Ferry Detectives Bureau joined the investigation when it was discovered that the operation extended into that village. The undercover officers of the Westchester County Sheriff's Department made buys of heroin during the investigation. The investigators of the other three departments were too well-known to the suspects to make buys.

On Friday night, May 11, 1973, at 11:30 p.m., Det. DeFalco and I, Det. Parra of Tarrytown and Det. Robert Cunningham of Dobbs Ferry, along with investigators of the sheriff's department put a plan into effect where Elton Waller and Roy Cole were followed as they left Valley Street and headed for Dobbs Ferry. They were followed, arrested, and a search was made of Barbara Combs apartment on Beacon Hill Drive, Dobbs Ferry by Dobbs Ferry officers and officers of the other departments. A second group of officers searched 1 River Plaza, Tarrytown and arrested Raymond Wood and George B. Tate. Elton Waller, 22 years of age, Raymond Wood, and George B. Tate, all of North Tarrytown, were charged with two counts of criminal possession of dangerous drugs, third degree, B Felony and two counts of criminal possession of dangerous drugs in the fourth degree, C Felony. They were held in the Tarrytown and North Tarrytown jails for transfer to the county jail the next day. Roy Cole, 24, was charged with possession of dangerous drugs, degree to be determined by the weights. Barbara Combs, 21, of Dobbs Ferry, was charged with one count of possession of a narcotic implement. Fred Rigsbee, 23, of Dobbs Ferry, was charged with one count of possession of a narcotic implement. Sealed indictments had been handed down for Elton Waller, Raymond Wood, and George B. Tate. Search warrants were obtained for the apartments. At a later date, I would locate Georgette McFadden, 23 years, of North Tarrytown, in reference to this investigation. She was charged with two counts of possession of a dangerous drug, third degree and two counts of sale of dangerous drugs, fourth degree. All drugs involved in the investigation were heroin. Officers in the raiding party from North Tarrytown, Lt. John Pankovic, Sgt. Stephen Kosletny, Sgt. Basil Gargia, Sgt. Floyd Variano, PTL. Vincent Butkovich, PTL. Thomas Smith, PTL. James Brophy, PTL. William Booth, PTL. Walter Schrank, and PTL. Joseph Lawlor. From Tarrytown Sgt. Williams McLaughlin, Det. James Weaver, PTL. Tony Rodriguez, Det. Douglas Dullin, and Der. Dominick Del Grande. From Dobbs Ferry Sgt. Kevin Costello, PTL. William Gelardi, PTL. Dennis Engel, and PTL. James Neal. Sheriff's department Sr. Inv. Dominick DeMarco directed his department's investigation.

The New York State Civil Service exam for Police Sergeant would be given on Saturday, June 16, 1973 at White Plains High School. I had attended classes for police promotion during the fall semester of 1972 and the spring semester of 1973, concluding the week of the exam. I had to block out of my mind that I had been on the sergeant's list from 1966 to 1970. I knew that I had to finish in the top three to keep the rank of sergeant. I have previously mentioned that I did not feel it was proper for people to be bypassed to reach me on the list if I was second or third. This is not an ideal way to take an exam. My church parish, when growing up, was Annunciation in Crestwood, but I would sometimes go to nearby Our Lady of Fatima. There was a shrine there. The day before the exam, June 15, 1973, I drove down to Our Lady of Fatima. I lit a candle and asked for help for the exam.

Everyone in our police department who had completed four years of service was eligible to take the exam and many other departments were also taking the exam that Saturday morning. The exam was very difficult. I took all of the time that was allowed, answering all of the questions that I knew first and going back to those I wasn't sure of later. After the exam, I knew that it would probably be many months before the state notified us of the results of the exam.

I was on duty the morning of September 12, 1973, driving the unmarked detective car when a police hotline alert was received from the Mount Pleasant Police Department. John Marsh of Old Chappaqua Road, Briarcliff Manor, had noticed two men leaving the home of his vacationing neighbor, Percy Knight, carrying a small grandfather clock and silverware. Marsh went out to investigate and the two fled by car. Marsh pursued them in his car but lost them. He did jot down the license number and a detailed description of the car and the men. He relayed this information to Mount Pleasant Police who issued the hotline alert at 12:00 noon, reporting the burglary of a private home, two males operating a stolen car, New York registration B-H-C-1, a green Vega station wagon. Sgt. Floyd Variano in a marked police car, Officer Lee Hayward and I were notified. At 12:10 p.m., PTL. Lee Hayward, at the traffic crossing of Depeyster St. and Broadway (school crossing), reported that the green Vega station wagon N.Y. registration B-H-C-1, a file I (stolen vehicle) from Mount Kisco, just passed him, heading south and turned down College Ave. at 12:20 p.m. Sgt. Variano and I reported that we were in pursuit of the file B-H-C-1 license plate containing two males, traveling north on Cortlandt St., then east on College Ave. and then south on Valley Street. I was in pursuit behind the file 1 when Sgt. Variano cut through the south end of the 100 College Ave. parking lot and headed the car off, forcing it to stop. We arrested the two men at gunpoint and recovered the stolen property from the burglary. The suspects—Benjamin Riggs, 28 years of age, of Mount Kisco, and Larry Sparks, 31 years of age, of New York City—were charged with possession of a stolen vehicle and possession of stolen property (proceeds of the burglary). There were warrants of arrest out on both men for various felonies. White Plains and Mount Pleasant had warrants for both men for burglary. Mount Kisco Police Department had a warrant on Sparks for robbery, first degree, and Ossining Police Department had a warrant on Riggs for robbery, first degree. The car was stolen from Mount Kisco the previous day. Both men were held in our lockup for arraignment. Mr. Marsh should be commended for his part. He felt, his marine corps background had something to do with the way he reacted. He added that a lot of people are afraid to get involved, but "I just care about people."

From October 14 to October 18, 1973, I attended the Narcotic Enforcement Officers Association of Connecticut, Sixth Annual Training School on Narcotics and Dangerous Drugs held at Kiamesha Lake, New York.

In the second week of November 1973, I received my test results from the New York state Department of Civil Services, Albany, N.Y. I was ranked first in my department and fourth in Westchester County. I thanked God. Pat and I were really happy. Todd, who would be four on the 19th of the next month, had a big smile. Melissa had a smile but sitting in her highchair at eight months I was not sure she really understood.

Tues. Jan. 8, 1974

N.T. Det. Spota promoted

DET. RICHARD SPOTA

Detectives

Elect Spota

—President

I was told that the board of trustees might not take any action until after the first of the year. I felt I could enjoy Thanksgiving and the holidays with that weight off my shoulders.

I was told that the Village Board of Trustees would act on my grade on the Sergeant's list at the Board Meeting of January 7, 1974. Before the meeting, I learned that there would be an attempt to stop my permanent promotion. I would be working the 4 p.m. to 12 midnight shift, so I would not be at the meeting. I remember giving Todd a hug that day while I was at home. I remember at that time thinking about the Assistant District Attorney, who told me after the grand jury probe into gambling in our area, that it would be very difficult for me to continue to work there. But I chose to stay there, work hard, and study hard for the next sergeant's test. As I hugged Todd, I thought about things that had happened. The state police that had protected the gambling operation had been convicted of same. But those who had not been apprehended were bragging that I would never get promoted. Every time we had raided a major part of the syndicate, it cost them approximately $25,000 to set up again. They had to make an example of me so that anyone else who might buck them would be dissuaded.

The board meeting would start at 8:00 p.m. on this cold winter night. As I worked the 4 p.m. to 12 midnight shift, people entered the Municipal Building for the meeting. Pat, her mom and dad, and her two younger twin sisters, all residents of the village, attended the meeting. One decent person, who at the time had a difference with me, addressed the board with his complaint. He may have been encouraged to do this by others. A second person who complained of me, assisting an officer in his arrest and throwing him in a cell did not tell the truth. An officer who worked the police desk that night stated that I was working when the arrest happened, but that I was having dinner at the time of the arrest. Many residents of the community came to the meeting. Some were victims of crimes that I was able to solve. Others were officers of the Westchester County Detectives Association. Det. Sgt. Carl Fulgenzi of the County Police spoke, as did Det. Sgt. Jack Kelly of the Mt. Vernon Police Department. Ralph Purdy, President of the

New York State Federation of Police spoke and was accompanied by his wife, who was pregnant at the time. James Tierney, who told of being robbed and beaten and how he felt when I apprehended the person responsible. I was told that Mr. Tierney got up again to say that he was the desk manager of the Tarrytown Y.M.C.A. where I worked out. He said that Det. Spota always paid his way and never walked into the Y.M.C.A and flipped his badge. Joseph Schwer of the Citizens Against Drugs Committee spoke and had committee members with him. Rita Hernandez and Gertrude Giusti were there. I was deeply moved when I was told that Rita Hernandez got up and stated that "Detective Spota didn't sleep until he got the man who killed my son." I know only too well how hard it was for her to talk about what had happened to Ricky. After 10 p.m., the board moved to make my appointment permanent. The overwhelming majority of this community were good, hardworking people who have nothing to do with organized crime. They had made a statement on that cold winter night. It truly was government of the people, by the people and for the people.

About six months after arresting the members of a heroin operation, on May 1973, we were receiving information from residents and drug users of a new drug ring. We spent approximately three months in a joint investigation with the Tarrytown Detective Bureau and investigators of the Westchester County Sheriff's Department. On the evening of Friday, February 8, 1974, at approximately 9:15 p.m. during a heavy snowfall, Det. DeFalco, PTL. Brophy, PTL. Hayward and I, along with Det. McLaughlin and Det. DelGrande of the Tarrytown P.D. proceeded to Beekman Ave., North Tarrytown, N.Y., armed with a search warrant. We were

72

joined by six investigators of the sheriff's dept. under Sr. Inv. Frank Conklin. Using a no-knock search warrant, we entered the second floor apartment at 174 Beekman Ave. We found heroin, LSD, methadone, amphetamines, and barbiturates hidden in the refrigerator, cabinets, closets, and other spots throughout the three-room apartment. We also seized hypodermic needles, syringes, and other narcotic instruments. We also seized a large quantity of marijuana. Arrested and charged with felonious possession of heroin, LSD, methadone, amphetamines, and barbiturates were Roger Mann, 24 years of age, and Matthew Lindsay, 24 years of age. Arthur Chambers, 24 years of age, and Robert Sperry, 25 years of age. Lt. John Pankovic and Sgt. Basil Garzia transported the prisoners.

The grand jury would hand down the following indictments at a later date. Roger Mann was indicted on two counts of unlawful sale of a controlled substance in the second degree. Mann and Lindsay were indicted for criminal possession of a controlled substance in the second, fifth, and seventh degrees—the first two were felonies and the last charge, a misdemeanor. They were also charged with possession of a hypodermic needle. Robert Sperry was indicted on possession of a controlled substance in the third degree, a felony and possession of a controlled substance in the seventh degree, a misdemeanor. Arthur Casey was indicted on possession of a controlled substance in the seventh degree and possession of a hypodermic needle. Under the new drug law, Mann, Lindsay, and Sperry faced possible life sentences. Casey could get two years.

On February 27, 1974, at 3:00 a.m., a 25-year-old Tarrytown woman was brought to police headquarters by a friend. The woman stated that she and her boyfriend were visiting some of the boyfriend's acquaintances at an apartment shortly before midnight. When her companion left the apartment to buy a pack of cigarettes, the woman was taken into the bedroom and raped by four men. When the companion returned several minutes later, he was told the woman had left. She was released by the men approximately two hours later. The woman was examined and treated at Phelps Memorial Hospital and later questioned by Det. DeFalco, myself, and a female investigator of the County Sheriff's Department Sex Crime Unit. At 1:30 p.m., on February 27, 1974, Ben Thompson and Raymond Washington were arrested at their homes by Sgt. Thomas Smith, PTL. Walter Schrank and myself charged them with rape in the first degree. At a later date, Kevin and Bo Caldwell would be charged with rape in the first degree.

On April 5, 1974, I completed the New York State Municipal Police Training Course in Police Supervision that was given at the Yonkers Police Training School. This state-mandated course must be completed when you are promoted to a supervisory rank. On June 7, 1974, 14 people in four communities, Port Chester, Yonkers, the Bronx, and North Tarrytown were arrested after a six-month investigation of gambling. The 15 million dollar operation was investigated by the Westchester County Sheriff's Department, the Tarrytown Police Department, the

North Tarrytown Police Department, the Yonkers Police Department, and the New York City Police Department. A policy "numbers" bank at the College Arms Apartments, 100 College Ave., North Tarrytown, N.Y. was raided by Det. DeFalco, PTL. James Brophy, PTL. Ron Biro, PTL. Gordon Ferguson, PTL. Vincent Butkovich, PTL. Edward Ciffone, and myself. The metal door to the apartment had to be smashed open. We seized over 900 "number plays" worth more than $3000 for the day, in addition to $700 cash, records, adding machines, and telephone recorders. The yearly take at the bank exceeded one million dollars. Arrested at this bank were Gabriel Soyar, 59 years of age, and his wife, Marie, 48, of 100 College Ave., North Tarrytown, N.Y. A total of 52 police and law enforcement agents took part in the investigation.

SHERIFF'S OFFICE

WESTCHESTER COUNTY

COURT HOUSE
WHITE PLAINS, N. Y. 10601

THOMAS J. DELANEY
SHERIFF
682-2112

CIVIL DIVISION
682-2199

JOHN P. O'BRIEN
UNDER-SHERIFF
682-2113

WARRANT DIVISION
682-6127

June 20, 1974

Chief John Jandrucko
North Tarrytown Police Department
28 Beekman Avenue
North Tarrytown, New York

Dear Chief:

We wish to express our sincere appreciation to Detective Sergeant Richard Spota for his efforts and assistance during a recent gambling investigation within Westchester County and the Bronx.

Through his cooperation, with men from other departments, we were able to effect the arrest of fourteen persons in four communities in a major gambling arrest.

Sergeant Spota is to be commended for his efforts in this investigation. His actions reflect favorably on your department.

Sincerely,

Thomas J. Delaney
Sheriff, Westchester County

/rmd

75

The other twelve persons were arrested in Port Chester, N.Y., Yonkers, N.Y. and the Bronx, N.Y.

On April 21, 1974, a sophisticated alarm system was bypassed at the Brunt & Brooks Pharmacy on Cortlandt St. and drugs with a street value of $15,000 were stolen. After an investigation, I had witnesses who could identify one of the men seen near the pharmacy on the night of the burglary. I obtained an arrest warrant on a trespass charge for the identified suspect. I met with Hastings Det. Harry Bloomer and Det. John Knapp, along with PTL. John DeSauza on June 11, 1974. The suspect had an M.O. (Method of Operation) for bypassing alarms at drug stores. We observed the suspect Michael Hatfield, 23, of Hastings, near his home at a Getty station. When he saw us, he attempted to flee. He attempted to throw away a paper bag, which contained a quantity of cocaine and several other drugs. Two of the drugs, Demerol and Dilaudid, had been stolen from Brunt & Brooks Pharmacy. We apprehended the suspect and the drugs were seized. He was charged with multiple counts of criminal possession of the drugs and possession of stolen property. Dobbs Ferry Police were able to identify drugs taken from a drug store in Dobbs Ferry. The sharing of information with the Hastings Detectives and Det. Robert Cunningham made the case possible. Michael Hatfield would receive a sentence of one year in the County Jail after being sentenced in Hastings Village Court at a later date.

We had an investigation and surveillance of a drug dealer who was involved in the sale of large quantities of high grade, uncut heroin. In June 1974, we obtained a search warrant for the suspected dealer and continued to surveil his operation. At 5:00 p.m., Det. DeFalco, PTL. Biro, PTL. Brophy and I, along with investigators of the Westchester County Sheriff's Department, tailed the suspect as he set up the delivery of heroin. He met several people and counted money. He then drove to the vicinity of 8 Ave. and 114 St. in New York City where he picked up the heroin. He then drove back to Westchester County into the parking lot of the College Arms Apartments on College Ave. We searched him, and he had four quarter pieces of pure heroin with a total weight of over an ounce. We charged James Lott, 35 years of age, of North Tarrytown, with criminal possession of a controlled substance in the third degree. Under New York State's new drug law, this was punishable by life imprisonment. The investigation would continue.

In September 1974, we had received information that a large amount of marijuana was being grown in our area. It was determined that the marijuana was being grown in a wooded area off Gorey Brook Road, not far from property owned by the Rockefeller Family. Tarrytown Detectives were notified because a key suspect lived in Tarrytown. Investigators of the Westchester County Sheriff's Department were brought into the investigation. We had obtained search warrants. After 4:00 p.m., we found that the marijuana was being harvested. Shortly after 5:00 p.m., PTL. Brophy and I tailed the suspect as he drove his red Gremlin around the grounds of Sleepy Hollow High School. Dets. Parra and Weaver of Tarrytown joined in the surveillance. We closed in on Edward Gordon, 20 years of age, of Tarrytown, N.Y. When we stopped him, we found a large shopping bag containing approximately six pounds of freshly harvested marijuana. A subsequent search of Gordon's apartment in Tarrytown turned up an additional ounce and a half of marijuana, as well as an assortment of pipes and paraphernalia. The suspect was charged with possession of a controlled substance in the fifth degree, a felony. The investigation would continue. If it wasn't for the anonymous information supplied by a good citizen, this operation may have gone undetected out in a vastly wooded area that was not open to view. Involved citizens can make a good contribution to law enforcement and the drug trade in particular.

I had met with, and had been working with, the Federal Organized Crime Strike Force. Det. DeFalco and I, along with members of our department that I had confidence in, along with Det. Sgt. Parra of the Tarrytown Police Dept. and officers he had working for him, worked together with the F.B.I. Agents of the Organized Crime Strike Force. When evidence had been gathered, the F.B.I. agent in charge of the Strike Force and I applied to District Attorney Carl Vergari for a wiretap. It was going to be set up in our community but, because of security reasons, was set up outside of our community. The wiretap would have to be manned seven days a week, including all holidays. The District Attorney would provide us with his investigators to assist in the manning of the wiretap. The officers I had working on this investigation knew that they would work on this in addition to their regular shift. They knew they were not to discuss what we were working on with anyone other than those officers assigned to this investigation. Everyone knew they had to be careful and cover their tracks, or the investigation would be blown. The F.B.I.'s jurisdiction covered all counties, as well as all states. We had been working well into November 1974 on this investigation. We were going to raid the Headless Horseman Sport Center in North Tarrytown one weekend, but something was amiss, and we waited until November 23, 1974. On that date, Det. DeFalco, PTL. James Brophy, PTL. Ron Biro, and I, along with Det. Sgt. Parra, Det. DelGrande, and members of the F.B.I. and the DA.

Investigators raided the Headless Horseman Sports Center. We found approximately $9,000 worth of slips for sport events and another $1,000 in numbers. This was also the headquarters for the football pool slips. Henry Bowman, 40 years of age, of North Tarrytown, was arrested on felony charges of promoting gambling and possession of gambling records. Phillip Kilgen, 28 years of age, of North Tarrytown, was charged with felony, promoting gambling and possession of gambling records. He was also charged with maintaining a criminal nuisance. Bowman would be released on $5,000 bail and Kilgen on $2,500 The suspects were in a rear room, taking bets over the phone and counting gambling slips. This investigation lasted three months. We were still running the wiretap.

We continued to work with the F.B.I. agents of the Organized Crime Strike Force. On Thursday, December 19, 1974, there were two raids. One at a barber shop in Tarrytown that had two persons charged and one in North Tarrytown at a stationery store at 95 Beekman Ave. operated by Alfonse and Christine Letti. The stationery store was clean. There were no betting receipts. This was the first time this had ever happened on a raid I was involved in. I had a sickening feeling in my stomach. If an investigation is done properly, this should not happen. It doesn't mean it can't happen, but it shouldn't happen. There were two police departments, the D.A.'s office and the F.B.I. involved in this investigation. It would be my responsibility to find out if there was a leak in my department.

On New Year's Eve, December 31, 1974, the North Tarrytown, Tarrytown Police Detective Bureaus, the Westchester County D.A.'s Investigators, and the F.B.I. agents who had continued the gambling investigation went into action. At 12:30 p.m., we raided the house of Francis "Pop" Mooney, 26 years of age, and his father, Anthony J. Mooney, 67 years of age, on Cedar St., North Tarrytown. They were both charged with felony possession of gambling records, first degree and two counts each of possession of bookmaking records, second degree and promoting gambling, second degree. They had over 600 policy plays and were handling bets on horse racing. I had told my men to search the room that was under the area where they were taking bets on the phone for extensive records. In the ceiling of that room PTL. Biro found those important records. At the same time of this raid, the other officers and agents raided a Sports Bank in Pelham, New York, and a wire room of the syndicate in the Bronx, N.Y., where persons were charged at those locations, John A. Jolston, of the Bronx, was arrested at the Flamingo Restaurant on South Broadway, Tarrytown and charged with two misdemeanors, possession of gambling records, second degree and promoting gambling, second degree.

On January 14, 1975, at approximately 2:05 a.m., two white males in their 20s entered the Embassy Bar on Cortlandt St. One of them displayed a gun. The barmaid, Amparo Vasquez, and two other patrons were ordered to lie on the floor. When the robbers could not open the cash register, Ms. Vasquez was ordered to do so. The duo escaped with $317.00 in cash. On February 2, 1975, Ms. Vasquez recognized one of the robbers at another bar, Blinky's on Cortlandt St. Police arrested Gene Conway of Riverview Ave., Tarrytown, and charged him with robbery in the first degree. He was later released on $15,000 bail. On Wednesday, February 19, 1975, at 2:07 a.m., after an investigation, I, along with PTL. James Brophy, arrested Richard Conway at his room at the Tarrytown Y.M.C.A. We brought him to North Tarrytown Police Headquarters where he was arraigned, and bail was set at $15,000.

Marie E. Lynch was walking on North Washington St. near College Ave. at noon time when a youth approached her, knocked her down, and grabbed her pocketbook. He fled west. When I arrived on the scene, there was no one visible running away from the scene. I searched a wooded area off College Ave. The woods sloped down into a valley area below. When I climbed down there, I observed three boys in possession of a pocketbook. The pocketbook contained personal papers and over $50 in cash. I radioed headquarters for assistance in taking the three boys to headquarters. A 16-year-old boy was charged with possession of stolen property. The other two boys, who were 14 and 15 years of age, were referred to family court.

A Westchester County Grand Jury would hand up indictments of four men arrested in gambling raids in November and December of 1974. Indicted on charges of possession of gambling records are promoting gambling, both felonies, were Henry Bowman, Philip Kilgen who was arrested on November 23, 1974. Francis Mooney and Anthony Mooney were indicted for possession of gambling records and promoting gambling, both felonies in connection with their December 31, 1974 arrests.

On Tuesday, February 10, 1976, the five-year federal investigation that we worked on with the Federal Organized Crime Strike Force ended. A Manhattan Grand Jury handed up sealed indictments against 13 men, 8 from Westchester, accusing them of operating a Bronx and Westchester gambling ring that grosses $2,000 a day for more than 7 years which totaled more than $4.5 million. The unsealed indictments charged that gambling was carried on in a barber shop in Tarrytown, N.Y., the Green Tavern Restaurant in Hastings-on-Hudson, and the Headless Horseman Sports Center in North Tarrytown, N.Y. The F.B.I. identified those indicted as John Monaco and Michael J. Picciano of the Bronx and Michael Evangelista of Manhattan, James Ostrander of the Bronx and Alfonso Letti, who operated a wire room at Al's stationery store, 95 Beekman Ave., North Tarrytown, N.Y. Arrested on this day were Lawrence "Black" Centre and Michael Cellini of Yonkers, Peter Vitchelli, and Henry Bowman of North Tarrytown. Det. DeFalco and I, with two F.B.I. agents, arrested Bellini, 40 years of age, at his furniture store, the Garage Sale, on Beekman Ave., North Tarrytown. Also arrested were Michael Delorn of Hastings-on-Hudson, Anthony Joseph Russell of Pelham, and William Murty, of New Rochelle, was still being sought. The F.B.I. stated that the gambling ring had been in operation since September 1, 1968, and that the F.B.I. became aware of it five years ago.

Notice had been given that the civil service written examination for the rank of lieutenant would be given on May 22, 1976. It was stated that there was no vacancy and appeared to be no vacancy in the future in our police department, but we would be authorized to take the exam because it would not be given again for two years. I had been continuing to attend classes in my off-duty time and would take an additional class in preparation for the exam. We had been investigating a group that was selling a high grade of Colombian marijuana and other drugs. We used an informant to infiltrate the group and make purchases for us. Shortly before midnight, Det. DeFalco, PTL. Biro, PTL. Ferguson, and I arrested Fred Corchaao, 19 years of age, of New York City, and Idolene Rankin, 32 years of age, of Ossining, N.Y. The pair had a pound and a half of high grade Colombian marijuana in their possession. Both were charged with felony possession and sale of a controlled substance.

We conducted an investigation of the sale of drugs that lasted for six months. There had been complaints from citizens about the sale of marijuana at a stationery store at the corner of Cortlandt and Depeyster Sts. Det. Sgt. Barney Parra of the Tarrytown Police Department had given me information early in the investigation of sales taking place at the stationery store. We used an undercover officer of the Westchester County Sheriff's Department to make purchases of drugs. Sealed indictments handed up in the case were opened up on Monday, March 8, 1976. On Monday evening March 8, we arrested the owner of the stationery store, Felix Colomer, age 39, on three counts of criminal sale of a controlled substance and six counts of criminal possession of a controlled substance. Colomer was a major supplier of marijuana to the area. Ronald J. Collier, 21 years of age, was charged with criminal sale and possession of a dangerous drug by both Tarrytown and North Tarrytown Police. Conlon sold phenobarbital in both North Tarrytown and Tarrytown and LSD in Tarrytown. Local officers working on the case were: Dt. DeFalco, myself, St. Floyd Variano of North Tarrytown, and Det. Sgt. Barney Parra of Tarrytown P.D. The investigators of the sheriff's dept. were under the direction of Chief Investigator Sal D'Orio.

The final two suspects in the investigation were arrested on Friday, March 12, 1976 by PTL. Gordon Ferguson and myself. Suspect one, an associate of Felix Colomer had made himself scarce since the earlier arrests. He was charged with two counts of sale of a controlled substance, two counts of possession of a controlled substance, all felonies, and two misdemeanor counts of possession of a controlled substance. He sold marijuana to an undercover officer. Tarrytown Police arrested Kent Banta, 20, Scarborough, and charged him with the sale and possession of LSD. This was a joint investigation of the North Tarrytown, Tarrytown P.D.'s and the Westchester County Sheriff's Dept.

We would conduct a two-month investigation of a woman who was observed collecting policy (numbers) bets in North Tarrytown and Tarrytown. We brought investigators of the sheriff's dept. into the investigation because the woman could recognize the local officers. We obtained a search warrant and raided the Apartment of Teresa Yoland a.k.a. Teresa Barrios. We charged her with promoting and possession of gambling records. She was additionally charged with assault for cutting PTL. Ron Biro with a large kitchen knife. The amount of numbers seized indicated a $2,000 a week business. Participants in the raid were PTL. Biro, PTL. Ferguson, PTL. Brophy, Police Matron Kathleen Biro, and myself of North Tarrytown, Det. Sgt. Baltasar Parra and Det. Dominick DelGrande of Tarrytown in addition to undercover officers of the Westchester County Sheriff's Dept.

I continued to attend my classes and study for the lieutenant's examination on May 22, 1976. I went to the shrine of Our Lady of Fatima Church the day before the exam to light a candle and ask for help. I was always amazed by people who would say an exam was easy after taking the same. I've never had an easy exam and this one was no exception. Towards the end of May 1976, about a week after the exam, I received a telephone call from headquarters that Lieutenant John Pankovic had a heart attack at his home and had died. Poncho, as we called him, was 50 years of age and had not complained about his health. His funeral mass was at my parish, Holy Cross Church. He left a wife, a son, and a daughter. I had worked with him a few days earlier and he was in good spirits.

On Thursday, July 8, 1976, the case we had worked on with the F.B.I. agents of the Federal Organized Crime Strike Force came to a conclusion. In Manhattan Federal Court, Judge Robert L. Carter doled out prison terms to ten men convicted of running gambling operations in Westchester and the Bronx, N.Y. Peter Vitchelli of North Tarrytown received the stiffest sentence. Judge Carter sentenced Vitchelli to three years in jail and fined him the maximum $20,000. Vitchelli, in the past, had served time on federal bribery and interstate racketeering convictions. Judge Carter sentenced Michael Cellini, of Yonkers, N.Y., to 18 months and a $20,000 fine. He described Cellini as the "Kingpin" and "financier" of the seven-year operation. The two men were among 13 arrested in February of this year accused of operating a $4.5 million numbers, horse, and sports betting operation between 1968 and 1976. Four of the 13 pleaded guilty to charges of operating and conspiring to operate the gambling ring. A jury found six others guilty of the actual operation, acquitted two and could not decide on the 13th defendant. The remaining defendants and their sentences were: Michael DeNicholas of Hastings, N.Y., was sentenced a year in jail and fined $5,000. The judge suspended all but four months of the jail term. Anthony J. Trujillo of Pelham, N.Y., was given a sentence of two years, but the judge suspended all but five months and placed him on probation for the remaining 19 months. William McCray of New Rochelle was denied a reduction in his sentence to five months in jail and 19 months of probation. Henry Bowman of Tarrytown, N.Y., was sentenced to two years in prison, but the judge suspended all of it and put him on probation for two years. Michael Evans of Manhattan was sentenced to a year in prison, but all 30 days were suspended

Michael Portini, 28 years, of the Bronx, N.Y., was sentenced to one month in jail and one year's probation on the condition that he register in a drug rehabilitation program when he is released from jail.

Michael Abzug, an assistant U.S. Attorney, said his office would decide whether to retry Lawrence Centre of Yonkers, N.Y. The jury could not decide on him.

"The following commendation was received from the Federal Bureau of Investigation. Special Agents of the New Rochelle office of the F.B.I. have brought to my attention the excellent performance of members of your department in regard to the recent arrest and conviction of persons involved in illegal gambling in Westchester and Bronx Counties, New York (N.Y.). The F.B.I. is extremely grateful for the assistance afforded the Bureau by your department in bringing the investigation of Peter Vitchelli, et.al. to a successful conclusion. I would like to convey to Detective Sergeant Richard Spota, Detective Carmen DeFalco, Patrolman James Brophy, and Patrolman Ronald Biro my personal thanks and congratulations for a job well done. Very Truly Yours, Wallace La Prade, Assistant Director in Charge."

UNITED STATES DEPARTMENT OF JUSTICE

FEDERAL BUREAU OF INVESTIGATION

In Reply, Please Refer to
File No.

1 Sheraton Plaza
New Rochelle, New York   10801

Chief John Jandrucko
North Tarrytown Police Department
28 Beekman Avenue
North Tarrytown, New York   10591

Dear Chief Jandrucko:

     Special Agents of the New Rochelle Office of the
Federal Bureau of Investigation (FBI) have brought to my
attention the excellent performance of members of your
Department in regard to the recent arrest and conviction,
of persons involved in illegal gambling in Westchester and
Bronx Counties, New York (NY). The FBI is extremely grateful
for the assistance afforded the Bureau by your Department
in bringing the investigation of ~~Peter Varlese~~ Et Al,
to a successful conclusion.

     I would like for you to convey to Detective Sergeant
Richard Spota, Detective Carmine De Falco, Patrolman James
Brophy and Patrolman Ronald Biro, my personal thanks and
congratulations for a job well done.

Very truly yours,

J. WALLACE LA PRADE
Assistant Director In Charge

In June 1976, we gave the last four drug abuse seminars for the school year at St. Teresa's school.

I had received information of a policy (numbers) bank operating in our area from Det. Sgt. Barney Parra of the Tarrytown Police Dept. I used an undercover C.I. (confidential informant) of mine to get additional information on the operation. After several months of surveillance and investigation, I obtained a search warrant from Acting Judge Joseph Frascati. It was a warm July day on Friday, July 8, 1976. Det. Carmen DeFalco and I had a van that we used for the raid. In the van with us were PTL. Ron Biro, PTL. Lee Hayward, and PTL. James Brophy. The element of surprise was always critical when hitting a gambling operation. If you are delayed or slow to get into a building or room, those running the gambling operation would have time to dissolve the bets, if they were written on submarine paper, or burn them if they were written on flash paper. On a prior day, the persons running the operation were acting suspiciously according to my undercover person. As we pulled up to the first building on the south side of Clinton St., we had several officers go down the hallway of the building to the right rear apartment. My group went down the alleyway on the right side of the building with our sledgehammer. As we got to the rear, we were almost as surprised as the people running the bank and wire room.

$6 million numbers 'bank' hit in N.T.

The rear door was open, because of the hot day. Nothing was lost. We got everything. We notified the uniform officers to back us up and take out the prisoners. PTL. Walter Schrank, PTL. Gordon Ferguson, and PTL. Gabe Hayes responded. Arrested and charged with felony promoting gambling and felony possession of gambling records were William Bank, 51 years of age, of Elmsford, N.Y., "Bub" Sanders, 66 years of age, of Tarrytown, N.Y., Leonard Farr, 41 years of age, of Yonkers, N.Y., and Lois Taylor, 35 years of age, of North Tarrytown, N.Y.

We seized huge amounts of policy slips, record books, and wads of cash. The suspects would be released on $5,000 bail each for court appearances on July 15. The raid was conducted with the help of Det. Sgt. Parra and the Tarrytown Det. Bureau.

In August 1976, the grades for the police lieutenant's exam were mailed out by the Westchester County Personnel Office. When I opened the envelope, I observed the grade of 97.9, which was first in my police department and second in the county of Westchester. This was a happy day. I thanked God and Our Blessed Mother for being so kind to me. Pat had told my mother about the exam results.

While I was home, at our apartment, my mom telephoned. She said to me, "If your father was alive, he would be very proud of you."

I didn't know at the time that this would be the last time that I would speak to my mother. On August 26, 1976, which was a very hot, humid day, I came home from work. Pat, Todd, and I were about to eat dinner when we received a telephone call from my cousin, Skip Farrell. He was at Lawrence Hospital in Bronxville. He said that Aunt Rita, my mom, had suffered an apparent stroke while working at Aires Real Estate in Yonkers. She had worked there for many years as a real estate saleswoman. They called Skip and my Aunt Loretta (Mom's sister) because they lived closest to the office. Skip had ridden in the ambulance with Mom to the hospital. Skip said that she was not responding at all. When Pat and I arrived at the hospital, we went up to her room. I was standing by her left and Pat was to her right. She moved her head, looked at me, and then turned to look at Pat. The doctor asked for my permission to do a spinal tap. When I saw her grimace from the spinal tap I had wished that I didn't give permission. George was on vacation upstate with Eleanor and was driving home, so I couldn't get his medical advice. Later that evening, while we were with her, Mom died. She was 68 years old and had worked up to the last day of her life. I was 37 years old and my dad had died 19 years ago, while I was in my teens. I had a very empty feeling, as we left the hospital. Even though Melissa was only three years old and Todd was six years old, at least she had known and loved her grandchildren.

The morning of her funeral was a hot, humid August day. We had taken Todd with us, but left Melissa home, because she was only three. My mom's sister, Aunt Loretta, was with us as we arrived at the front of Annunciation Church in Crestwood. Aunt Loretta was older than Mom and did not like the hot weather. As I glanced up at the priests standing in the doorway, I saw Father Menna standing there. His parish was near Boston, Massachusetts, and I had not called him. When I opened the door to the limo, it felt as if the temperature had dropped 20 degrees from early morning. I said to Aunt Loretta, "I know your sister is alright now."

She said, "Why?"

I answered, "The first two things she would ask God for were to let Father Menna be at the church for Richard and let the temperature drop for my sister." The greatest gift I had received from my mother was her faith. She would always say to pray to the sacred heart of Jesus and Our Blessed mother. In the following days, I would think of my Irish Catholic mother and my Italian Catholic father who were married in 1937. Of how they were treated by some people because at that time they had married outside of their own ethnic group. I know where they both are now, and I know that the people there are all very kind to them.

On September 13, 1976, at the Board of Trustees meeting, my promotion to lieutenant was to be proposed and voted on. I had received word that there would be an attempt to stop the promotion. I would also be working the 4 p.m. to 12 midnight shift so that I could not attend the 8:00 p.m. meeting. I think that by now members of the community thought that it was the normal thing to do, to attend the board meeting if I was up for a promotion. Approximately, two dozen of them did attend the meeting. Many of them had been there at the last such meeting. God Bless these good, decent people. Pat, her mom and dad, and her younger twin sisters were there. Trustee Philip E. Zegarelli, Chairman of the Police Committee, made the motion for my promotion and read a very kind statement of my accomplishments, honors, and awards. Phil was a young former, naval officer who was not your typical politician. He had good integrity, strong beliefs, and was willing to fight for them. At this point, a trustee said that the board should not act immediately but should consider the matter further. "I think we're rushing this."

During the investigation with the F.B.I., he became aware of photos taken of him carrying a crap table. He had told me that I took the pictures. I had told him that they were taken by the F.B.I. during a surveillance, but that yes, I was working with them. His brother had been subpoenaed to a grand jury probe that I had worked on as a rookie in 1963. After he finished, Trustee William McBride interjected that the appointment should be acted on immediately, and Spota should be either accepted or rejected at this meeting. The audience burst out in applause at McBride's statement. The opposition to the appointment quickly faded as all the trustees voted to approve my promotion to lieutenant, effective, October 1st for the spot that was vacant since the death of Lt. John Pankovic in May. After the approval, the onlookers again burst out with applause. Then a hush fell over the large room as the board declared a moment of silence for my mother, Rita, who had died some two weeks ago.

13 September 197_

It is the strong, unanimous, and unqualified opinion and vote of the Police Committee and the Chief of Police to fill the vacancy of the post of Lieutenant with Detective-Sargent Richard Spota. Detective Sargent Spota has been with this Police Department for 15 years and has, more then any single policeman established an exemplary record of investigations and convictions especially in the fields of narcotics and illegal gambling without equal. It is felt that the filling of this key position will in effect strengthen and revitalize North Tarrytown's Police Department. And this department is in need of not only this type of police officer and personality but of a good internal and personnel shake-up.

The opportunity for change and revitalization exists now and now is the time to go forward. The people of North Tarrytown want these steps taken. In time other Police Department changes and additions will be decided upon and implimented.

Richard Spota received one of the very highest scores county-wide on the most recent lieutenant's examination and was the only member of this department to pass. This too is indicative not only of his own personal high eductional standards but also the daily application of high moral models and ethical examples in his everyday police work routine. He has been praised, recognized and credited by other local Police Departments as well as by the Sheriff's Department, District Attorney's Office and the Federal Bureau of Investigation - one does not attain these honors by sitting back and letting illegal events and incidents to take place unchallenged nor by doing the very minimum of police work. This village owes much to the timely and effective work of Detective Sargent Spota and his promotion to Lieutenant is greatly deserved.

Born in the Bronx, N.Y. and raised in Crestwood, he is married to the former Patricia Kofka and they reside locally in North Tarrytown. The Spota's have two children, A son, Todd and a daughter, Melissa.

I now proudly and without reservation nominate Richard Spota to the rank of Lieutenant of the North Tarrytown Police Department.

Philip E. Zegarelli
Trustee and Police
Commissioner

"where the Headless Horsemen rode"

Chapter Four

At the present time, I will continue in the detective bureau but work on the shift opposite the other lieutenant so that there will be a Lieutenant on both the 8 a.m. to 4 p.m. and 4 p.m. to 12 midnight shifts.

On September 3, 1976, there had been a burglary at the Elsvari Restaurant at the corner of Beekman Avenue and Teresa Street. A wristwatch and cash were stolen from the restaurant. A window in the door was broken and entry made through same. I located glass fragments that were matched to the broken pane. Fingerprints were lifted off the glass and the prints were matched to the suspect. On September 19, 1976, David Cobb, was arrested and charged with the burglary. Cobb would be indicted by the grand jury for burglary, third degree, petty larceny, and criminal mischief. Cobb would, at a later date, be sentenced to one and a half to three years in prison for the burglary.

In November 1976, the trial of Barbara England, who we had accused of killing her husband, Clarence, the year before (1975) began. The trial would last ten days. Barbara England, age 31, was accused of shooting Clarence England with a 20-guage single barrel shotgun in their apartment at Hudson Street, North Tarrytown, N.Y., Mrs. England had testified at the trial that she and her husband had been arguing and fighting for about an hour before the gun discharged. She stated that her husband had struck her several times. Mrs. England stated that she had received bruises on her upper right arm and upper right quadrant of her body. Dr. Louis Fazio, Chief Physician for the County Corrections Department, substantiated Mrs. England's claim that she had bruises on her upper right arm and upper right quadrant of her body, but he did not find any head injuries. Mrs. England had claimed that her husband had hit her on the head with his shoe. Assistant District Attorney Robert Ryan said that the doctor's testimony fit perfectly with the prosecution's contention that the shooting was no accident. Ryan stated that Mrs. England's right arm and shoulder area were bruised and sore, not by an assault by her husband, but by the kick of the 20-gauge shotgun. He added that the kick of the shotgun had caused the bruises.

After final summations by the attorneys and instructions from the judge, the jury deliberated for more than ten hours. The jurors asked the judge if a person could make a spur of the moment decision to shoot another and be guilty of first degree manslaughter. The judge told them that a person must intend to inflict serious physical injury and that the person must act without justification to be guilty. Mrs. England's fear that her husband would kill or seriously injure her and her daughter, Bethany, age 8, would constitute "justification" if the jurors believed her. Less than an hour after Judge Walsh's response to their question, the jurors said that they had reached a verdict. At approximately 2:30 p.m., on Wednesday, November 17, 1976, the jury of seven women and five men delivered a guilty verdict on both counts of manslaughter in the first degree and criminal possession of a dangerous weapon. Barbara England would be sentenced by Supreme Court Judge John J. Walsh on December 10, 1976. She could receive a mandatory prison term of one to 25 years.

An Assistant D.A. had told me that I could pick up subpoenas that I had needed for the trial at his home in the evening. He lived locally, so this would save me a trip to White Plains, N.Y. While at his home, he told me of the house next door to his that was for sale. It would need a lot of work. I noticed the swing set in the yard. Todd was six and Melissa was three. This would be great for them and they would have their own bedrooms. I was in the process of selling my mother's house, which would have been too small for us. I'd discuss it with Pat when I arrived home. I was sure she would appreciate not having to take two small children and our dog up and down the stairs of our fifth floor walk-up apartment. We were able to get a mortgage. When I would finish a shift 9 a.m. to 5 p.m. or 4 p.m. to 12 p.m. I would go to the house and work for as long as I could. Usually, I would paint, repair, plaster, etc. It's amazing what you can learn to do when you have a goal and a limited budget. Pat, her mom, and Aunt Helen would put in as much time as they could. After the closing was finished, we were able to move into our home in March 1977. Todd and Melissa had their own rooms and a yard to play in.

On March 21, 1977, a woman initiated a fraud when she opened a savings account at the First National Bank using the name of Lydia Marten, Tarrytown, N.Y. On March 24, 1977, an unidentified man deposited a stolen check for $3,500 into the account. On March 28, 1977, the female returned to the bank and withdrew a total of $3,000. The bank did not discover the fraud until March 30, 1977. Det. DeFalco and myself conducted an investigation and we were able to identify the woman as Jeanette Hooper, 27 years of age, of New York City. We obtained an arrest warrant, charging her with grand larceny. On April 15, 1977, we went to the N.Y. City Probation Office at 100 Center Street where she was to appear. We arrested her and brought her back to police headquarters. She was placed in the women's jail. She was to be arraigned in court that evening.

We learned that she had escaped from jail between 6:50 p.m. and 7:08 p.m., Friday, April 15, 1977. We learned that a taxicab took her to Lenox Ave. and 38 St. in Manhattan. It was believed that she moved a bed in her cell near the cell door and reached outside of the cell. She then twisted the brass knob and opened the door. We learned that she had been arrested 18 times in several states since 1970.

She had been charged in eleven cities, including Washington DC and New York. The charges ranged from possession of stolen property, grand larceny, fraud, and possession of drugs. Her stiffest sentence had been five years' probation. She had to know the banking business very well to pull of the most recent crime. This was the first time we knew of a female prisoner escaping from the woman's jail. Making the case against her wasn't an easy task but finding her would be even more of a challenge. This was going to be a long night. The night would turn into days and then weeks of searching for her. For several weeks, we interviewed friends and relatives of the suspect and surveilled places in Manhattan and the Bronx that she would frequent. We had developed information that she had a 9:30 a.m. appointment on May 1l, 1977, at St Luke's Hospital in N.Y. City. She was to have a prenatal checkup there. We watched the area, but she did not show up for the appointment. We learned that she had been a patient at St. Luke's Hospital in the past and had used the name Paulette Hobson. She had used an address at 880 Boynton Ave. in the Union port section of the Bronx, N.Y. It was now afternoon, and we were tired from going day and night, trying to find her. I felt we had to at least check out the new address. We had brought a police matron with us in the event in case we might have arrested her at the hospital.

We checked in with the 43 Precinct who covered the area. Officers of the anti-crime unit came with us to the address. The apartment building was brick and the hallways were clean and well cared for. We knocked on the door, but she didn't answer. I went to a neighbor's apartment while some of the officers stayed in the hall. The neighbors let me use their telephone. I called her apartment. It was actually her parents' apartment, but they were away. When she answered the phone, I told her who we were and that we had a warrant for her arrest on the escape charge. I asked her to check our identification through the peephole in the door and let us in. She said that there was no one there by that name. A New York City Police Officer said he would go downstairs to get a key. As I left the neighbor's apartment, Det. DeFalco came down the hallway and told me that she was dead. The officer who had gone to get the key had told Det. DeFalco that she had fallen from an outside terrace to the grass 12 stories below. We learned that while I was on the phone she opened the sliding glass out to the terrace. She then climbed from her terrace to the one next door. A seven-foot plywood wall separated them.

Then she was trying to jump from the 12th floor terrace to the 11th floor terrace when she spotted a boy on the terrace below. She said, "Little boy, could you let me in? My husband is mad at me." She was dangling from a concrete slab in a beige raincoat and moccasins. She then fell to the grass 12 stories below. Doctors from Jacobi Hospital were immediately summoned in an attempt to save the baby, but to no avail. She was wrapped in canvas and taken away by City

Morgue personnel. Several hours later, we would drive back to the Westchester County. We were very quiet while driving back. I thought to myself, if we hadn't worked so hard, she would be alive. I also thought that all she had to do was open the door and come with us. But she tried to escape one last time.

At approximately 5:00 a.m., on June 25, 1977, a man broke into a home on North Washington Street. He crept into the bedroom of a female teenager who was sleeping. He jumped on top of her and told her to lie still. The girl began to scream, and the man ran out of the house.

Det. DeFalco had been promoted to sergeant and assigned to the uniform division. Det. Vincent Butkovich was now working with me in the detective bureau. We gathered as much information and evidence as possible. I had taken the victim with me on several occasions. We drove to areas in the Tarrytown, Greenburgh, and White Plains. The girl observed many persons on the street in all communities, but to no avail. Det. Sgt. Barney Parra of the Tarrytown Det. Bureau gave me the name of a suspect based on the information we had supplied on the crime. This person was on parole. I spoke with his parole officer, Andrew Farese. He told me when and where he would be meeting with the person. On July 5, 1977, at approximately 7:40 p.m. I had the victim in the unmarked police car with me. As in the past I told her to let me know if she recognized anyone in connection with the crime. As I drove by Franklin Courts in Tarrytown, she observed a male talking to another male. She told me, "That is him."

I asked her if she was positive and she said, "Yes." At that point, with the assistance of the Tarrytown Police Dept., we arrested Ronald Sloan, 27 years of age, of Tarrytown, N.Y., on charges of attempted rape, first degree, and burglary, second degree. Sloan was on parole from a Colorado penitentiary. He had been released in April in Colorado after serving a sentence for rape and burglary there. His M.O. (method of operation) in previous crimes was the same as in our crime. He was held in lieu of $50,000 secured bond or $25,000 cash at his arraignment.

At a later date, he would be indicted on charges of sexual abuse, burglary, and criminal mischief by the grand jury in our case. After a four-day trial, at which the victim and I testified, the 12-member jury found Sloan guilty of burglary on January 31, 1978. Westchester County Court Judge Lawrence Martin sentenced Sloan to five to ten years in State Prison on February 24, 1978. The district attorney's office said that Sloan's sentence will run in addition to any which may be imposed by Colorado courts if Sloan is found guilty of parole violation. The young lady in this was very courageous, a good witness, and a credit to her parents and family.

Det. Butkovich and I investigated a burglary at the Fraternal Order of Eagles that occurred on September 8, 1977. A knife that was used to jimmy open the bathroom window in the rear of the hall was left behind. It was taken to be checked for fingerprints. The prints lifted off the knife matched those of a local 17-year-old. We charged him with the burglary on September 16. The youth had always been honest with us. He had a disability, and we had tried to help him in the past. He admitted breaking into the club eight days earlier. He was being held in lieu of bail. He would spend the week at the County Jail and was returned for arraignment on September 24, 1977. As PTL. Joseph Lawlor was leading the youth from the courtroom back to a jail cell, the youth broke free and ran out the rear door of headquarters. The door opened out, but not in without a key. He apparently ran toward Sleepy Hollow High School and the wooded area near the Tarrytown Lakes. Members of our department, Tarrytown Police to the south and Mt. Pleasant Police to the east searched for him. Conrail Police met me with their helicopter at Kingsland Point Park. The pilot and I checked the area. PTL. Whalen observed him on Broadway, but he ran into the woods. Our police dog and Mt. Pleasant's police dog were called in to search. They were wading through swamp areas around the Tarrytown Lakes. I was concerned that the youth in a frightened state would get injured somewhere along the line. The chief called off the search by 6:00 p.m. After I landed in the copter, Det. Butkovich and I started to check out the youth's former residence. White Plains Police aided us, I started a surveillance in White Plains that lasted for 24 hours. I had Det. Butkovich, Sgt. Brophy and PTL. Whalen with me. I had received information on the youth's possible whereabouts. Sgt. Brophy and PTL. Whalen observed the youth at a restaurant he was believed to frequent. They arrested him at 7:05 p.m., Friday night, September 30, 1977, near White Plains Hospital. Det. Butkovich and I were watching another spot on the east side of White Plains at the time. The youth didn't resist and apologized for the trouble he had caused. He said that he had escaped because he didn't want to go back to jail. The officers with me should be praised for their alertness during the long hours of waiting at various locations.

I testified at a felony hearing concerning the burglary on October 13, 1977. Judge Maroney ordered the case to be held over for the Grand Jury. He reduced the bail and imposed a curfew on the youth and warned him to adhere to it. He was told to live at home with his parents. Det. Butkovich and I would stay in touch with the youth and provide support for him.

At approximately 11:30 p.m. on November 2, 1977, Det. Butkovich and I received some information from an informant concerning a large quantity of cocaine. The informant stated that it would be necessary to act immediately to seize the cocaine before it was diluted, packaged, and shipped out. This would be one of the few times we acted without a search warrant, because of the time element. Shortly after midnight, on November 3, 1977, Det. Butkovich and I, along with PTL. Biro went to the second floor apartment of Francisco Espinosa. We crashed through the door of the apartment and seized Espinosa with the cocaine in front of him on the table. The five ounces of pure cocaine had a street value of $50,000 after packaging and cutting. We charged Francisco Espinosa, 28 years of age, with criminal possession of a controlled substance in the first degree, an A-1-Felony. Espinosa, a native of Columbia, South America, was married to a local woman.

We also seized two books with the addresses of people who were Espinosa's accomplices and customers in the United States and Columbia. Espinosa's bail was set at $100,000. A local woman put up her home as collateral and the bail was reduced to $50,000. We believe the woman received a $5,000 payoff for her efforts, which saved Espinosa's partners some money and kept the source of their funds secret. We testified before the grand jury and Espinosa was indicted for an A-1-Felony. A-1-Felonies are the class of serious crimes, such as murder. The suspect covered his tracks by appearing to be just a driver for a beer distributor. This was a completely legitimate job, but the well-tailored suits in his closet were quite stylish. They weren't the sort of garments you would expect a truck driver to wear, but he apparently didn't get them with his truck driver's paycheck. He made his money as a courier in the cocaine trade, distributing the expensive white powder in Westchester and Rockland Counties. We had contacted the undercover narcotics officers we worked with and D.E.A. The person working for us was one of a very few who could give us the flights and airports where the drug was coming in for distribution by Espinosa.

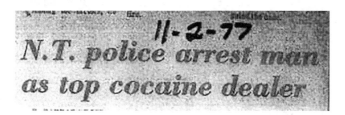

11-2-77
N.T. police arrest man as top cocaine dealer

We had identified the person who was above Espinosa in the Columbian operation. Espinosa's attorneys attempted to have our search declared illegal. When I was testifying in Westchester Supreme Court, I observed people from Columbia enter the courtroom. After the hearing, a Westchester Supreme Court Judge ruled on September 13, 1978, that our search was valid. The ruling would clear the way for Espinosa's trial. At approximately 5:00 a.m., on the morning of September 20, 1978, I was awakened by a telephone call from a detective in Queens, New York. He told me that Espinosa went to Elisa's Hideaway, a bar at 69th St. and Woodside in Queens, N.Y. As he left the bar, he was shot in the stomach with a 38-caliber bullet. He was taken to Elmhurst Hospital where he died at 1:00 p.m. He did not divulge any information to police before he died. I learned that he had been asked about our upcoming trial the night he was shot. The truth was that Espinosa was given the opportunity to cooperate with police prior to the trial, but he refused. The detective from Queens told me that this was the 35th drug related homicide there. He said that the Columbians would kill anyone facing a long jail term who could help put away the hierarchy in the drug trade. He said that Det. Butkovich and I were in danger. The detective told me that they would kill the informant that we had in this case. On October 16, 1978, our informant was found dead in the informant's apartment. The police in the area, where the informant lived, believed it to be a drug overdose. We met with them and gave them the information we had.

We had been working on the investigation of a policy (numbers) bank for several months. A bank is a drop point for the runner who collects the bets. Because of the large number of runners involved and the fact that some of them may recognize us, we had investigators of the Westchester County Sheriff's Department working with us on the case. On the morning of Friday, November 18, 1977 we had obtained a search Warrant for the Cortlandt Lounge at Cortlandt and Clinton Streets. The fact that this appeared to be a bar helped to conceal the runners bringing in the work (bets) every day. Friday was a good day to raid a bank because, in addition to having the regular bets for Friday, there would be bets placed and collected for Saturday and Sunday. We would aim to raid the bank late in the morning to early in the afternoon.

The most work would be there at that time, but we had to make sure it was not transferred somewhere else in the afternoon. I had Det. Butkovich, Sgt. Brophy, PTL. Biro, PTL. Ferguson in plain clothes with me and investigators of the sheriff's department in a van. As we entered the Cortlandt Lounge, I observed William Bentley, the key figure in the operation, run toward the right rear of the lounge. He had a wastepaper basket with him, I ran after him as he entered a bathroom and locked the door. I kicked the door in and seized Bentley and the basket. It was full and packed with policy slips. We seized nearly 50,000 policy plays valued at more than $50,000. Arrested and charged with felony promoting gambling and felony possession of gambling records were William Bentley, 52 years of age, of Greenburgh, New York. Bentley had served 15 days in the county penitentiary last year for an arrest we made. Also arrested was Charles Simpson, 47 years of age, of Ossining charged with one count of felony possession of gambling records and Theodore Becker, 68 years of age, of Tarrytown, New York, charged with felony possession of gambling records. The betting slips that were seized ranged from 60 cents to $13 for each number play. The work (bets) represented the collection of 14 numbers runners.

Sheriff Thomas Delaney, who arrived at police headquarters after the raid said that it was "rare" to knock off a numbers bank of this size. I would testify at a hearing for the raid on Thursday, December 15, 1977. After the hearing, Judge Maroney ruled that the case be sent to the grand jury. It was estimated that the bank handled $22 million in numbers annually.

On January 11, 1978, we arrested Henry Bowman, the owner of "The Garage Sale" a used furniture store on Beekman Avenue for second-degree sale and third degree possession of a controlled substance. Bowman sold 1,000 "black beauties" amphetamines to an undercover officer of the Westchester County Sheriff's Department. Bowman is on parole from the 1976 federal gambling conviction that we worked on. He had prior gambling convictions in 1969, 1971, and 1974. The 1,000 black beauties have a street value of $3,000. At a later date, Bowman would be convicted in Westchester County Supreme Court. He would receive the mandatory sentence of six years to life imprisonment for the drug sale. He will not be eligible for parole for six years. Det. Vincent Butkovich and I, along with Det. Sgt. Baltasar Parra of the Tarrytown Police Department, worked on the case. The investigators of the Westchester County Sheriff's Department who worked on the case were under the direction of John Nault.

In January 1978, Det. Butkovich and I were investigating a large gang of nomadic "gypsies" who has swindled a number of Westchester County residents in flimflams in recent weeks. We were able to get information on the gypsies from some fellow members of the Westchester County Detectives Association who specialized in investigating and gathering information on this group.

On December 29, 1977, two females who were feigning to be new neighbors, entered the home of Eleanor Guzman, on Depeyster Street. Once inside the home, the women began a routine that was intended to confuse the occupants of the house. One asked for a glass of water to take a medication, while the other woman looked around for valuables. The pair then went to the second floor apartment of Mrs. Guzman's cousin, Joseph. Joseph Guzman asked them to leave. One woman went downstairs and was believed to have left the house when the door slammed. The second woman continued to double talk with the Guzmans. The first woman had, in fact, stayed in the house and took $2,000 from a cash box on the first floor and another $40 from a bureau. The gypsies have an uncanny knack for finding money that is hidden in the house. Their methods of pretending to be new neighbors or pleading for assistance of some sort can be easily recognized. However, they often succeed, because they choose their victims carefully, usually taking advantage of the elderly. I had shown photos of some of the gypsies to the Guzmans. They were able to identify one of the women, the one who actually took the cash. We obtained an arrest warrant for Vercha Kertin of Brooklyn. She was to appear in Harrison Justice Court on another burglary charge. We arrested her there and charged her with burglary and grand larceny. She additionally was to face burglary charges in Yonkers, New York. We brought her back to our headquarters for booking and arraignment. That evening at Vercha Kertin's arraignment, a man who referred to himself as the "King of the Gypsies" appeared on her behalf. Judge Thomas Maroney set bail at $5,000 cash and $10,000 secured bond. The "King" identifying himself as Mr. Edwards became upset at the bail amount. Judge Maroney told him, "You may be King of the Gypsies, but I run this court."

Det. Butkovich and I investigated a burglary that occurred on March 14, 1978, on Peirson Avenue in the Philipse Manor section. Jewelry, silverware, and two handguns were stolen from the residence. Charles Michaels of Yonkers, New York, one of the several possible suspects I was investigating, used a handgun to commit suicide on March 24, 1978. I learned of the suicide on April 2, 1978. A ballistics test of the handgun Michaels used to commit suicide was made by the Yonkers P.D. The test revealed that this was one of the guns stolen in the March 14th burglary of 37 Pierson Avenue. Det. Butkovich dusted Michaels's apartment for fingerprints. We had received information that Frank Conger might be involved in the burglary. A subsequent check of the fingerprints in Michaels's apartment showed that Conger had been there and had possibly handled some of the stolen goods. Det. Butkovich and I attempted to arrest Conger at his home in the Bronx, New York, but we found out that he was being held on Riker's Island awaiting sentencing on charges of armed robbery and may also be connected with the theft of a van in New York City. I would arrest Frank Conger after he was sentenced for an armed robbery in another case in State Supreme Court in White Plains, New

York. He is being held at the county jail in Valhalla, New York. He will be arraigned in our court at a later date.

I had been notified that the department's lieutenants would be able to take the examination for police chief that would be given on April 29, 1978, by the New York State Department of Civil Service. I had continued to attend classes in my off-duty time. I again lit a candle at Our Lady of Fatima the day before the exam. I don't believe that a person would receive any help if one does not work hard, study hard and long, and does not prepare himself. On the morning of the examination, after receiving my question booklets, I checked to see the number of questions. There were 125. There were 30 questions on dangling participles in the English grammar section. I said a "Hail Mary" and then took the exam. I took all of the two and a half hours allowed for the exam. I left questions that I wasn't sure of and came back to them later. After the exam, George Mullins and the other attorneys that run the P.T.S. (Police Tutorial Service) School researched some of the questions that were on the exam. At a later date, they said that some questions were not found in any police administration books; they may have come from a naval officer's manual. On a few very difficult questions, even the attorneys who run the school differed on a few of the possible answers.

Det. Butkovich and I continued to give drug abuse seminars for the remainder of the school year. On several occasions, we had a former substance abuser with us. He was able to connect will with the students and give them a different perspective and describe how hard it was to overcome his addiction. We always stressed that if a person had a drug problem and came to us for help, we would do all in our power to help that person. There were different programs we could get them into. But if someone had a drug problem and continued to sell drugs, we would do all we could to arrest that person. We would address the parents of youths and show them what signs to look for if a parent suspects that his or her child is using drugs.

Dating Game Serial Killer

In June 1978, I was contacted by and met with New York City detective Don Tasik. They were trying to find Ellen Hover, who was last seen at her Manhattan apartment on July 15, 1977. She was the daughter of Herman Hover, a scriptwriter and owner of Ciro's—a Hollywood hot spot frequented by celebrities. Her godfather was Dean Martin.

The detective told me they had a psychic who was helping to locate Ellen Hover. The psychic was well-regarded by the police. She had helped to locate missing persons in other cases. The psychic believed that Ellen was by the water in Rockwood Hall, behind Phelps Memorial Hospital, near the Hudson River.

We were checking the wooded area on June 14, 1978. There was a tree that had a bra tied up on the branches. I had contacted the District Attorney's Office. Assistant D.A. Carl Falcone responded. The medical examiner was notified. At the base of the tree were some rocks and solid dirt. Digging with my hands, I began to find bones. After removing her skeletal remains, the M.E. would be able to identify the body through dental records. We would begin a long investigation. I had Detective Vincent Butkovich of our department work with me. In a book in Ellen Hover's apartment, she had written how she was meeting a man named John Berger. She had told friends that he was a photographer whom she had met on an unemployment line. She was 23 years old. I received information that John Berger had a job in New Hampshire at a camp, counseling teenaged girls. Det. Butkovich and I drove to New Hampshire. When we got there, we were able to ascertain that John Berger was actually Rodney Alcala. Rodney Alcala was a photographer, who was a contestant on the TV show, *"The Dating Game."* He was a suspect in the murder of 23-year-old Manhattan flight attendant, Cornelia Crilley. Det. Butkovich and I drove back from New Hampshire and went directly to New York City to interview people. We did not sleep. There was too much work to be done. Ellen Hover's family stated that they could not go through the emotional turmoil that came along with meeting us and going through the investigation would be tiring. We followed every friend and spoke with many people regarding Alcala. A major breakthrough in the case came when we interviewed the young lady that Alcala had taken out. She told us about going out with Alcala to a place in Westchester County where he photographed her. She agreed to get in our unmarked police vehicle in New York City and show us the area.

We did not say anything. She gave us directions from New York City into Westchester County. She continued to tell us which route they were on until we came to Rockwood Hall on the Hudson. We walked with her through the woods until she showed us the spot where he took her and photographed her. She took us to the exact spot where I had dug up the remains of Ellen Hover. I told her what happened to Ellen Hover right where we were standing. We had many questions for her. I told her that if Alcala contacted her, to contact us and not go with him! We drove her back to New York City. She knew she was lucky to be alive! We continued our investigation and followed every lead. We set up surveillances. At one point, detectives in Los Angeles, California, contacted me. They were building a murder case against Alcala in California. We discussed our cases. They asked to meet with us. They flew in from California. They were building a good case against Alcala. They believed that we had an excellent case as well. We agreed to attempt to put the two cases together. Alcala went back to California. I called them to give them some information on him.

At this point, they found him with a very young girl that he had tied up and was raping. He jumped out a window while they tried to save the girl's life. We all knew at this point that the "Dating Game Serial Killer" was an out-of-control monster. The California courts would not allow us to put our cases together. He would be brought to trial in California and was convicted of several murders there. He has been on death row in California since then.

We continued to investigate this case. Cornelia Crilley, a 23-year-old T.W.A. flight attendant was raped in her upper east side apartment in 1971. She was strangled with her own pantyhose. She had moved into her apartment the day before she was murdered. I had Det. Butkovich working with me on the investigation. We were able to connect Rodney Alcala to the rape and murder of Cornelia Crilley.

We continued to make drug arrests, and we continued to make arrests of person involved in gambling operations.

In the first week of August 1978, the grades for the chief's examination were mailed out by the County Personnel Office. I was at home with Pat when the mail was delivered. Pat's mom was visiting with us. Pat and I saw the envelope from the county Personnel Office in the mail. Pat asked me if she could open it. I said, "Okay." As Pat opened the envelope and took out the yellow sheet with the exam results on them, she said, "Oh, my God."

I said to myself, "Oh, no." I knew that was a tough exam.

Spota places 1st on chief's test

Then she said, "104.7." I was number one in the county. Pat, her mom, and I were all excited. I would receive a call from a Gannett newspaper reporter. He had the results of the chief's and lieutenant's examinations. The reporter asked me about the points above 100 that I received. I explained to him that although I had over three years' active duty in the Navy, I did not receive the 2.5 or 5 points given for veterans, because I did not serve during a war. I did receive .4 of a point for my years of service as a police officer, as did everyone else who had passed the exam. I said that I would like to thank the administration for giving me the opportunity to take the exam, village residents for wishing me well, and my family for tolerating me. I added that my only regret was that my parents weren't alive to see the results with me.

For several months, the department's sergeants and lieutenants worked on a draft of a new set of rules and regulations for the police department. We worked on stricter enforcement of departmental standards, development of clearer lines of authority, and formulation of a clearer definition of the police officer's powers and responsibilities. The new rules and regulations were voted on and passed by the board of trustees and made part of the Village Code.

In December 1978, I was promoted to the rank of executive lieutenant. I would continue to head the detective bureau, but I would also be responsible for the administration of the department and the deployment of the uniform personnel. I would be working in uniform when I was not acting as head of the Detective Bureau. The department's other lieutenant would continue to work opposite me on the other shift. It was time for me to buy some new police uniforms. Since becoming lieutenant, and with this position, I realized it was time to shave the moustache and trim the hair. Your appearance is much different in uniform than when you worked on drug and organized crime cases.

We would wrap up a drug case that we had been working on for three months. At 4:30 a.m., on December 21, 1978, we raided a third floor apartment and arrested Richard Cline, 36 years of age, and Richard Solis, 24 years of age, of White Plains, New York. They were each charged with three counts of possession of a controlled substance and possession of a hypodermic needle. We seized a variety of drugs including barbiturates, Valium, Elavil, and some 100 pills of various drugs. Solis had 15 previous arrests on charges of larceny, burglary, robbery, and forgery. Cline had twelve prior arrests on charges of larceny, burglary, and possession of dangerous drugs. Participating in the raid in plain clothes were Det. Butkovich, myself, Sgt. James Brophy, Sgt. Lee Hayward, and PTL. William Patten. Patrolmen James Whalen, Ron Biro, and Gordon Ferguson were in uniform.

On Friday, March 23, 1979, shortly after 4 p.m., we raided a numbers bank on Beekman Avenue. Arrested at the Day and Night Delicatessen were Renaldo "The Godfather" Rodriguez, 40; Andres Hernandez, 47 years of age; Roberto Hernandez, 53 years of age; and Orlando Buck, 40 years of age. Each was charged with promoting gambling in the first degree, a felony, and possession of gambling records, also a felony. Buck was additionally charged with possession of marijuana, a violation. The bank accepted bets from customers throughout lower Westchester. As we were making arrests, the store's telephone kept ringing with persons trying to place bets. Confiscated were a large amount of policy "number bets," two adding machines, and two calculators that were used in the operation. The delicatessen was owned by Umberto Santos of Main Street, Port Chester, who would be charged with Alcohol Beverage Control violations stemming from the raid. The Westchester County District Attorney's Office was asking that bail be set at $5,000 cash or bond for each man arrested. The officers involved in the raid were Det. Vincent Butkovich, Sgt. James Brophy, PTL. James Whalen, PTL. Ron Biro, PTL. William Patten, PTL. Gordon Ferguson, and myself. The raid culminated a three-month investigation by our department.

On April 15, 1979, the office of the Sleepy Hollow Cemetery was burglarized. We were investigating an incident in which 150 gravestones were overturned at the cemetery. We found two typewriters and office materials that had been taken from the office. The items were hidden in a wooded area behind the cemetery off Gory Brook Road. We connected two suspects to the burglary after finding their fingerprints on an adding machine inside of the toilet. All stolen property, except for a watchman's clock, was recovered. We arrested a 15-year-old and a 17-year-old for the burglary. The 15-year-old's case would go to family court and the 17-year-old's case would be tried in Village Court. Additional fingerprints were found on the items recovered in the wooded area. PTL. James Whalen, Deputy Sheriff Al Peffers of the County Crime Laboratory and myself conducted the investigation.

On April 18, 1979, an alert patrolman observed two males, as they left a house on Munroe Avenue in the Philipse Manor section of the community. At 2:30 p.m. PTL. Gordon Ferguson observed one male carrying a yellow pillowcase leaving the rear of the house. PTL. Henry Mockler and I responded to the scene and, with PTL. Ferguson stopped the suspect's vehicle. The pillowcase contained an extensive amount of jewelry, silverware, clocks, and vases. The owners of the home and a relative would later identify the items. The driver of the vehicle and the male carrying the pillowcase, of Mount Vernon, N.Y., were both charged with burglary, criminal mischief, and possession of stolen property. We were investigating the possibility that the aforementioned two males may have been involved in another burglary committed the previous week.

An elderly woman was in her home on Devries Avenue in the Philipse Manor section of the community when a man broke a window on the first floor, entered the house, and began ransacking the house. When the man went upstairs, he was confronted by the lady. He ordered her to return to her bedroom, but she ran down the stairs and out of the house to a neighbor's house. The neighbor, Theodore Muldoon, told his 13-year-old son to guard the woman's front door and told his son's friend to guard the woman's rear door. Mr. Muldoon then entered the house as the man was coming out. As the man started to run, Mr. Muldoon grabbed him and pinned him against the wall inside of the front door. Mr. Muldoon put his hand on the man's throat and warned him not to move. When we arrived, we arrested Edward C. Hurst, 29 years of age, of Yonkers, N.Y., for burglary. The suspect was concealing a four-inch knife on his person. Talk about profiles in courage. At the time, Mr. Muldoon had a prosthetic leg and the woman also had a lot of guts.

In April 1979, Chief John Jandrucko notified the Mayor and the board of trustees that he would retire on October 7, 1979, at age 65. Lieutenant Michael O'Shaughnessey and I had both passed the exam for chief of police. The mayor and board had discussed the promotion with me. One trustee stated that he wanted to interview me alone. I met with him in the board of trustees' room. He started by telling me that the family didn't want me. I said, "You mean your sister and brother-in-law, whom I had arrested for bookmaking.

He replied, "No. The Family (The Genovese Family)."

As startled as I was I replied, "No, I'm sure they don't want me." He told me he was a born again Christian and what he had done wrong was in his prior life. That he attended Mass regularly and was completely changed. He said, "I worked for Pete Vitchelli (who runs gambling in this area of New York)." I replied that I had thought he worked for Polsino, because when I arrested him in 1968, he had your name and phone number on his person. He replied, "I bet with Polsino, but I always worked for Vitchelli." He added that his family had run a bar in Tarrytown. "I brought the money up here to take care of everyone back there, but when you came here, we knew it would end." As I listened to him in his loud tone of voice, I couldn't believe that this conversation was happening.

Others in positions of power had no use for me. I would never make an excuse for what I believed in and even if it cost me this promotion I wouldn't compromise my integrity. He asked me about the Police Community Relations Committee that I wanted to form. I explained that a police department should reflect the community it serves, and that the department has no minorities. That we must develop mutual respect and understanding between the police and the people they serve. He asked me whom I would appoint to that committee. I mentioned several minority members of the community and others. At this point, I didn't know what to expect as he looked at me. He said, "I know all that I have to know about you now."

At 8:00 p.m. that night on Monday, April 16, 1979, the board of trustees conducted their regular meeting. They had the certified promotion list for chief of police. The opening for chief of police was brought up. Trustee John Malandrino questioned the wisdom of appointing a new chief six months before the current chief was to retire. He stated that he felt I was more than qualified but could not see the advantage of naming a new chief so quickly. Mayor Philip Zegarelli countered by pointing out that my promotion would provide for a smooth period of transition, adding that it was incumbent on the board to make a quick decision. Trustee James Timmings noted that by delaying its decision the board ran the risk of losing Spota to another municipality in search of a police chief. The motion was put to a vote. By a unanimous vote of the board of trustees, I was named chief of police. The appointment would take effect on October 7, 1979. When contacted by the Gannett Newspaper reporter, I stated, "I would like to thank the mayor and the entire board of trustees. I know they, the community, and the many dedicated men in the department want us to have the finest police department possible, and we will work to that end."

Spota named N.T. chief

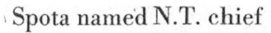

I would continue to be executive lieutenant from this date, April 16, 1979, until October 7, 1979. In addition to my regular duties, I had a great deal of work and planning to do before October 7, 1979.

For the remainder of the spring and throughout the summer, I would spend my off-duty time planning the reorganization of the department, who would be promoted to fill vacancies created by my promotion to chief in October 1979. I would start to write a policy and procedure manual that would take at least a year to complete. I had contacted the Training Division of the Nassau County Police Department for their help in this matter. The Nassau County P.D. is one of the best organized and trained departments in the state. A part of the manual, but something I had to have in place by October 7, 1979, would be a Performance Evaluation

Report for all members of the department and instructions on how to use and evaluate same. I was glad that we had completed the new rules and regulations for the department, that would be one less thing to do. I would complete the draft of the Police Community Relations Committee, the General Concepts, the purpose, and the appointment of a broad cross section of the community as members of the committee to start in October 1979. The delegation of authority and responsibility to the supervisors of the department for the specific areas they would be in charge of in order for the department to run properly. I would contact the New York State Division of Criminal Justice Services and ask them to do a study of the department, its equipment, the facility, and what is needed to operate as a first rate police department. I would become the chief of police of an all-male, Caucasian department. I would lay out plans in a legal, ethical, and moral way for this department to reflect all of the members of the community it serves.

In the last week of September 1979, I was acting chief of police, because the chief was on vacation. As I was driving to headquarters at approximately 8:51 a.m., I received a call over the police radio from Lieutenant O'Shaughnessey. He stated that he had received a call from the Sleepy Hollow Cemetery that three elderly women from New Jersey were sightseeing at the historic cemetery and reported seeing a corpse on the ground. He said that it was probably a mannequin. I was in the area, so I responded. As I got near the section in question, I looked up from the road and observed a fully clothed corpse on the grass next to a grave. A grave had been opened for a burial and a stone grave marker was pushed onto a coffin that was in the adjacent grave. The coffin then was opened and the body of Helen Waters, who had died four years ago at age 80, was removed. Her son, Gordon, who died on September 25, was to be buried in the open grave in two days. Approximately one foot of dirt had covered Helen Waters' coffin before her body was removed. I had Det. Butkovich and Sgt. DeFalco, who I had working in the detective bureau, notified. The District Attorney's Office was also notified. The body was well-preserved as I observed it on the grass. I tried to contain my anger that anyone would do this to someone's mother.

When I was contacted by the media, I said, "No crime will be tolerated in this community, especially a crime that's as sacrilegious, insidious, and horrendous as this. The detectives lifted fingerprints from objects near the grave and corpse. They began interviewing approximately 15 youths known to frequent the cemetery grounds after hours. Helen Waters' corpse was placed in a new coffin and reburied before her son's funeral. Her son was buried in the adjacent grave as scheduled. Sgt. Dellalco and Det. Butkovich worked around the clock on the investigation. The other officers of the department were very upset over what had happened. On October 3, 1979, Sgt. DeFalco and Det. Butkovich arrested Lloyd Quinnn, Victor Mallet, of Franklin Courts Apartments, Tarrytown, N.Y., and John Miren, of North

Tarrytown charging them with felony counts of body stealing and criminal mischief. All had prior arrest records.

At a later date, John Miren and Lloyd Quinn would plead guilty to the charges before County Supreme Court Justice Lawrence Martin. Miren would be sentenced to a year in jail. Quinn would be sentenced to five years' probation. Victor Mallet would be found guilty after a trial. Mallet would be sentenced to three years in jail. Youthful offender status was denied for Miren and Quinn.

Friday, OCT. 10, 1961

3 teens charged in animal's death

Police suspect cult practices may be involved

By Richard L. Williams
Staff Writer

viction, could result in all court proceedings being sealed from public inspection.

Two of the suspects live in North Tarrytown, and the third lives in Verplanck, police said. Spota said the teens attend public schools in their communities.

Sleepy Hollow High School Principal Ira Oerstatcher could not

Sgt. James Whalen said the case could be far-reaching.

"There are untold numbers in this group," he said. "It's a problem that not only North Tarrytown is going to face, but also the rest of the county and the rest of the nation."

Whalen said the group's logo has been painted on several build-

105

Chapter Five

On October 7, 1979, I became chief of police. I had been 39 years old when the marks for the chief's test had come out in August 1978, and I was now 40 years old. I began moving into my new office, taking pictures of Pat, Todd, and Melissa with me. Todd was nine years old and Melissa six years old. I guess it was unique seeing Todd and Melissa visiting my office. I was putting my law books on the two bookshelves behind my desk. I brought some awards and items I had received from my family. I hung up the framed commendation from Bobby Kennedy. I also hung up a picture of Vince Lombardi with this message above him, *"All right, Mister, let me tell you what winning means. You're willing to go longer, work harder, give more than anyone else."* I strongly believed in that message. Also, Vince Lombardi bore a striking resemblance to my father. I put a statue of Our Blessed Mother that Filomena Fallacaro, our village clerk, had given to me and that Father Menna had blessed in my office.

The statue belonged there because if it weren't for Our Blessed Mother, I wouldn't have been there. I had a new marble pen and pencil set that Pat and the children had given to me for my desk, Pat's mom and dad gave me a beautiful brass desk lamp, and her twin sisters, Jean and Joan, gave me a brass ashtray. I would join the Westchester County Chiefs of Police Association, the New York State Association of Chiefs of Police, and the International Association of Chiefs of Police. I declined an interview with the media on the changes I would me making in the department so that I could meet with the uniformed officers and detectives first. This meeting would take place the first week. I had contacted George Mullin, an attorney and head of the P.T.S. School, one of the best law enforcement schools. He agreed to give classes to the department on Article 35 of the Penal Law Defense of Justification—the use of physical and deadly physical force. L considered this subject to be most important for the department. You must know when and where you may use deadly physical and physical force. You may only have a split second to make this decision and you must make the correct decision. There was a lot of work to do, and I would spend the weekends to make sure everything was finished. I completed an organizational chart for the department so that clear lines of authority and responsibility were established.

In my first week as chief of police, I met with the entire department. I explained to the officers what I expected of them and the organizational changes in the department. Lt. Michael O'Shaughnessey would be in charge of scheduling the department personnel and would be acting chief in my absence.

I recommended that Sgt. James Brophy be promoted to lieutenant to fill the vacancy created by my promotion. He would set up a department training program and, in addition, he would qualify all officers in firearms twice a year at our firearms range. I would transfer Sgt. Carmen DeFalco from the uniform division to Det. Sgt. and head of the detective bureau where he would work with Det. Butkovich under the unconsolidated laws of the state of New York, a chief may transfer an officer to detective or plainclothes duty, however, a pay increase must be voted on by the board of trustees, which I would recommend. I would create a Juvenile Aide Bureau. There were several candidates for the position. This person would be responsible for setting up drug education programs in our schools. The Juvenile Aide Officer would be responsible for handling cases that would be sent to family court. We would recruit minority applicants for the department and help prepare them for the civil service exam for police officer. I would try to establish a Department K-9 Unit and have the officer and K-9 certified in the searching for drugs. I would recommend the purchase of a three-wheel Cushman type vehicle for the department's civilian parking enforcement officers. Sgt. Lee Hayward would be in charge of the department's vehicles and equipment.

With a limited budget, we could not immediately replace all of the department vehicles, but Sgt. Hayward, with a community service program from the General Motors Plant, would have all the marked department vehicles painted the same color, a national police blue. He would help outline the needed equipment that I would include in my detailed budget request for the fiscal year (next budget year) June 1, 1980, through May of 1981. Sgt. William Booth would be in charge of the department plant facility.

I stated that all officers would pay their own way in the community. This would include even a cup of coffee. The officers would not be obligated or indebted to anyone and people will have more respect for us. There would be no sacred cows either in the department or the community. A person receiving a traffic ticket or summons should be prepared to "plead guilty or not guilty" and not try to have tickets fixed. There would be a biannual evaluation of all officers by their superiors. I would evaluate the lieutenants, the head of the detective bureau and the juvenile aide bureau. The lieutenants would evaluate the uniformed sergeants and the uniform sergeants would evaluate the patrol officers. I would have a final review of all performance evaluation forms after they were signed by the officers and their superiors. I had copies of the evaluation forms to show members of the department. The evaluation categories include appearance, tact in dealing with the public, integrity, attitude, quantity, and quality of work, common sense, efficiency, job knowledge, and sick time. The sick time would be noted on the day of the week and the part of the work week that it occurs.

There was a section for a superior to write up an officer for a formal department commendation. I had completed that section of the department policy manual. All of the categories for medals (bars) had been included. I had set up a committee with an officer of every rank to meet twice a year to evaluate the commendations and vote on them. Once a year, we would have a department awards program dinner. There were questions during the meeting about the Police Community Relations Committee I was setting up. Some officers wanted to know if it was going to be a civilian review board. I answered, "No." I had made up forms for officers that might be brought up on department charges. The officer would have the option of waiving a disciplinary hearing and pleading guilty. If this occurred, the officer would be disciplined by me. This would not prolong the disciplinary process; the officer would once again become a productive person after correcting his mistakes. That is unless the charges warrant a dismissal of the officer. In case of the latter, formal charges would be drawn up and the officer would face a hearing and trial. I mentioned to the department that there were things relating to integrity that would bring a dismissal of the officer. No officer would ever again find himself walking a beat around the clock in the snow, because he had made an organized crime arrest. With the officers who wanted to remain with the department, we would work together to build the finest police department possible.

To make the department reflect the community it serves would be a full time, continuous project. To appoint new officers to the force, they must be on a county civil service exam list and be in the top three of the list. We would encourage and help minority candidates prepare for the examination. The department, at full complement, would have 27 full-time officers. The civilians working for the department would total 12. They would include parking enforcement officers who I would assign to the three-wheel Cushman, so they could cover a much larger area in a more effective manner, thus relieving officers to be able to perform more police duties. There would be eight traffic positions covered by civilians and two police matrons for female prisoners. In the area of civilians, I could make an immediate impact on appointing minorities. I would hire Vilma Lesmo, a female Hispanic, to secretarial duties. Part time employees could not exceed 17 hours a week, but these appointments would be beneficial to the community and the department. Vilma Lesmo being bilingual would type information for the Hispanic community, police officer exam information, and notices. The Auxiliary Police would be under my authority. The approximately 20 volunteers of this group were invaluable to the department. They helped with crowd control at church crossings on Sundays and various other functions. Like the all-volunteer fire department, they were dedicated, unselfish members of the community who served without any financial remuneration.

The following are the general concepts and purpose of the Police Community Relations Committee:

Community Relations — General Concepts

The primary objective of the department's community relations program is to emphasize the mutual interdependence of the police department and the community at large in the maintenance of law and order and in the prevention of crime, to develop mutual respect, and understanding between the police and the people they serve; to promote an atmosphere conducive to greater public cooperation and, as a consequence, greater police effectiveness.

Such understanding and cooperation are greatly facilitated through a continuous on-going interchange of information and views. Consequently, the attainment of sound police-community relations involves the opening and maintenance of a series of channels through which communication can be maintained with all members of the community interested in its lawful development.

The chief of police and his men hold the key to the accomplishment of this objective. Their leadership initiative and personal commitment are necessary if meaningful police-community dialogue is to be established. They must encourage people in the community to feel free to discuss grievances, real or imaginary. They must cultivate avenues of friendly communication with individuals and groups in the community and solicit and maintain their interest in the law enforcement process. School authorities, business leaders and local press, the clergy, leaders of block associations, and other neighborhood organizations represent some of the sources through which the chief of police and his men can develop a community-wide spirit of cooperation with the police. These contacts may be maintained on a formal or informal basis and can be the "sensory preceptors" which enable them to anticipate problems, or become readily aware of them, and initiate appropriate corrective and preventive remedies. Areas of misunderstanding can, thus, be detected and corrected before they erupt into major crises.

Fundamental to police-community relations is good police work based on a policy of equal treatment for all members of the community. It is the responsibility of the chief of police to make this basic philosophy of the police community relations a reality.

A favorable public attitude toward the police must be earned. It is influenced greatly by the personal conduct and personal attitude of each member of the force; by his personal integrity and courteous manner; by his respect for the due process of law; by his devotion to the principles of justice, fairness, and impartiality.

By precept and example, the chief of police must set the standard for performance by his subordinates. The personal conduct and personal attitude of each member of the department in the performance of duty reflects the effectiveness of his leadership.

Purpose

The Purpose of the N.T.P.D. Community Relations Committee:

To promote community support for law enforcement efforts.

To encourage and increase cooperation between the police and the people they serve.

To develop specific programs in accordance with true needs, interests, and resources of the local community that will support the maintenance of law and order and the prevention of crime and delinquency.

To develop an understanding of police objectives and of the difficulties and hazards confronting the police officer in the performance of his duties.

To develop an awareness of the powers and limitation of powers of the police—what the police can and cannot do.

A recognition of the individual citizen's responsibility in maintaining and preserving the peace.

To develop an insight into the police departments operations, especially its humanitarian, protective, and preventive services.

The Committee Members

Can help make the police department personnel aware of the public's point of view and more sensitive and responsive to the needs, feelings, and attitudes of the community as they pertain to police services. Citizen criticism of the department, legitimate or unfounded, aired in the open, hospitable setting of a committee meeting in which key police department personnel participate, can be the foundation for developing a constructive program of mutual understanding and cooperation.

An informed community relations committee can be a vital medium for public education. It can interpret to the community, in a meaningful way, police policy and techniques, especially as they relate to operations in the public focus: at demonstrations, strikes, public assemblies, or parades.

The committee, through education and persuasion, can also foster compliance with local ordinances which prohibit activities that are socially tolerated in other jurisdictions.

The committee can be a strong force in counteracting negative stereotyping. They can stimulate ways and means by which local citizenry get to know police department personnel as individuals and cultivate an appreciation of the police officer as a necessary and vital member of the community. Conversely, the face-to-face relationships of the community relations committee allow police department personnel to gain a better understanding of the local citizen and his problems.

In our pluralistic society, two important by-products of the community relations committee can be improved inter-group relations, and reduction in racial tensions. Broad public involvement in neighborhood crime prevention efforts create opportunities for the interaction of representative religious, racial, and ethnic groups of diverse social, economic backgrounds. Such intercommunity dialogue promotes an advancement of tolerance and understanding.

R.J.S.

The following were my original appointments to the police community relations committee, representing the Van Tassel Apartments (a large apartment complex in the center of the village) Robert Kargoll, Margaret White of the College Arms Apartments (located in the south end of the village) and representing the Black Community, Leon Solis, Luis Matos, and Umberto Leon representing the Hispanic community, Mary Ward of the Webber Park section of the village, Debbie Lovecky of Philipse Manor, and to also serve as Secretary of the committee, John Reiners of the Sleepy Hollow Manor section of the community. Fire Chief Frank Gallagher representing the fire department, Capt. Reginald Cardwell of the Auxiliary Police, Jack Lynch, Chief of Security at General Motors, William Barron, assistant principal of Sleepy Hollow High School representing the Public Schools of Tarrytown, Harry Donsky, editor and general manager of the Daily News, Edna Belanich representing the North Washington Street area of the village and Lenny Intoni, Jr. of the village's Civic Businessmen's Association. The police department officers on the committee were Lieut. Michael O'Shaughnessy, Sgt. Lee Hayward, PTL. Gabriel Hayes, President of the department's P.B.A., and myself. If a resident or a group had a problem, the committee representative could provide a direct line to the police. It was a forum in which the community and the department could make an attempt to iron out problems and misunderstandings in a less emotional environment. The committee would meet on the last Thursday of the month at 7:30 p.m. in the courtroom. The first meeting was held on October 25, 1979. Each member of the committee would make a report on his/her area of representation or concern. Solutions to the problems would be discussed and implemented whenever possible. A good exchange of ideas would be freely discussed.

Margaret White, a committee member, was appointed to the position of village trustee, replacing a member who was leaving. She became the first black person to hold this position. We had become good friends. We would discuss how we were going to attract qualified minority candidates to take the police exam that would be given by the County Personnel Department every couple of years. Alone, we would agree that the candidates would have to possess outstanding qualifications so as not to reflect adversely on his or her race.

The community relations committee would, at times, work late into the night until all members concerns were addressed. The second meeting would be held on the last Thursday in November 29, 1979. It was understood that if a member had a problem that could not wait for the next meeting that he/she could telephone or meet with me.

A short time after becoming chief of police, I received a transfer request. The officer requesting the transfer had many fine attributes that you look for in a police officer. Additionally, he had a Hispanic background and was fluent in Spanish. With a large Hispanic population, he would be a good fit for our community. I recommended Manuel Caixeiro to the board of trustees and his transfer was approved. When Hispanics in the community had a problem, they were grateful to have a police officer converse with them in their native language.

Police bring food

North Tarrytown Auxiliary Police Officer Luis Matos unloads a box Sunday contains some of the total 4,000 food items the police auxiliary collected during the past several weeks for Rosary Hill Home. Hawthorne. Auxiliary Captain Reginald Cardwell, center, helps along with Police Chief Richard Spota. Cardwell also presented the home with a $255 check. Sister Kevin and Sister Patricia of Rosary Hill look on.

One thing about transfers must be made clear. I would never approach an officer from another department about transferring to my department. If an officer came to police headquarters, requesting an interview for a transfer, the proper paperwork would be filled out by the officer. If the officer met the criteria for the department, his/her current department and/or the Westchester County Personnel

Office would have to approve the transfer. The officer must be a good officer first and then any additional attributes the officer may have would be evaluated accordingly.

In the fall of 1979, the auxiliary police conducted their drive for items of food to be given to the Rosary Hill Home in Hawthorne. The home was completely run by Sister Kevin and her nuns for terminally ill cancer patients. I went with Capt. Reginald Cardwell and the auxiliary police on a Sunday to help bring some of the more than 4,000 items of food. The nuns reminded me of the nuns who taught me at Annunciation School. Then, nuns gave tender loving care to the patients, day in and day out.

They were not subsidized by any organization. I know there are many worthwhile causes, but there are none that are more deserving than the nuns at Rosary Hill Home in Hawthorne.

From the first day that I became chief of police, I let everyone know that no racial epithets or racial slurs would be permitted. I did not have anyone referring to another using a racial slur or epithet. The only time a slur or epithet was used was in the form of a joke or reference. At that point, the person guilty of this would be brought immediately into my office. The person would be told that an ignorant person thinks in terms of a group, an intelligent person thinks in terms of the individual. If one uses that word again, he/she will face disciplinary charges. This was not acceptable and would not be tolerated. The few times that this happened, it ended and did not occur again. If everyone in this world did not use racial slurs or epithets, this would be a far better world. It is the responsibility of the person at the top of every organization to have no tolerance for this type of conduct.

The supervisors and officers working the front desk in police headquarters had been advised by me not to let anyone in to see me, concerning a summons. However, early on, a body shop tow truck operator did manage to get by the desk without revealing his true reason for wanting to speak with me. As he entered my office, he pulled out a stack of parking summonses, stating that he had let them pile up before coming to police headquarters with them. I usually don't lose my temper, but I shouted to him, "Get out! Get out!" One of the officers asked me where I wanted him to go (the holder of the summonses). I said, "Out the front door, make a right turn and into the courtroom to pay the summonses."

I had gone to Eastchester to pay my respect to an Eastchester detective whose mother had died. When I was leaving, the detective said lo me that he had seen my brother in his room at Lawrence Hospital in Bronxville, N.Y. He added, shaking his head, "Boy, that cancer is terrible." As I left, I realized that George didn't want to trouble me, so he had entered the hospital without telling me. As I arrived at the hospital, one of the doctors asked to talk with me. He said that George had been checking the X-Rays of some of his patients. He looked at one X-Ray and asked the X-Ray technician, "Who is this poor S.O.B.?"

The X-Ray technician responded, "That's you, Dr. Spota." I visited with George in his room. With his usual honesty, he explained his illness to me. He told me what he would go through before he died. George's wife, my sister-in-law, Eleanor, had died two years earlier. She had survived her five-year period after her mastectomy and had died of a heart attack in her sleep. They had been married a long time and her death affected George immensely, although he would not talk about it. Sometimes, you wonder why the worst things happen to the best people. George had a colostomy after Eleanor's death, but the cancer had spread. George had a strong influence on my life since the time our father had died while I was in my teens.

On Sunday, December 16, 1979, I received a telephone call from police headquarters, shortly after noon, that there was a stabbing at 400 North Broadway. When I arrived at the scene of the two-family house, George Mangieri was lying in a pool of blood in his bedroom. He was pronounced dead at the scene. He had been stabbed repeatedly on the left side of his chest. The murder weapon, an 11-inch carving knife, was recovered at the scene. After the preliminary investigation, Virgil Sanford, 50 years, was charged with murder in the second degree. Sanford was George Mangieri's son-in-law. He lived upstairs in the house with his wife and daughter. Mangieri lived on the first floor. Sanford had been unemployed for the past two years. At this time, it would have been "pure conjecture" to state a motive.

George Mangieri had operated a bar next to his house from 1933 until he retired in 1975. His nephew operates a florist there now. George Mangieri was one of the most loved persons in the area. As word of the murder reached the residents of the community, there was an outpouring of shock and grief. As a friend of his, James Halpin, a fellow bar owner, stated, "George Mangieri was a legend of North Tarrytown, just like Ichabod Crane."

College students at home on spring break or for the holidays would always go to see George. George had his own set of rules. If you got out of hand, you were restricted from the bar for two weeks. He would never let anyone get drunk. If you had no money, he would still serve you. If you needed money, he would lend it to you. George would charge five cents for a beer and fifty cents for a mixed drink. If the patrons started to get out of hand, he would put everyone out and lock the door. Almost everyone who heard about the murder had something good to say about George Mangieri. No one could understand why someone had killed him. The officers involved in the investigation were Det. Sgt. Carmen DeFalco, Det. Vincent Butkovich, PTL. Gordon Ferguson, William Patton, John Quartuccio, Gabe Hayes, and Richard Kiggins.

On December 11, I attended the Municipal Police Recruit School (Police Academy) graduation held at the State University at Purchase. PTL. Joseph Lanzo of our department was in the graduating class. PTL. Lanzo was honored for receiving the highest mark for written material in his graduation class. He received a $50 bond from the Westchester County Policemen's Benevolent Association. The award was presented to him by Lt. Arthur Johnson of Briarcliff Manor P.D. on behalf of the Westchester County P.B.A. A job well done by PTL. Lanzo that reflects favorably on our police department.

During my first Christmas season as chief of police, the department unequivocally understood that no member would accept anything from the citizens of the community. However, through delivery men, some persons had left gifts at headquarters. I'm certain that most of the gift givers only meant well and were not trying to buy influence or favor. As I put the giftwrapped packages in my unmarked police vehicle, I felt awkward thinking that some people might think I was receiving, not returning, the gifts. But after I returned them, I was certain that there would not be a recurrence the following year.

Having more bars and clubs per population than any other community in the county could mean hold-ups at holiday time. Liquor stores were always a favorite target. Based on intelligence, information, and common sense I would assign officers to plainclothes duty in private and unmarked vehicles during this time of the year. We would do this when certain burglary patterns were prevalent.

In January 1980, I would assign two police officers, James Whalen and Ron Biro, to work in plainclothes on organized crime surveillances. They would conduct the investigations during the time when they were off-duty from their regular shifts. They would be coordinated by the detective bureau.

There was planning for several months to celebrate the passage of the Olympic Torch through North Tarrytown on its way to the Olympic Village and Games at Lake Placid, New York. Mayor Philip Zegarelli had appointed several committees to help plan and carry out this special occasion. On February 3, 1980, the mayor, board of trustees, the Olympic Torch Committee, representative organizations and a variety of ethnic groups, some in colorful native dress, gathered at the Union Church of Pocantico Hills for a special service. The church is opposite the entrance to the Rockefeller Family Estate. It is a beautiful stone church well known not only for some of its famous parishioners, but for its Chagall windows. In the parish hall, following the service, Mayor Zegarelli awarded Olympic flags and torches to the members of the various committees.

On the day the runners and the torch came through the community, February 4, 1980, a replica of the flame was on Broadway, Route 9, and Beekman Avenue. Our six-year-old daughter, Melissa, and Christopher Maceyak led the runners down Broadway to the Sleepy Hollow Restoration. One of the committees had chosen Melissa and Christopher for the run. Melissa and Christopher were born on the same day at Phelps Memorial Hospital. They had been in the window of the maternity ward together when they were born. The Olympic Torch runners carrying the torch, the Olympic officials, those at the ceremony at the Sleepy Hollow Restoration and all of the persons who worked as hard for this day were rewarded with an unforgettable day. Everyone will remember and cherish this truly magnificent day for years to come. On this cold, clear, winter day, the Olympic Flame would continue to burn on Broadway until the end of the games.

I would be working on my detailed budget request for the next several months. There would be budget hearings in the beginning of April. The fiscal year was Jun I through May 31. The department needed many things to bring it up to standards, not the last of these were additional officers, vehicles, equipment, expanded space for evidence control, interrogation, and many other items. I would have all of my supervisors submit to me items that were needed in their area of supervision.

Usually cities and towns in the county have a large tax base, but many villages have a limited tax base and, therefore, chiefs of police in those communities must be creative. All grants must be applied for and researched extensively.

Through the winter and spring, I would try to visit George either at Lawrence Hospital or when he was at home.

On Saturday mornings, I would help coach Todd's dad's Club (Little League) team. I had done this for several years.

In April and then May of 1980, George's condition was getting worse. He came home from the hospital several times only to return. One day, while we were alone in his hospital room, he looked at me and said, "We've both been very stupid. We both could have made a lot of money." I was surprised to hear him say this. But then, he smiled at me and said, "But I would have never respected you if you had."

George was one of those rare MDs that took care of patients whether or not they could pay him. His closest friend, Dr. Carmine Dente, DDS, told me that George would make house calls and charge ten dollars if you had the money to pay him. If a person did not have money, he still took care of the patient. He would never overcharge a health provider and would almost always charge the minimum amount. Dr. Dente added that George was the most intelligent person he had ever known in all areas of life. He added then, after he (George) had finished medical school, he would always be called out to hospitals on a much more frequent basis than older doctors, because of his ethnic group. Towards the end of May 1980, my niece, Jerrylyn, called me on the phone and asked if I could put George somewhere, because she was worried about her parents, Jerry and Lena, who would come up from Long Island and take care of George while he was home. She said that they were really worn out and that she was worried about something happening to them. I contacted the Rosary Hill Home and was able to have George taken there by ambulance. George had been there less than a week when I received a call from Sister Kevin while I was in my office at police headquarters. She said that it was time. I rushed out after calling Jerry and Lena, picked up Pat, and proceeded to Rosary Hill. I didn't take time to change out of my uniform. When we arrived at George's room, in Rosary Hill, Sister Kevin was with him. We told him that Jerry and Lena were on their way. George hung on until they arrived. Pat, Lena, and I stayed with George. Jerry stayed outside of the room. Jerry and George were extremely close all of their lives and Jerry didn't want to see this happen. After George died, Sister Kevin closed his eyes. A large number of people came out for his wake. One of his very special young patients told his parents he had to see Dr. Spota. Tommy had Down syndrome and he loved George very much. George had many special patients and there was always a special love and admiration between him and the patients. Besides the fact that he was a war hero, something he would never talk about, he was the real hero of our family. It was nice to see many of the nuns who had taught me at George's wake. One of the priests said it best when he recalled a woman on the morning of George's funeral saying that this was a sad day for Crestwood. He said that we as Catholics are taught to believe that this should be the happiest day of Dr. Spota's life, as he receives his eternal reward. I knew that Jesus would really enjoy having George with him.

In June 1980, I would formally request a complete study of the police department by the New York State Division of Criminal Justice Services, Bureau for Municipal Police, Albany, New York. Personnel from D.C. I. would stay at police headquarters for an extended period of time to conduct the study. They would examine every facet of the department. All records, files, the plant facility, vehicles, equipment, and anything related to the operation of the department would be made available to them. They would independently conduct the study and, upon the completion, would issue a printed document containing their recommendations. I realized that this study was needed in order for us to have a truly professional, well-run police department.

An investigation and surveillance of an auto parts store on Beekman Avenue was begun in December 1979 and continued until June 18, 1980. One month after the store had opened, we received information that the store was a front for drug sales. I had officers Whalen and Biro conduct the surveillance in conjunction with Det. Sgt. DeFalco and Det. Butkovich. When it was established that drug sales were being made at the store, we brought in county undercover personnel under the supervision of Insp. Sal D'Orio and Lt. John Nault. This was done because using a search warrant alone, even if successful, would result in only a possession charge, while the charge of sale of a controlled substance would result in a much stiffer penalty. It was observed that the owner of the store would pull down a solid metal gate over the storefront when he was going to make a sale of drugs. He also kept old car tires stacked up high in the doorway to conceal whatever was going on in the store.

Parts dealer arrested as drug seller

A raid was conducted at 2:30 p.m. on June 18, 1980, at the N.T. Auto Parts store on Beekman Avenue. The owner of the store, Robert Briggs, 28 years of age, had a spoon of heroin in his possession. It was potent enough to be further diluted. He also had a supply of Valium pills in his possession. Officers Biro and Whalen found glassine envelopes (used for packaging heroin) and a weighing device for drugs in the van of Briggs. Based on an indictment by the county grand jury, that was signed on June 13,

Briggs was charged with two counts of criminal sale of a controlled substance and four counts of criminal possession of drugs. He was additionally charged with two counts of possession of drugs for the drugs seized with the search warrant during the raid. Briggs could receive up to 25 years in prison if he was convicted on even one of the sale charges. The detectives and officers involved in the case did an excellent job.

Shortly after 9:00 a.m., on August 2, 1980, a call was received at police headquarters from a resident of Millard Avenue in the Philipse Manor section. The person making the call, Richard Winfrey, said that he had been out all night and found his father, Irving Winfrey, age 49, dead. Irving Winfrey was found shot to death in his upstairs bedroom. Irving Winfrey had died of gunshot Wound to the head and chest. He was President of Scott Personnel Inc., a Wall Street area employment agency. Winfrey had founded the firm with a former partner in 1961. Winfrey was divorced from his first wife and lived at the home address with his son, Richard, from that marriage. The Winfreys had lived in North Tarrytown for seven years. Irving Winfrey had been separated from his second wife, Barbara, since early that year. She and her daughters from a previous marriage had moved out of the house.

Det. Sgt. Carmen DeFalco and Det. Vincent Butkovich, along with other officers would begin an intensive investigation. Members of District Attorney Carl Vergari's staff would assist in the investigation. When an investigation of a major crime is undertaken, it is always advisable to contact the D.A.'s office as soon as possible, because if an arrest or arrests are made, the prosecutor will be an assistant D.A. It is far better to do more investigative work and collect as much evidence as possible. You can never have too much evidence, but you can lose a trial by not having enough or by improper investigative practices.

The investigation of the Winfrey murder was continuing with the detectives and other officers assigned to the case pursuing all leads and interviewing everyone who could be a suspect or provider of information.

Sunday August 3, 1980

N.T. resident
found fatally
shot at home

The organized crime investigation was also continuing. This was one of the reasons why I had assigned Officer Whalen and Biro to investigate organized crime. A major case such as the Winfrey murder would take almost all of the detectives' time. On August 27, 1980, a search warrant issued by Supreme Court Justice Isaac Rubin in White Plains, New York was executed on Dominick Satelli, a 56-year-old retired employee of General Motors. The officers searched the apartment of Satelli and confiscated more than 250 policy play and $1,000 cash, possibly his take for the day at 11:20 a.m. Satelli was charged with two counts of promoting gambling and two counts of possession of gambling records. PTL. James Whalen and Ron Biro conducted much of the investigation along with Det. Sgt. Carmen DeFalco and Det. Vincent Butkovich. They were assisted on the arrest by PTL. Manny Caixeiro, PTL. Robert Morrison, and PTL. Richard Kiggins. Maryanne Harkins of the District Attorney's Rackets Bureau assisted in the investigation along with Asst. D.A. Carl Falcone, who headed the rackets bureau.

On August 29, 1980, another collector was arrested at 11:25 a.m. after a search warrant issued by State Supreme Court Justice Isaac Rubin, was executed. Erskine "Bub" Sanders, 60 years of age, Tarrytown, was arrested while on lower Cortlandt Street. Sanders had been collecting bets from "runners" while he sat in his parked car. He had 341 bets "plays" in his possession. Sanders was charged with two counts of promoting gambling and two counts of possession of gambling records. PTL. Ron Biro, James Whalen, Det. Sgt. Carmen DeFalco, Det. Vincent Butkovich, PTL. Richard Kiggins and Robert Morrison participated in the investigation and made the arrest. Asst. D.A. Maryanne Harkins of the D.A.'s Rackets Bureau assisted in the investigation.

On September 2, 1980, the owner of a North Tarrytown stationery store was arrested, after a raid at her store turned up gambling records that indicated that more than $250,000 in bets were handled there annually. Christina Letti, 68 years, the proprietor of Letti's Stationery Store, 95 Beekman Avenue, was arrested and charged with three counts of promoting gambling and two counts of possession of gambling records. Det. Sgt. Carmen DeFalco, Det. Vincent Butkovich, PTL. James Whalen, PTL. Ron Biro, PTL. Richard Kiggins, and PTL. Robert Morrison entered the store before 7:00 a.m. with a search warrant issued by Supreme Court Justice Isaac Rubin. They seized records indicating policy and horse racing bets totally $7,000 for the week. I commended the fine police work of the officers involved in this and the two previous arrests in the previous week.

2nd N.T. gambling arrest

Suspected gambler arrested

N.T. man charged with gambling

I stated that organized crime in this area may ultimately defeat me, but it would not coexist with me.

A story on illegal gambling followed the arrests in an article in the *Gannett* newspapers. Several employees of General Motors gave their opinions of the raids both pro and con. Carl Falone, Asst. D.A. in charge of the rackets bureau of D.A. Carl Vergari's office stated that gambling is the grassroots money of organized crime such as loan-sharking and wholesale purchasing of drugs. I stated, "There is no such thing as an independent bookmaker." Most local bookmakers establish a certain money limit to reduce their risks of a loss. Bets over that limit are usually financed and laid off by someone above them. In the Bronx, New York, Westchester and Rockland counties the current head of the Genovese Crime Family set up the territorial areas that bookmakers are allowed to operate in. There are no exceptions. Illegal gambling cannot operate without police protection. It is up to the chief of police to set the tone for the area that he is responsible for. When organized crime cannot control the police chief, they get people elected to office who will reflect their opinions. To play it safe, they will sometimes have people from both major parties on their payroll.

The investigation of the murder of Irving Winfrey had continued from August 2, 1980, until the third week in October 1980. Most of the people connected with Irving Winfrey, his first wife, Lanic Sattler, his second wife, Barbara Winfrey, and a man who had a cocktail with Winfrey at the Hilton the night of the murder had been eliminated as suspects. His first wife had been at home with her husband at

.ne time of the murder. His second wife, Barbara, had called Winfrey from her home that night. The man who met Winfrey at the Hilton for a drink and had driven him home had also been eliminated. The evidence had been presented to a grand jury. The arrests would take place the next day, October 24, 1980. One of the persons who would be charged in the murder, Richard Winfrey, came to police headquarters on October 23, 1980 and told the officer working the desk that he wanted to speak with me. As he waited in the front of police headquarters, I called Chief Asst. D.A. Tom Facelle and told him that Richard Winfrey was at police headquarters and wanted to speak with me. I did not want to make any legal mistakes at this point in the investigation, nor did I want to give Richard Winfrey any indication that he would be arrested the next day.

As Richard Winfrey entered my office, I had him sit down opposite me. I asked him if I could help him. He asked if he could take possession of some of his father's jewelry that was in the possession of the detectives. I told him that I would speak to the D.A., but that I did not think it would be a problem. I knew if everything went right tomorrow that he would be in jail and it would not be a problem. He left my office satisfied that he would take possession of the jewelry, and I believe he was also satisfied that nothing was going to happen to him. The grand jury had indicted Richard Winfrey for murder in the second degree and criminal possession of a weapon. They had also indicted Merrill Willis of the Bronx, New York, of murder in the second degree and possession of a weapon. Willis and Winfrey were both 19 years of age. On October 24, 1980, we had set our plan for the arrests. At 6:47 p.m. Sgt. William Booth and PTL. Robert Morrison both in plainclothes arrested Richard Winfrey as he left his home in Philipse Manor with two female companions. The female companions were not implicated. Winfrey was brought to police headquarters and booked for murder, second degree, and possession of a .22 caliber magnum rifle. At 10:00 p.m., Merrill Willis was arrested in front of his Bronx apartment house by Det. Sgt. Carmen DeFalco, Det. Vincent Butkovich, and Investigator Donald Rabb of the D.A.'s office. He was taken to police headquarters for booking. The motive for the murder was that Richard Winfrey wanted to collect an inheritance of over $150,000 from his father's estate. Richard Winfrey had promised Merrill Willis $10,000 to kill his father. There were inconsistencies from the beginning in Richard Winfrey's statement to us.

Winfrey had told us that he had spent the night of the murder at a friend's house in the Bronx, New York. That friend, Robert Gruber, had given a different story. Winfrey had spent the night at a parking lot of Gimbel's in Yonkers, New York. A Yonkers' police officer who had found him there stated that, "He was sweating like crazy." The investigation and surveillance had been conducted in Westchester County and the Bronx where Merrill Willis lived and other areas of the Bronx. The detectives had gone to Pennsylvania to search a wooded area for shells that matched the Z2 caliber rifle to no avail. They also went to Van Cortlandt

122

Park in the Bronx, where Bronx teenagers held shooting practice. Gruber had given a statement to us that he had gone to the Winfrey house with Richard Winfrey and Merrill Willis on the night of the murder. He stated that he waited in the car while Willis and Winfrey went into the house. He stayed in the car for approximately 30–40 minutes. He heard "firecracker like sounds." When Winfrey and Willis returned to the car, carrying a rifle, Willis demanded $10,000 from Winfrey then added, "I can't believe I shot him." Winfrey told him that he could have anything he wanted but the car. Gruber was scared out of his wits.

He realized that Winfrey and Willis knew that he knew too much. He cooperated with us. The detectives, Det. Sgt. Carmen DeFalco and Det. Vincent Butkovich and other members of the department working in plainclothes had done an outstanding job on the investigation, along with Asst. D.A. Carl Falcone and members of D.A. Carl Vergari's staff. As we wrapped up late on the night of October 24, 1980, I was thankful that the arrests had gone down without anyone getting injured. The residents of the community would also be relieved that the murder was solved. There was no way that I could have relieved their fears during the investigation by indicating that we had found out who committed the murder. To do so would have jeopardized the investigation.

In November 1980, I received a call from my niece, Jerrylyn. She told me that her father, my brother Jerry, had a heart attack and died immediately. He was in their home in Syosett, Long Island, at the time. I couldn't believe that just five months after George had died that Jerry was gone too. Pat and I traveled to Long Island for the wake and the funeral the next day. Jerry had been the oldest of my brothers and sister. When he would worry about me working on a case, he would tell me that I didn't have to see everything that happens. I would miss him and it hurt more coming so close to George's death. Jerry and George were always together, long before I was ever born. I wondered how much of a toll George's long bout with cancer took on Jerry. I had tried to block out of my mind all that had happened to George and now it was back all over again. I was thankful that Jerry had seen his four grandchildren and had gotten to know and love them.

During the holiday period of December 1980, I would again have police officers in plainclothes patrol the areas of our extensive number of bars and clubs for possible holdups. The detectives would coordinate the assignments. We would continue this until after New Year's Day. The bars, clubs, gas stations, places where checks were cashed, and homes were always a target for robberies and burglaries during the holiday period. By doing this, we would again be successful in preventing crimes.

On the morning, of February 11, 1981, at approximately 9:15 a.m., an informant came into police headquarters and spoke with one of our police officers. The informant stated that Adam L. Sobolof, 22 years old, told him that he had mutilated his parents in their home in the Town of Greenburgh, Westchester County, New York. Det. Vincent Butkovich called Greenburgh Police Headquarters with the information. Greenburgh Police rushed to Balmoral Crescent, Greenburgh, New York. At the time, PTL. James Whalen spotted a four-door, yellow Ford that was believed to be operated by the suspect. It was parked by a house in the Philpse Manor section of our community. PTL. James Reddy positioned his police vehicle in a place where he could also observe the vehicle. Det. Butkovich, with PTL. Morrison parked his unmarked vehicle and observed the house and car. I positioned my unmarked police can where I could observe the house. I had PTL. Gordon Ferguson with me. We heard a hotline report from Greenburgh P.D. that told of the slayings. The license plate on the yellow Ford, 58-WSR, had been transmitted by us to the state computer in Albany for verification of ownership. The computer in Albany had broken down, so we could not verify the information of the license plate. We wondered if we were sitting on the right vehicle. We hadn't seen the suspect in fact enter the house. The unconfirmed license plate and the fact that we had not observed the suspect enter the house made it difficult for us to consider entering the house. We were at a disadvantage. The suspect could open fire before we had determined if he was Adam Sobolof. We observed the house and car until almost 1:00 a.m. At that time, the car began backing out of the driveway. PTL. Whalen recognized the suspect, because he hung out in our area. The four police vehicles cut off Sobolof's vehicle on Bellwood Avenue near the upper mills of the Sleepy Hollow restoration. As he opened his car door, he faced a row of guns. He was ordered to freeze and put his hands on the car roof. No one relaxed until we saw that he did not have a weapon. With PTL. Whalen so close to Sobolof, we did not want to fire unless absolutely necessary. Sobolof was wearing sneakers with blood on them, but he had changed out of the bloody clothes he was wearing during the crime. He was now wearing a clean, blue denim shirt and pants. He was taken to police headquarters and charged with murder in the second degree. The medical examiner said, "The bloody attack was carried out with a blunt instrument, possibly a hammer or a pipe." Det. Butkovich's quick call to Greenburgh Police Headquarters may have saved the life of Sobolof's mother, Michelle. She was revived by an emergency medical team and was fighting for her life. Sobolof's father, Jerome, the owner of a successful liquor store in Manhattan, was found dead in a separate, blood-splattered bathroom on the upper floor of their split-level house. His mother was found in the other bathroom on the second floor. Blood was thickly smeared on the walls and ceiling of the upper level hallway. Both of the Sobolofs were covered with so much blood that you could not tell immediately where they were shot, stabbed, or beaten over the head. When we arrested Adam Sobolof, he had a wild look in his eyes, but he did not show any remorse. On his right forearm he had a tattoo with the words

"Snake killer."

N.T. police star in crime thriller

Mother recovering from hatchet attack

The arrest did not end the case for us. We brought possible witnesses to headquarters. There was one last person that had been with Adam Sobolof. We were worried that the person may have been killed. We were relieved when that person came to police headquarters. Friends of Adam Sobolof stated that he was heavily into drugs, usually Mescaline, a powerful psychedelic. He had been arrested and charged with stealing $10,000 worth of liquor form Capital Distributors Corp. of Greenburgh this past October. He was out on $1,500 bail. His friends stated that Sobolof was obsessed with a punk-rock song by the group Talking Heads. The song is called, *"Psycho Killer."* Adam Sobolof was turned over to the Greenburgh Police at approximately 12:10 p.m.

Going into 1981, we continued to upgrade equipment and police vehicles. I had created a Youth Bureau (Youth Services Division) shortly after I became chief of police. This should be a full-time position. That requires taking an officer out of the patrol division and into plainclothes. That officer would apply for a grant that would offset some of the expense of the Youth Bureau. One of the most important duties of the youth officer would be to instruct the students in the elementary schools, the middle school, and the high school in substance abuse prevention. Education at the earliest possible age in substance abuse and drug awareness is the most important step in preventing drug abuse.

The duties of the youth officer are as follows: the youth officer shall be directly responsible to the chief of police and is particularly charged with the appropriate handling of youth cases. He shall be responsible to the supervisor in charge of the detective division for conduct, observance of rules and regulations, assignment when deemed necessary and for the exchange of pertinent information as required to affect the smooth, efficient workflow of the department as follows:

The youth officer shall communicate regularly with personnel of schools, churches, social agencies, and other civic groups, as well as police departments in neighboring communities regarding youth matters.

The youth officer shall handle all cases involving juveniles and present such reports as may be required by the chief of police.

The youth officer shall cooperate with detectives and the uniformed force in cases involving youths.

The youth officer shall perform such other duties as may be assigned by the chief of police.

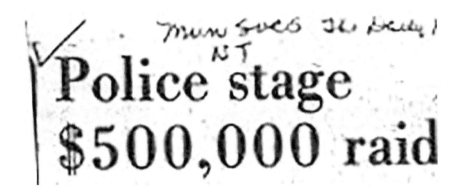

The youth officer shall be responsible for maintaining records and files pertaining to his activities. The youth officer shall be responsible for preparing a juvenile case that must go before the family court.

In January 1981, convicted gambler, Renaldo Dominguez, resurfaced. He was operating the Village Cleaners at 186 Cortlandt Street. An investigation was begun after information was received that this was a front for a gambling operation. After a thorough investigation, the Village Cleaners was raided. Shortly after noon, the officers found countless policy bets and $1,000 in cash. Ledgers were found along with 21 colorful posters of *"The Godfather"* idol Marlon Brando. Dirty clothes were collected at the cleaners but were sent to another dry cleaners. Det. Sgt. Carmen DeFalco said that the only thing that resembled dry cleaning was a White shirt dumped in a bucket of bleach. Renaldo "The Godfather" Dominquez, was part of an organized crime group in the area. He had convictions for arrests by us in March and May 1979. The officers did a good job on this case. The arrest and investigation was done by Det. Sgt. Carmen DeFalco, Det. Vincent Butkovich, PTL. Ron Biro, James Whalen, PTL. Manuel Caixiero, PTL. Richard Kiggins, and FTL. James Reddy.

We had been investigating a narcotics operation since the beginning of the year. It was centered around the GM Plant and a local bar. We were doing the investigation and surveillance with the help of the Westchester County Department of Public Safety. The investigation had started from the bottom up with small time dealers under surveillance. We worked the investigation with the intent of getting the top man in the operation. On August 14, 1981, Det. Vincent

Butkovich, Etl. Gordon Ferguson, PTL. Manuel Caixeiro, Sgt. Paul Grutzner, and I had a surveillance of the main gate at the General Motors Plant. There were several routes that the suspect could take to the plant. It was a Friday afternoon and the workers were arriving for the second shift (night shift at GM). Sgt. Paul Grutzner of the county police and I were in an unmarked vehicle when we observed the suspect drive into the main entrance of the plant. We sped after him, notifying the other officers that we were in pursuit of the suspect. Sgt. Grutzner and I caught up to the suspect's vehicle in the GM lot. As the suspect opened his car door, we drew our guns, identified ourselves, and told him not to move. The suspect ran and tried to reach the water (Hudson River). I was wrestling with him on the pavement and Sgt. Grutzner was trying to handcuff him.

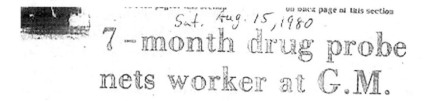

Sat. Aug. 15, 1980

on back page of this section

7 - month drug probe nets worker at G.M.

I put my gun to his head and Sgt. Grutzner handcuffed him. The suspect, Arturo Londono, 34 years, of Astoria, had a large quantity of high-grade cocaine on his person. The value of the cocaine was $7,000 to $10,000. The other officers had arrived at our spot and Londono was taken to police headquarters. He was charged with possession of a controlled substance in the third degree, possession of a controlled substance in the seventh degree, and criminally using drug paraphernalia, second degree. This was a multimillion-dollar operation. Londono had a relative in Columbia who was part of the Medien drug cartel. If convicted, Londono could receive 15 years in prison. Londono's cocaine buyers included GM workers. General Motors had cooperated completely with the investigation. In an investigation of this type, it is always advisable to trade the small fish (drug pushers) in, until you can go to the top echelon of the operation. The purity of the cocaine, in this case better than 90% pure, is an indication of how high up the person was in the operation.

In March 1981, the New York State Division of Criminal Justice Services Bureau for Municipal Police released its completed study of the police department. The report, which was well over an inch thick, recommended sweeping changes. It cited a cramped police headquarters and inadequate staffing. It called for civilians to handle traffic control and a record keeper to record police officers for patrol. Purchase of new police vehicles and new portables were among the 15 recommendations in the report. The report stated that the department needed 31 police officers, which was eight more than the present force of 23. They recommended eliminating the foot patrol. They said that 35 police officers would be needed if the foot patrol was not eliminated. A juvenile officer was recommended. We had been able to obtain a grant for the partial funding of a juvenile officer. I had anticipated making the appointment and the creation of a Juvenile Aide Bureau. The civilian traffic control officers were recommended to replace the two police officers directing traffic at the General Motors Plant. They recommended a records clerk to free officers from clerical duties. A new records system was recommended. A back-up crew for school crossing guards was recommended. When the civilian crossing guards were ill, police officers would fill in for them and approximately 500 man-hours a year were used for this function. On the department's organization, the report suggested, using senior patrolmen to man the desk at police headquarters freeing up the sergeants for supervisory work. During the 8 a.m. to 4 p.m. shift, lieutenants would be used as division commanders, one to oversee patrol and crime investigations and the other to oversee the desk, records, crossing guards, parking enforcement officers, and traffic control. The report suggested shifting posts and altering the way the village was divided for supervision during the three shifts, 5 a.m. to 4 p.m., 4 p.m. to midnight and midnight to 8 a.m. Their recommendation for the elimination of foot patrol was based on the proven theory that foot patrol is your most expensive form of patrol. The least amount of area is covered by a foot patrol officer. Everyone likes to observe a police officer on foot patrol, but you must assign officers where they are needed for the most productivity.

On police headquarters, they recommended a larger area to interview prisoners, for record keeping, for an evidence room, and the detective bureau. They suggested expanding police headquarters into the water department office on the first floor. They stated that the department needed a new radio communication system.

I concurred with virtually everything in the report. Because of our tax base, it would be impossible for me to obtain funding for all the changes. People resist change, but we must make these changes to move the department forward. We had begun to make some of the recommendations in the report. I would apply for every grant available for the department. I would put items into my yearly detailed budget request. Some would be attained in the next budget, others in future fiscal years. All of my supervisors would work hard in their areas to help bring about the needed changes. Having spent a considerable amount of time in the detective bureau, I knew what was needed for a new detective bureau and an evidence room. The detectives and new youth officer would work to bring about these changes.

In September 1981, Richard Winfrey and Merrill Willis went on trial for the murder of Irving Winfrey. Asst. D.A. Joseph West was the prosecutor for the trial in Westchester County Court, White Plains, New York. The judge was Lawrence N. Martin, Jr. The key prosecution witness was Robert Gruber. He testified that Winfrey and Willis had left him in a parked car near the Winfrey home on the night of the murder. He stated that they were gone for 30–40 minutes. During that time, he heard "firecracker sounds." He added that when Winfrey and Willis returned to the ear, they were carrying a rifle. Winfrey told Willis, "You can have anything you want except the car." Willis demanded $10,000, then admitted, "I can't believe I shot him."

Richard Winfrey testified that Willis shot his father for money. He said that he did not report it to the police until 9:00 a.m. the next morning, because Willis threatened to kill him and his mother. Merrill Willis testified that he had waited outside the house, petting a dog and was dozing while Winfrey was inside with the rifle at the time of the shooting.

It was brought out that the dog, a basset hound that belonged to the Winfreys, was in fact at a neighbor's house. It was testified that the Z2 magnum rifle used to kill Irving Winfrey was purchased at a Yonkers gun shop by Merrill Willis. In his summation to the jury, Asst. D.A. Joseph West stated that Richard Winfrey set up his father for the killing and that Merrill Willis pulled the trigger. He said that there was no evidence that Merrill Willis, a Bronx resident, knew how to get to Richard Winfrey's house. Merrill Willis had never been to North Tarrytown, New York, before the murder. The prosecutor stated that he had proven an intentional killing took place and that the testimony of Gruber, Winfrey, and Willis placed the two defendants in the house with a rifle at the time of the murder. He added that the photo he was holding up was a graphic portrayal of murder. The photo showed Irving Winfrey, a defenseless man, lying in his bed, shot twice. He had a bullet wound in the head. The 22-caliber magnum rifle was fired from between two to three inches from the deceased. He stated that one shot could be an accident, but that two shots were not an accident. The trial had lasted a week. On the night of Thursday, September 24, 1981, the jury of nine women and three men deliberated for almost six hours before returning their verdict at 10:30 p.m. They found Richard Winfrey and Merrill Willis guilty of murder in the second degree. They faced 25 years to life in a state prison.

In the evening of Monday, December 14, 1981, it was snowing. A 1975 Firebird, that was driven by Geraldine Smith, 41 years of age, of Ossining, N.Y., was traveling north on Route 9 (Broadway) when it was involved in a rear-end collision. After the accident, Ms. Smith was standing near the main entrance of Sleepy Hollow Cemetery. She was searching for an insurance card at approximately 6:25 p.m. when she was struck by a car being driven north on Route 9. One of her legs was cut off and the other was mangled. The driver of the car stopped for a moment, but then sped away. At the hospital, doctors had to remove the mangled leg. A police hotline alarm was sent out with the limited information we had about the suspect's vehicle. Geraldine Smith had been treated at Phelps Memorial Hospital in North Tarrytown, N.Y., Montefiore Hospital in the Bronx,

N.Y., and at the Westchester County Medical Center, Valhalla, N.Y. Geraldine Smith had been a witness for us in the murder case of Richard Winfrey and Merrill Willis. I visited her at the Westchester County Medical Center. She showed me where both of her legs were severed. Before I left her at the hospital, I told her that we would get the person who had done this to her. I was furious to think that someone had severed her legs and then left her there to bleed to death.

Woman loses leg in hit-run

For several days, I would not leave the detectives alone concerning this case. I knew that we had little to go on other than some broken parts of the vehicle that struck her. We were fairly certain that the vehicle was blue. Officer Richard Kiggins and Robert Morrison had recovered a Dodge emblem and some grillwork on Route 9 that was from the vehicle that struck Geraldine Smith. They worked with Det. Sgt. Carmen DeFalco and Det. Vincent Butkovich. Sal Donzella, who owned a body shop in our community, identified the parts as belonging to a blue Dodge Coronet. He spoke with me and said that he had a contact in the auto industry that would contact him if parts were ordered for the particular vehicle in New York. We had given out the additional information that we had to other police agencies. The public, through the media, knew we were looking for a particular vehicle in connection with this case. Every call that came in, no matter how far the information was off from what we had, was investigated. I knew I was driving the detectives crazy in having them run down every lead that came in. If Geraldine Smith died, this would be a homicide. If the suspect's car was repaired or demolished before we found it, the case would probably never be solved. I couldn't rest at all. If the detectives and officers were out checking leads when additional information came in, I would check out the information. The amount of calls that were made to police headquarters about blue vehicles with front-end damage was unbelievable. I know in praying I said that we could no let someone commit such a horrible crime and get away with it.

On Wednesday, December 16, 1981, we were still checking out every possible lead and information that we had received. After 4:00 p.m., I received a call from Sal Donzella. He stated that he had received a call from his contact in the auto parts industry. The contact had stated to him that parts had been ordered for a 1973 blue Dodge Coronet. The parts matched some of the broken parts that were recovered at the crime scene. The body shop was located on Ogden Avenue, the Bronx. I quickly went into the detective bureau and told Det. Vincent Butkovich and PTL. Gordon Ferguson about the information I had just received. I told them that we had to get to the body shop in the Bronx, N.Y. before 5:00 p.m., because it might close at that time and the vehicle could be gone before the next day. Det. Butkovich drove the unmarked detective vehicle with myself in the front seat and PTL. Gordon Ferguson, our youth officer, in the rear seat. Det. Butkovich sped down to the thruway entrance and got on the New York State Thruway going south. He had the detective vehicle going at almost top speed with the gas pedal to the floor most of the way down the thruway and to the Major Deegan Highway. The area of the Bronx we were traveling to, the Fort Apache section, was just north of Yankee Stadium. We got off the Major Deegan at the exit near Yankee Stadium and proceeded until we were traveling north of the stadium onto Ogden Avenue. It was almost 4:50 p.m.

"Will the shop be open? Will the vehicle still be there?" I asked out loud. As we drove along Ogden Avenue, it became apparent that most of the buildings on the street had been leveled or burned down. On the west side of the street, there was a narrow wooden structure. Could this be the M&M Auto Body Shop? We alighted from the unmarked police car. Det. Butkovich and Officer Ferguson were in plainclothes. I had a jacket and raincoat on over my police uniform and my two gold stars on each side of my white shirt collar. I did not have time to change completely into plainclothes, because of the time constriction that the shop could close at 5:00 p.m. and the vehicle may be removed. I opened the door to the building, and we entered. It was dim inside the building. As we looked down a narrow section of the building, a single light could be seen toward the end of the structure. There were three men standing around a 1973 blue Dodge Coronet. The front end of the Dodge was damaged. I asked who was in charge of the shop. One of the men said he was. I asked where the owner of the blue Dodge was. The owner of the shop said that he didn't know the man. I explained to him that the vehicle had struck a woman, severing her legs, and that if she died, the driver of the vehicle would be charged with a homicide and that anyone helping him would be charged accordingly. The shop owner said that he knew a woman who knew another woman who was a friend of the owner of the Dodge. I asked where the woman he knew lived. He said that she was at a house on 135th Street (upper Harlem, Manhattan).

I didn't know if the shop owner was telling the truth or not. He appeared to be possibly telling the truth. I asked him if he would come with us to the building. He agreed to come with us. We called back to our police headquarters to send a flatbed truck to the body shop so that we could secure the Dodge, and have it brought back and held for evidence. We drove to 135th Street. When we got to the apartment-type building, the shop owner agreed to come in with us. We went upstairs to a second floor apartment. There were several women in the apartment. The shop owner introduced us to the woman in charge who knew the owner of the Dodge's girlfriend. I explained to her what had happened and that we were only interested in the driver of the vehicle. She said that the man's name was Carlos and that he was coming to the apartment tonight to see the girlfriend. She gave us a description of him. I told her not to have anyone contact him before he arrived. It was before 6:00 p.m. Det. Butkovich, PTL. Ferguson and I stayed in the unmarked police car and surveilled the building. As we waited, we observed a lot of different activity on the street. After waiting for an hour and a half, I told Det. Butkovich and PTL. Ferguson to stay in the vehicle while I went upstairs to see if the suspect had been in contact with the apartment. They told me in the apartment that he had not contacted the apartment. I returned to the police car and waited. One man entered the hall of the building, and we checked him out to make sure it wasn't the suspect. It wasn't the suspect. We returned to the unmarked police car. Could someone at the body shop have contacted him? Could someone at the apartment house have contacted him? We hoped that this had not occurred. At approximately 8:15 p.m., a man fitting the description of the suspect entered the hall of the building. Before he got to the inside door of the building, we ran into the building and stopped him. The man, Carlos Daniels, age 50, was arrested by us and charged with the felony, leaving the scene of a personal injury accident. We drove back up the Major Deegan and N.Y. State Thruway with the suspect arriving at police headquarters where Carlos Daniels was booked on the charges. Daniels had been convicted of forgery of a public record in April 1971, selling dangerous drugs in July 1971, possession of a dangerous weapon and possession of dangerous drugs in June 1974. He had been sentenced to 3 to 25 years in prison in August of 1974 but was paroled in October 1979.

Yellow paint chips from Geraldine Smith's Pontiac Firebird were found on Daniel's blue Dodge that was brought back to police headquarters on a flatbed truck. Det. Butkovich, PTL. Ferguson, PTL. Richard Kiggins and Robert Morrison, along with Det. Sgt. Carmen DeFalco had all done an excellent job on this case. We would submit Sal Donzella's outstanding involvement in this case to our department awards committee for consideration for the departments' civilian award. I can't think of a better example of a civilian helping the department solve a major crime. I told Geraldine Smith and her family what had transpired. I told her about the civilian award and department dinner that we would have in 1982. I asked her if she would like to attend and present the civilian award to Sal Donzella. She had a big smile on her face and said that by the time of the dinner she would have been fitted with her prostheses and that she would walk up to present the award. If anyone is writing a book on profiles in courage, he should take a good look at this courageous inspiring lady. Carlos Daniels was indicted by a Westchester County Grand Jury for the felony that carried a maximum sentence of four years in prison.

69 get commendations at N.T. police awards dinner

Chief Richard Spota, left, with Geraldine Smith and Sal Donzella at awards dinner

One of the units that I thought would be beneficial to the police department and the community was a canine unit certified in narcotics detection. I had two officers who were interested in being involved with this. An older police vehicle would be transformed into a K-9 vehicle. The officers and the K-9s would have to train every week after they were certified. They would be able to search for lost children and adults with a memory related disease. The K-9s could search for a bomb or enter a place where a suspect had a deadly weapon. I am an animal lover, particularly dogs, but if it comes down to an officer losing his life or a canine, I would have to go with the latter. Many of the canine officers in Westchester County would train together once a week usually in a wooded area. As the information about the canine unit was discussed for budgetary and other reasons, it was brought to my attention that there might be some opposition from members of the black community. Because of the things that had happened to blacks in Alabama and other areas in the 1960s, I could understand their concern. We decided to have a demonstration of the canines with their handlers (police officers) for the public. I felt that if everyone understood the training and purposes of the canine units, then any fears would be addressed. Many of the K-9 officers in Westchester agreed to participate in the demonstration. It was held on a weekend in a wooded area of the Tarrytown. My K-9 trainer, Noel James, was very highly regarded. At one point, during the demonstration, he said, "My skin color may be black, but I bleed red blood." He continued to put the canines through their demonstration. He carefully explained the purposes of the dogs and what they would be used for. A friend of mine, Greenburgh Police K-9 Officer Sam Washington and his canine, Bandit, participated. Sam, who is black, walked over to some black men who were standing near me and said, "What's the matter with you guys? You're not making enough money with the numbers?"

I can be naive at times and treat all criticism as legitimate. I knew there were politicians who did not like me because of my work on organized crime and the continuation of that work as chief of police. I've never registered in a political party. I would always vote for the best person, regardless of political party. Some law enforcement executives I know would stay away from canines, because of possible criticism. I believe that if the officer and the canines are continuously well-trained, and if their purpose is clearly defined, that they can be an invaluable asset to the police department and the community. I was glad that we had the demonstrations. The members of the community could clearly observe the outstanding work and discipline of Noel James and all the canine units. We would have two canine units. PTL. Walter Schrank and Mike and Officer Richard Kiggins and Muggs, both were German shepherds. It was a pleasure to see them train and work. It was always heartwarming to see youngsters pet and hug Mike and Muggs after a demonstration.

Gun probe in North Tarrytown helped nail NYC rob suspects,

At approximately 6:50 a.m., on Tuesday, March 9, 1982, a man who was jogging on Gory Brook Road found the body of a male, black, approximate age between 20–30 years. The responding officers, Richard Kiggins and Robert Morrison, observed the man, who had been shot several times, once in the head. He was dressed in jeans, sneakers, and a jacket. Dr. Louis Rob, the county's associate medical examiner, was called and arrived at the scene. Det. Sgt. DeFalco, Det. Butkovich, and Carl Falcone, Chief of the Rackets Bureau of the Westchester County's D.A.'s Office also responded. Tarrytown Police Detectives also responded, in an effort to help us identify the body. No one could identify the murder victim. Gory Brook Road is located in the northeast part of the community. This is a paved road that turns into a dirt road and continues through a heavily wooded area that is often used by joggers or persons taking a walk through the scenic area. The body was found over 100 yards from where the paved road ends. The road runs parallel to the Old Croton Aqueduct. The road takes its name from the bloody skirmishes of the American Revolution, of which Westchester was neutral territory. On Wednesday, March 10, 1982, after the detectives were frustrated in their efforts to find relatives or friends of the murder victim, we released the victim's name. He was Branton Coley, 21 years of age, of New York City. He had been murdered with a shotgun. He also used the names Coley Branton and Coley Nitty. He had a heart-shaped tattoo on his right arm. He had an extensive arrest record. Was he murdered and his body dumped at the location, or was he murdered there? Most people who live outside of this general area do not know of the wooded area. It would be very important to find his family and friends, so that we could find out whom he was connected with.

There are cases such as this that remain unsolved for long periods of time. Many cases such as this are solved when someone in serious trouble with the police has valuable information about a murder and are willing to provide that information if it will help them get a lighter prison sentence for a crime that they have been charged with.

A five-month investigation of drug sales ended on June 10, 1982, with the arrest of Rene J. Catalan, 26 years of age, of North Tarrytown, N.Y. A vehicle driven by a female friend of Catalan's was stopped at 9:10 p.m., by PTL. Manuel Caixeiro and PTL. Frank Hrotko. Rene J. Catalan, a passenger in the vehicle was arrested and charged with two counts of fourth degree criminal sale of a controlled substance. A North Tarrytown arrest warrant had been issued for Catalan based on sales he had made to an undercover police officer.

N.T. man indicted on 24 cocaine charges

Det. Sgt. Carmen DeFalco and Det. Vincent Butkovich had investigated Catalan for drug sales of cocaine. This arrest should have an impact on the community. The information that was gathered showed that Catalan was a main supplier to children of elementary school age. He sold the drugs in the area of Valley Street and College Avenue. Village Justice Thomas Maroney set bail at $5,000 each at Catalan's arraignment. Catalan faced a maximum of 30 years in prison on the two counts.

A six-month investigation of a suspected drug dealer ended with the arrest of Juan Suarez, 31 years of age, of North Tarrytown, N.Y. He was arrested on June 3, 1982, by Det. Sgt. Carmen DeFalco and Detective Vincent Butkovich who coordinated the investigation along with PTL. Robert Morrison and the Narcotics Unit of the Westchester County Department of Public Safety Services. Suarez, who was arrested on Clinton Street, North Tarrytown, was charged with eight counts of third degree criminal sale of a controlled substance, eight counts of third degree criminal possession of a controlled substance, one count of fourth degree criminal possession of a controlled substance, and seven counts of seventh degree criminal possession of a controlled substance. A sealed indictment was handed up by a county grand jury after the purchases were made from Juan Suarez. Suarez was selling cocaine heavily and continuously. There was no known prior criminal record for the defendant who was a citizen of the Dominican Republic. Suarez posted the $5,000 bail and was awaiting trial in County Court. Intelligence information and surveillances must be continuous to rid our area and Westchester County of drug dealers.

When I became chief of police, I had said that the Police Department Awards Committee would meet twice a year to vote on commendations for the officers. The voting would take place at the end of each performance evaluation report period (twice a year). Officers would receive bars corresponding to the commendation they received and a certificate suitable for framing. Unless you head a large state or city department, the amount of promotions that a chief can make are limited. But there is no reason for not recognizing outstanding police work performed by your officers. A lieutenant, sergeant, detective, a patrolman, and I had met and voted on the commendations. The first annual department awards dinner was held on Thursday, December 2, 1982, at Holy Cross Hall in North Tarrytown, N.Y. I invited the members of the Police Community Relations Committee to the awards dinner. The members of the Police Community Relations Committee had continued to meet one evening a month and were responsible for helping make the police department better and more responsive to the community. At this first awards dinner, we would start by awarding three civilian awards to persons who had made significant contribution to our law enforcement programs. For the first award, I asked Geraldine Smith to come up to the podium to present the first civilian award. She had not been fitted with her prosthesis yet due to some complications. As I introduced her, she came up in her wheelchair and received a standing ovation from everyone at the dinner. Sal Donzella received his award from Geraldine Smith for his outstanding involvement in her case. Sal Donzella, a physically large man who is known as a tough businessman, was clearly moved to see this courageous lady come up to present the award to him. The second civilian award went to our police canine trainer, Noel James, for all the work he had done to help our two department canines, Mike and Muggs and the officers, PTL. Walter Schark and Richard Kiggins. The third civilian award went to Jack Lynch, Chief of Security of General Motors. He had helped Sgt. Hayward to have GM repaint our old police vehicles and paint our new police vehicles the national police colors. With my limited vehicle and equipment budget, Chief Lynch had helped us to have great looking and running vehicles through a community service program of General Motors. Twenty-one of our officers would receive 66 awards at the dinner. Det. Sgt. Carmen DeFalco and Det. Vincent Butkovich received medals for their outstanding work in solving the murder of Irving Winfrey and in helping to obtain convictions in the case. Medals were also given to them for their work that led to the arrest of two suspects in the armed robbery of the New York Daily News plant in Brooklyn, N.Y. Patrolman James Reddy and James Whalen were given medals for the arrest of Adam Sobolof in the murder of his father and the attempted murder of his mother. Det. Butkovich and PTL. Gordon Ferguson received commendations for the arrest of the hit and run driver in Harlem, two days after Geraldine Smith had her legs severed. PTL. Ronald Biro received three separate awards for life saving. Sgt. Stephen Kostelny, who had retired live days previously, and Sgt. Gabriel Hayes both received the lifesaving award. They saved the life of a man who was stabbed at a bar with a 12-inch cut across his abdomen. They pushed the victim's intestines in place and rushed him to the hospital. As each officer received his award, James Halpin, a Former freelance photographer for the Associated Press and the Gannett Westchester papers took a picture of the presentation. Each officer would receive a photo of the presentation. Many of our officers received multiple awards. At each awards program, one officer received the departments Best Dressed Award.

The officers of the department had truly given a 100 percent. Outstanding police work, I was very proud of them. On Friday, July 8, 1983, I would deliver the keynote address to the 66th session of the Police Recruit Training School (Police Academy Graduation) at the Humanities Building Auditorium of the State University of New York at Purchase, N.Y. I had been asked to speak by Commissioner Daniel P. Guido of Westchester County. Dan Guido is a very gracious man of impeccable integrity He is one of the leaders in law enforcement that I admire very much. The graduating class represented many of the 33 town and village police departments of Westchester County, the six cities of the county, as well as other departments outside the county. My address to the class would be on police corruption. After Comm. Guido introduced me to the class, I told them that as a former graduate of the school, I was very pleased to be there that day. I asked the class what was the most important attribute that a police officer must have. Several attributes were mentioned by class members before one of the officers said, "Integrity," the correct answer. I told them it matters little what other attributes you have if you do not have integrity.

One of the most significant moments in any police officer's life comes when he or she puts on a uniform and a badge. From that point on, the officer realizes that he or she has been given a unique form of power in order to carry out many of society's most dangerous, unpleasant, and often unrewarding tasks. Police agencies must reassure the public that they will not abuse the power with which they are endowed by society. The coexistence of police corruption and crimes such as gambling and drug peddling has, in some cases, virtually destroyed the confidence of citizens in the police. Because vice is so profitable, the vice laws provide enormous opportunities for police corruption. Organized crime takes in over 150 billion dollars annually. The reasons for the mob's success are clear; their tactics and techniques are well known. Organization and discipline, vows of secrecy and loyalty, insulation of its leaders from direct criminal involvement, bribery and corruption of law enforcement and public officials, violence and threats against those who would testify or resist the criminal conspiracy, all have contributed to the protective curtain of silence that surrounds its activities. Police corruption destroys respect for the law itself. Corruption indicates that the police themselves, who are sworn to uphold the law, hold it in contempt. Citizens ask why they should obey the law when it is clear that some police officers do not. When a doctor, lawyer, or teacher is expelled from his or her profession for unethical conduct, few people conclude that all members of the profession are blameworthy. But many people do conclude from police scandals that all police are corrupt.

The path of political corruption at all levels of government winds through American history. Inevitably, what has happened in government has spilled over into policing, because our entire criminal justice process is heavily influenced by the wishes of mayors, city council members, prosecuting attorneys, and judges. However, frequently, it is asserted that politics and law enforcement do not mix, frequently they are forced to. Given this environment, it is not surprising that police should become cynical about their work. If the police become accustomed to seeing assignments made on the basis of political considerations, integrity can easily be damaged.

In connection with gambling in particular, police corruption is a perennial threat. Drug trafficking goes on more covertly than gambling. Generally, payoffs to the police by those involved in the drug trade are not regular. Most frequently, the payoff occurs when the opportunity presents itself. Drug dealers are engaged in a crime that frequently involves much larger sums of money in individual transactions, man does gambling.

In departments in which corruption is rife, officers frequently must show that they are willing to engage in illegal conduct in order to be accepted by the group. It proves the officer's solidarity with the group. The officer's peers will breathe more easily once they know that he or she can be trusted. Typically, the corruption of a new police officer is a gradual thing. It begins with the free cup of coffee, the free meal, the discount police price on merchandise, and the Christmas present. Patrol officers may learn that as long as they don't "rock the boat," they need not worry about discipline. Their main reward in the corruption process is being allowed to take their duties lightly. Tolerance of corruption extends even to the honest officer. Even though he or she may refuse corrupt rewards, he or she will keep silent and pretend not to see the corruption of others. Police officers are required to perform tasks that in a perfect world would be performed by social workers, psychiatrists, physicians, and lawyers. Under those circumstances, the illegal gains come to be seen as part of what society owes the police officer for handling society's troubles.

On training, I urge you to take advantage of the various schools and seminars that will be available to you. Take police science and criminal justice courses.

Graduating rookie police officers told integrity means everything

Work out a schedule so that you can study at least a half hour to an hour a day. Not only will this help you to make critical split-second decisions while on patrol, it will help prepare you for promotional exams in the future. I use loose leaf law books. The changes in the law will be sent to you every September. The five books are:

1. Penal Law
2. Criminal Procedure Law
3. Family Court Act
4. Vehicle & Traffic Law
5. New York State Extracts

Stress—Law enforcement is one of the most stressful professions. If you are not already in a fitness program, get into aerobic type programs and exercise.

Diet—Follow a good diet. Eat the proper foods.

Spiritual—Last and most importantly, don't be afraid to pray and ask for God's help, because with God on your side, who can your enemies be.

I wish all of you nothing but the best in your law enforcement careers.

This address was received well by the graduating class. Chief Frank V. Comito, of the New Castle Police Department, President of Westchester County Chiefs of Police Association, appointed me Chairman of the Communications (Police Radio) Committee for 1983. He wanted me to attempt to get funding from the state for Groups 2 and 3 of Westchester County for a new police radio system. Most of the jurisdiction in Westchester County and all the police departments that make up the areas in Group 2 and 3 had radios. They were installed more than 40 years ago. The Mobile Radio District (MRD) Program had suffered many setbacks since it began about 12 years ago. The fiscal responsibility for the program had shifted from the Federal Government (FEMA— Federal Emergency Management Agency) to the state government during the Carter administration. When the program started, it gave a new police station a radio console, transmitting police car radios and handheld portable radios. The new radio network would provide two local channels and added new countywide and statewide channels. All of the police departments in Group 2 and 3 of Westchester County and many other police departments in the county could not communicate with each other and could not communicate countywide.

During high-speed police chases, major fires, poor weather, train derailments, prison uprisings, and chemical spills, it is a must to be able to communicate with the other police departments. Most of the police departments in Westchester County and the other counties in the state could not fund new radio communications with their limited budgets. I had told Chief Comito that I did not have that much expertise in the area of radio communications. I think he felt that I would work hard for the bottom line, getting the job done. This would take a team effort statewide to get funding again in the state budget. The studies that were given to me on what was needed for Group 2 and 3 MRD showed that $150,000 and $200,000, a total of $350,00, was needed for the project. After consulting with the communication division of D.C.J.S. (New York State Division of Criminal Justice Services) and getting lists of what was needed from all the police chiefs in the county that needed MRD funding, I found out that the old figure of $350,000 was antiquated. The new figure would be over a half a million dollars more, $850,000. We had not been able to get funded based on the old figure. How would I be able to ask for over half a million dollars more? All of the police chiefs knew that there would be a serious disaster if we did not get a new communication system.

Chief Ronald Goldfarb of the Ossining Police Department had Sing Prison in his community. Both of us, and many other departments that were within a ten-mile area of the Indian Point nuclear power plant, were expected to respond to a possible disaster at the site. Chief Goldfarb and I knew that a nuclear evacuation plan without adequate radio communications would be a true disaster. This would be a critical point that we would have to make at hearings. I was appointed to the Communications Committee of the New York State Association of Chiefs of Police and the N.Y.S.L.E.T.C. (New York Statewide Law Enforcement Telecommunications Committee). The N.Y.S.L.E.T.C Committee would meet in Albany at least four times a year. This statewide committee is composed of five chiefs of police. Each of us represented an area of the state. I would represent the southern region of the state. The other chiefs represented the northeast, central and western regions of the state: Chief Harlin R. McLlwen of Cayuga Heights, N.Y.P.D., Chief Thomas J. Roche of Gates, N.Y.P.D. western N.Y., Chief Rocky Fermano of Solvay N.Y.P.D., and Chief John McClellan of Oneida N.Y.P.D. The four aforementioned chiefs were open, friendly, very knowledgeable in communications, and a pleasure to work with. Lt. Joseph Gallelli and a deputy superintendent of the New York State Police represented that agency on the committee. Capt. Walter Fitzgerald represented the N.Y. City P.D. Irv McAndrews represented N.S.D.C.J.S. Communication Division on the committee, and there was another civilian representing A.P.C.O. on the committee. I found all of the above great to work with. We would work hard to get the funding for the

MRD districts in the state.

Into the fall and winter of 1983, we continued to lobby for the funding from the state for the M.R.D. program. We asked and received support in the form of letters to Gov. Cuomo from Westchester County Executive Andrew P. O'Rourke. We contacted members of the state senate and the state assembly. Senator John E. Flynn of Yonkers would support our efforts. Chief Harlen McEwen and other chiefs who were members of N.Y.S.L.E.T.C. would speak at hearings in upstate New York. I was scheduled to appear at a hearing on police radio communications at the World Trade Center in New York City. The hearing would be chaired by the Lt. Gov. Alfred Del Bello. We made arrangements for most of the police chiefs in Westchester County who needed the M.R.D. Program to be funded for their police departments to attend the hearing. During the hearing, Lt. Gov. Del Bello, who was sitting opposite from me, was talking about radio communications going into the 21st century. When he finished, I respectfully said, "Governor, most police departments in Westchester County are not into the 20th century, as far as radio communications are concerned."

He looked at me and said, "You've made your point, Chief." I thought the hearing had gone well, but we would have to wait to see if the M.R.D. Program would be included in the upcoming year's 1984 budge. There was still a lot of work to be done.

In December of 1983, I was elected Vice President of the Westchester County Chiefs of Police Association for 1984. I had been on the Board of Directors.

On January 19, 1984, at approximately 2:50 p.m., Grace Van Bergh arrived home at 24 Evergreen Way in the Sleepy Hollow Manor section of the community. She parked her ear in the garage and entered the house. She observed two men on the second floor of her house. The two men ran out of the front door and sped south in a getaway car. Mrs. Van Bergh ran to a neighbor's house and called police headquarters. Det. Gordon Ferguson, our youth officer, and I were in police headquarters when the call came in. We both ran out to the rear parking lot of headquarters and got in our unmarked police cars, driving up to Broadway (Rt. 9). Det. Ferguson spotted the suspects' vehicle driving south by us on Rt. 9 at a high rate of speed.

N. Tarrytown police chief, detective nab suspects

N.T. Police Chief Spota catches
2nd burglary suspect in 2 months

141

Det. Ferguson spotted a TV in the rear of the car and tried to stop the car, but the vehicle made a right onto College Avenue with our two vehicles in pursuit. It was snowing and the roads were extremely slick. As we pursued the vehicle down College Avenue, by North Washington Street, the three vehicles slid down file hill and went up in the air like a skier on a slope. As the three vehicles came back to the ground, the suspects' vehicle continued down the steep section of College Avenue, skidding to a stop before coming to the next intersection at Valley Street. The two men jumped out of the vehicle and ran in different directions. I pursued one on foot through the Margotta Courts apartment house property until I apprehended him at gunpoint. Det. Ferguson chased the other suspect and apprehended him at gunpoint. We had Fred Parez, 26 years, and Charles G. Slatter, 31 years, both of Yonkers, N.Y., in custody at 3:07pm. As we approached the suspects' car, we observed a German Shepard in their car. There were two televisions, silverware, coins, a radio, and jewelry in the car. Mrs. Van Bergh would later identify all of the property but the jewelry. After we brought the suspects back to headquarters, they were charged with burglary and criminal possession of stolen property. Det. Ferguson and I were both surprised that all three vehicles had gone down the snow-covered slope, were airborne, and returned to the pavement without crashing into one another's vehicles. The arrests were made possible because Mrs. Van Bergh had enough presence to immediately get out of her house, as she did not know if anyone was still in the house, go to her neighbor's house, and call police headquarters with a description of the suspects and their vehicle.

On the morning of March 7, 1984, Roger Thiele, of Sleepy Hollow, surprised a burglar who was in his house. The burglar reacted by clubbing Thiele on his head with a hard object. The burglar fled the house, driving Thiele's car. Thiele did not have a good description of the burglar, but he described a shoulder bag the burglar was carrying. PTL. Manuel Caixeiro, who responded to the burglary call, found Thiele's car abandoned nearby. PTL. Nick Bizzaro, Det. Gordon Ferguson, and I joined in the search effort. I was going to attend a meeting of the Westchester County Police Chiefs Association at noon, but I wanted to recheck all the areas where the burglar could be hiding. Traveling south from Sleepy Hollow Manor on Riverside Drive into Philipse Manor, there is a wooded area between the Hudson River and the railroad tracks. I decided to cheek the west side of the train station again. That is where you wait for southbound trains. I drove down the road that is between the Hudson River and the train station. There is a beach club there on the river. As I neared the area adjacent to the station, I observed a black male carrying a bag. I got out of the unmarked police car and the male began running onto the train platform going south. He had sneakers on. I had shoes on, but I overtook him toward the end of the platform. I brought him back to where my car was parked and notified police headquarters. PTL. Manuel Caixeiro was the first to respond to the scene. The suspect had several watches stolen from Thiele's house—jewelry and $300 in cash. The suspect originally gave us an alias. We identified him as Robert "Jamal" Good, 33 years of Mt. Vernon, N.Y. He was wanted by Mt. Vernon and County Police on two burglary warrants. I expected other police departments to tile similar charges. PTL. Walter Schrank and PTL. Joseph Lanzo, through some good police work, were able to link Good to a car that was ditched off Riverside Drive. That car had been reported stolen in January of that year by Ralph Purdy of Greenburgh. Ralph Purdy was President of the New York State Federation of Police. After the paperwork, I left for the Westchester County Police Chiefs meeting. I was late and had a torn raincoat from the chase. As I was driving to the meeting, I thought to myself that I always thought that God gave me the gift of speed for athletics. Maybe I was wrong about that.

In March of 1984, we found out that the MRD Program funding had not been included in the state budget. Gov. Cuomo was going to different areas of the state to hold hearings on the proposed budget. Chief McEwen would attend the hearings in upstate New York. I attended the hearing held by Gov. Cuomo in Westchester County in Greenburgh, N.Y. I had prepared a text of the MRD Program that I would speak about at the hearing. There were many speakers before I would get a chance to address the governor, almost every one of them asking for some type of funding. Gov. Cuomo told most of them that they would not get it. Some students from the state universities asked for a reduction in their tuition. The governor told them, they were not going to get it. As I waited to speak, I did not think my chances were too good. While watching the governor speak, I thought to myself, I wish my father had lived to see this good Italian Catholic who had become governor. Dad would have been as proud, as my mother had been when John F. Kennedy was elected president.

When my turn came to go to the microphone, I introduced myself. "My name is Chief Richard Spota. I am Vice President of the Westchester County Police Chiefs Association and Chairman of the Radio Communications Committee. I am a member of the Communications Committee of the New York State Association of Chiefs of Police Communication Committee and the New York Statewide Law Enforcement Telecommunications Committee.

I am here to ask for funding for the MRD Program that is desperately needed here in Westchester County." The governor interrupted me and asked if Joe Dominelli (Executive Director of the N.Y. State Association of Chiefs of Police) had told me of a bill that he (Gov. Cuomo) had funded in his budget.

I said, "Yes, Governor. He did."

As I continued to speak the governor stopped me again and said, "Chief, I think I can help you get the funding." I had several paragraphs to go, but I stopped, thanked him, and gave a copy of my statement to his son, Andrew. As I put my coat on and started walking up the aisle, the governor called me from the stage.

"Chief, thank you for coming here today."

I replied, "Thank you, Governor."

It was after 5 p.m. when I arrived back at police headquarters. Our police department awards dinner was that night, and I had not signed the commendations. After signing them, I went home. Pat was sick with pneumonia. Her mother was at our house taking care of her. I spoke with Pat to see how she was feeling. She was really sick. It was almost 7 p.m. I took Todd and Melisa with me to the department awards dinner. Todd was 14 and Melissa had just turned 11. They enjoyed being with the children of the other police officers. Pat's mother had enough to take care of at our house, so Todd and Melissa would spend the evening with me at the awards dinner.

Our second annual police department awards dinner was held at Holy Cross Hall, North Tarrytown, N.Y. Five awards were received by civilians and 30 awards went to our police officers.

Carol DeFalco was working in the North Tarrytown Pharmacy in the summer of 1983 when a customer handed her a $20 bill that made her suspicious. She said that it was too green, too bright, and it was smooth. She walked to a rear room as if to look for change. She telephoned the detective bureau. Det. Sgt. Carmen DeFalco, her husband, arrived at the pharmacy. He questioned the man and brought him to headquarters. At police headquarters, a search revealed 20 $20 bills, all bearing the same serial number. The secret service was notified and took the man into custody. Similar bills had been passed in Atlantic City, New York City, Las Vegas, and New Orleans. The arrested man was later sentenced to five years' probation and fined $5,000 in Federal Court. The case led to the seizure of the counterfeiting plates in Baltimore, MD. Secret Service agents said that the plates were excellent. It took a very alert person to spot the counterfeit bill. As I presented the award to Carol DeFalco I said, "This was an outstanding case of civilian involvement."

Det. Sgt. Carmen DeFalco received a meritorious police service award for his part in locating a woman who had threatened to commit suicide. Officer Ron Biro was commended for his direction for the Stop-WI Program, directing roadblocks and programs aimed at strict enforcement of the drunk driving laws. There were 113 drunk driving arrests made in North Tarrytown for 1983. Officers Manuel Caixeiro, James Whalen, and Frank Hrotko were honored for their successful search for a knife and other evidence discarded by a suspect in a robbery of a service station, PTL. Robert Morrison and Det. Gordon Fergison were honored for their part in a four-month investigation that led to the arrest of a suspected drug dealer.

Officer John Cappello was given the Life Saving Award for saving the life of a stabbing victim through the use of first aid techniques. Our best dressed award had been instituted last year to help motivate the officers to look as sharp and well-groomed as possible. The winners, in a tie, were PTL. Joseph Lanzo and PTL. Frank Hrotko. All of the officers receiving awards tonight had worked hard and were doing excellent police work. I was proud of them.

It was now April 1984, and we had not been told that the MRD Program would be included in the state budget. Late in the afternoon on Monday, April 2, 1984, I received a call from Senator John E. Flynn who was in Albany. He told me that they were trying to get the MRD Program funded, but it still had not been approved. He said that he would call me back later that night at home and let me know the outcome. Senator Flynn went to Mass every morning. He is one of the hardest working persons in Albany. Late Monday night he called me back. He said that $853,365 had been approved for the Groups 2 and 3 of the MRD Program. We were both elated. I thanked him. This had gone down right to the wire. Most of the communities in Westchester County could not have funded this program in their limited budgets. I was particularly happy to be able to tell Chief Comito the good news. He had asked me to work on this project. He had been looking forward to the day that this program would be funded. His department would receive new radio equipment. Chief Comito had cancer and he was looking forward to the completion of this program.

We continued to encourage people to study for and take the exams for police officer—town and villages of Westchester County. When certified police officer lists were established after the exam, they usually would be established for several years. If you were going to make an appointment from a list, you could make a choice of one of the top three grades on the exam.

State to fund police radio network

.... North Tarrytown Police Chief Richard

In June of 1984, I had background investigations done on the top three candidates on the list for police officer. After interviewing the top three candidates, I told the members of the board of trustees that the three candidates were outstanding, and I wished we could appoint all three. With only one opening, I realized that I could get fiscal appropriations for one candidate. Before this list would expire, I would be able to get two of the three candidates appointed as police officers due to openings created in the police department. When I made a recommendation to the board of trustees on a proposal that required fiscal appropriations, I had to have at least four of the seven members voting in the affirmative for the proposal to be approved.

The candidate I was recommending for appointment as a police officer was Jimmy Warren, Jr., 25 years of age. He had scored a 97 on the civil service exam. He had graduated from Sleepy Hollow High School where he played football and was an all-county wrestler. After graduation from high school, he enlisted in the Navy and served five years, rising to the rank of aviation petty officer, first class.

He had seen duty in the Philippines, Japan, Portugal, and Spain. He was a member of the all-Navy wrestling team. After going through several Navy leadership schools, he enrolled in the external degree program of the State University of New York. He had transferred to Gupton Jones College in Atlanta where he graduated summa cum laude in 1982. Since graduation, he had served as a director of Lee's Funeral Home in White Plains, N.Y. He lived in North Tarrytown with his wife, Diana, a son, James David, one and a half, and a daughter, Diana Marie, three years of age.

I had a private meeting with Jimmy in my office. I asked him if he would have any problem with being the only black police officer on the force at the time. He assured me that he would not have a problem with that. I told him that I was a fan of the Brooklyn Dodgers when I was a youngster. I told him that I remembered the time in the 1950s when Branch Rickey brought Jackie Robinson into baseball as a member of the Dodgers. I said that I couldn't believe that here in the mid-1980s, I would be having a similar conversation with him. Margaret White, a good friend of mine and a former member of the board of trustees, had discussed and worked to encourage minorities to take the police exam. Margaret, the first black person to serve on the Board of Trustees, continued to serve on my Police Community Relations Committee. Margaret always reminded me that as important as it was to have a police department that reflected the community it served, the wrong person or persons would adversely reflect on the community. I told Jimmy that I knew that he was the right person to assume this responsibility. I assured him that as long as I was here, this department would do everything it could to attract more quality minority candidates.

North Tarrytown hires 25th police officer

North Tarrytown Police Chief Richard J. Spota hands out awards to Detective Vince Butkovitch, Officer Robert Morrison, Detective Sergeant Carmen De Falco and Officer James H. Whalen

5 civilians, 30 officers honored at police dinner

The candidates must always be as good or better than the other candidates. One of the most important decisions a chief of police can make is the selection of new police officers. That officer would be with the department for at least 20 years, barring unforeseen circumstances. On Monday evening, June 21, 1984, I attended the board of trustees meeting with Jimmy Warren. I was recommending his appointment as police officer. The mayor, Philip Zegarelli, shared my thoughts with having the police department reflect the community it served with top quality candidates. The original vote for Jimmy Warren's appointment was five "yes" and two "no." The two negative votes had nothing to do with race or discrimination, but with fiscal constraints in not filling the position of an officer who was seriously injured when struck by a car and retired. To the credit of the board, they changed the vote to unanimous. I explained the reasons of the vote to Jimmy during the meeting. Jimmy Warren was appointed, effective July 2, 1984, and would attend the police academy shortly after that. After the meeting, Jimmy and I went back to my office. I spoke with Margaret White on the phone. I asked her if she would like to speak with our newest police officer. I know she wanted to congratulate Jimmy and wish him well. This was a happy night, but there was a lot more work to be done.

At the December 1984 meeting of the Westchester County Chiefs of Police Association, held at the Pleasantville Country Club, I was elected president of the Association for 1985. I would utilize the remaining weeks of 1984 to make appointments to the many committees of the Association and name the chairman of each. I would name two new committees. The Organized Crime Committee Chairman would be the special agent in charge of the New Rochelle Office of the F.B.I., and the Youth Affairs Committee, with one of the chiefs who had been involved with the Juvenile Bureau before becoming chief as its chairman. I would have all the committees and their chairmen printed up so that this could be handed out at the first meeting in January 1985.

When 1985 began, there was one thing that I had hoped I would not have to do as President of the Westchester County Chiefs of Police Association. That was to lead the county police chiefs and commissioners at a funeral for a slain police officer. I didn't mention this to anyone. I had hoped it wouldn't happen. My wish did not come true. On February 24, 1985, a Westchester County Department of Public Safety Police Officer, Gary Stymilowski, was shot and killed while making a traffic stop, as this fine young police officer was checking out the driver of a car on the parkway.

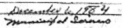
The animal would also kill a woman and scalp her, using her scalp as a disguise to avoid apprehension. The case enumerates the reasons why I believe that there should be a death penalty for murder in the first degree. A cold-blooded killer such as the one who killed Officer Gary Stymilowski must know that he will face swift and certain punishment for his act. On that cold winter day, I would assemble with the other police chiefs and commissioners to pay our respects at a church in Yonkers for our fallen brother. We were joined by thousands of police officers from throughout this state and adjoining states. It was heart wrenching to see the agony that Officer Stymilowski's parents were going through. Every officer attending the funeral knew it could be him or her inside of that casket. As well-trained as our officers are, going through the police academy, there is realistically almost no way to prepare for an unexpected attack such as this. As we saluted Officer Stymilowski's casket, my mind drifted off to thinking of other slain officers' funerals. Please, God, let this be the last one.

On February 25, 1985, I would finally receive approval for the expansion and modernization of police headquarters. The board of trustees would vote for the project and an architect's plan for same. The current one small room detective bureau would move into the area that had formally been occupied by the water department, which was adjacent to the main desk area of headquarters. There would be a separate area for interviewing juveniles, an evidence room, and other necessary changes. The changes would comply with the recommendations of the

D.C.I.S. study done on the department. The old detective room would be opened up to include the state-of-the-art front desk of headquarters and communications area. A training room would be built in the area where the old front desk of headquarters was now located. The cost to the village would be $42,000. The state grant that I had obtained of $537,821 would pay for the communications equipment, a console, computers, and other needed equipment. The building costs would go out for competitive bid to be completed before the new equipment would be installed. Sometimes, there is resistance to change, but a police administrator must adhere to his goals in order to have a first rate police department. These necessary changes took longer than they should have, but I appreciated their approval on my birthday.

On March 8, 1985, I was sworn in as President of the Westchester County Chiefs of Police Association at a dinner held at the Mamaroneek Beach and Yacht Club, Mamaronock, N.Y. Pat, Todd, and Melissa attended with me, along with other family members and friends.

Our Dinner Committee Chairman, Chief Joseph Del Bianco of Mamaroneck Village Police Department, did an outstanding job. Monsignor Cyril Potocek of Holy Cross Roman Catholic Church in North Tarrytown gave the invocation. State Senator John E. Flynn swore in myself and the other officers. State Senator Suzi Oppenheimer swore in the board of directors. I began my address: "Msgr. Potocek, Sen. Flynn, Sen. Oppenheimer, County Executive O'Rourke, County Legislator Sandy Galef, Comm. Dan Guido, Director of the Bureau of Municipal Police, N.Y. State Division of Criminal Justice Services, Mayor Philip Zegarelli of North Tarrytown, Trustee Dr. Steven Salman of North Tarrytown, fellow chief administrators, law enforcement associations, family and friends, this is a very humbling experience for me. As I look out at Chief Charles McLaughlin, our Secretary, who taught me in the N.Y. State Supervisory School, I can remember him waving his finger at me saying, "Son, are you taking your notes?" I thank Senator Flynn, not only for being here tonight but for his instrumental role in getting our M.R.D. funding. I thank County Exec. O'Rourke for his assistance in that project. I thank Comm. Dan Guido for his allocation of $512,000 in this year's state budget for the M.R.D. Group 7 funding and statewide law enforcement training for the year.

"In view of the recent tragic murder of Officer Gary Stymilowski two weeks ago, we must renew our efforts to invoke the death penalty for murder in the first degree. We have an outstanding slate of officers in our association. We have 25 committees from the Arson Task Force to the Youth Affairs Committee. Each committee is chaired by a chief or commissioner, with virtually all of our members serving on numerous committees. We have a wealth of law enforcement talent in Westchester County. This county will no longer follow, but we will lead this state in law enforcement."

Mayor Philip Zegarelli came up to the podium to read a proclamation naming March 8, 1985, in honor of me. As he was making his kind remarks that were on the proclamation, my mind drifted back to the time as rookie police officer testifying before the grand jury on organized crime; the person who came out of the grand jury after being subpoenaed and telling me that "We don't want police officers like you."

I said to myself, "Maybe now there are people who do want a police officer like me." The presentation touched me. I appreciated it.

On Thursday, May 16, 1985, we had our annual North Tarrytown Police Department Awards Dinner at the parish hall of Holy Cross Church, on Beekman Avenue. A total of 44 awards were given to 17 of our officers, two Tarrytown police officers, and four civilians. As the master of ceremonies, I made the presentations to the officers and civilians. Patrolman Walter Shrank and Joseph Lanzo received the Meritorious Police Service Award for rescuing residents from a burning home and an adjacent home in January. Patrolman Lanzo received a second Meritorious Police Service Award for arresting a burglary suspect and observing stolen property in the suspect's apartment while interviewing the suspect. That January arrest led to the solution of three other burglaries. Patrolman Lanzo received a third meritorious Police Service Award for an arrest of loiterer who was carrying a handgun and ammunition. This arrest occurred while Patrolman Lanzo was off-duty.

Patrolman Lanzo and Shrank were additionally awarded Excellent Police Awards for their March chase of a stolen car. The car was later abandoned by the driver. They searched for the driver to no avail but later traced him through evidence that was in the stolen vehicle.

Patrolman Shrank and rookie Patrolman Gregory Camp received Excellent Police Duty Awards for the arrest in October of a burglary suspect. Sergeant William Patten, Patrolman Camp, Tarrytown Officers Dennis DeCuffa, Rory Capra, and Frank Papp were given Excellent Police Duty Awards for the investigations and arrest of several people involved in a knife fight. Auxiliary Sergeant Melvin Effort and Officer Roberto Guzman and Louis Matos were given civilian awards for their part in the incident.

Police officer Richard Kiggins received a Meritorious Police Service Award for arresting a kidnapping suspect and rescuing his alleged victim in January. Patrolman Kiggins received an additional award for his involvement in the investigation of a bomb that was in a wall safe in a home. Detective Gordon Ferguson and Patrolman Robert Nevelus received Excellent Police Duty Awards for their part in the bomb case.

Patrolman Nevelus and Patrolman Ronald Biro received Meritorious Police Service Awards for arresting a suspect and recovering stolen property. Detective Ferguson received an Excellent Duty Award for this involvement in a mugging-burglary in September. Patrolman Mario Bizzarro and Manuel Caixiero were given Excellent Police duty Awards for the mugging-burglary case. Chief Spota, who arrested the suspect in the mugging-burglary, was given a Meritorious Police Service Award.

Chief Spota and Detective Ferguson received a second Meritorious Service Award for their chase and arrest of two burglars.

Patrolman Biro and Patrolman Donald Pellegrino discovered a quantity of stolen radios and electronic equipment in May. They received Meritorious Police Service Awards. Patrolman Bizzarro received another Excellent Police Service Award for helping apprehend two burglary suspects. He received a Meritorious Police Service Award for apprehending two suspects in a knife fight in September.

Patrolman Robert Morrison received an Excellent Police Duty commendation for his part in the arrest of burglary suspects in March. A Civilian Award was given to James Rutte for his involvement in the aforementioned case. Patrolman Caixiero received a Meritorious Police Service Award for his involvement in a kidnapping and robbery in March. Patrolman Morrison received a medal of Commendation for his work on that case.

Sergeant Lee Hayward and Patrolman Morrison received Life Saving Awards for administering first aid to the victim of a self-inflicted wrist wound in May. Phelps Memorial Hospital had commended the two officers. Patrolman Morrison received a Meritorious Police Service Award for his work on a November drug arrest. Detective Vincent Butkovich received a Meritorious Police Service award for a four-month investigation which resulted in the solving of numerous burglaries in July. He received an additional award for preventing a fire from spreading in June.

Patrolman Frank Hrotko received a Meritorious Police Service Award for quelling a near riot when a suspect threw a firecracker into a baby carriage in September. The infant was injured in the incident. Patrolman Hrotko received the Best Dressed Officer Award. A number of supervisors voted for him.

The Departmental Awards Committee comprised of Chief Spota, Sergeant Hayward, Detective Sergeant Carmen DeFalco, and Lieutenant James Brophy meet at the end of each six-month period to review the recommended award applications. A member of the awards committee is recommended for an award in which he cannot participate in the decision.

North Tarrytown board OKs police department project

151

In June 1985, I started the Suicide Prevention Screening Program for prisoners in our department. I had observed how the old methods of booking a prisoner and placing him or her in our jail were not a guaranteed deterrent in stopping a prisoner from committing suicide. We have cameras monitoring the cell blocks that the officer at the desk in police headquarters can observe. We have officers checking on the prisoners and police matrons checking on the female prisoners. But an investigation I had conducted proved that a prisoner could get in a position in a cell and commit suicide without the officer being able to observe the prisoner on the camera at the police desk. This could happen after an officer had made his regular check on the prisoner. Working with the State Commission of Correction and the Office of Mental Health, a questionnaire was developed. Working with Patricia Doyle, a program administrator at the Westchester County Department of Community Mental health, a program and screening form was adapted. The screening form would be used by the booking officer to identify information and factors that might make a person a high-risk candidate for suicide. At that point, a suicide watch would be put on the prisoner. Not having extra manpower or a large budget to work with, I received approval to train our off-duty auxiliary police officers for the suicide screening program. They were trained and approved for this purpose. Our department would be a part of a pilot program in the county and state. Patricia Doyle and her co-workers worked many hours with us on the program.

There are many good, decent people who make mistakes and get arrested for the first time. This is a traumatic and depressing situation for the person arrested. Officers using the screening form can find out if this person is a high-risk candidate for suicide. It is not only my responsibility as chief of police to make sure my officers arrest persons committing crimes, but it is my responsibility to make sure those persons do not harm themselves or commit suicide in our jail. As President of the Westchester County Chiefs of Police, I would make all of the police chiefs and commissioners aware of this pilot program at our meetings. I would have Patricia Doyle of the Westchester County Department of Community Mental Health at the meeting of the Westchester County Chiefs of Police Association to explain the program. The standard questionnaire is designed to help officers determine whether a prisoner is suicidal. It asks whether the prisoner has experienced a loss of a job or a family member within the last year had psychiatric problems or a history of alcohol or drug abuse, has attempted suicide, is showing signs of depression, is making suicidal statements, or is under the influence of drugs or alcohol. My officers are trained to automatically put a prisoner down as a high-risk if they believe any of the signs are there. To those who would criticize new programs that may become state-mandated or the cost of the program, I would state that it is better to have this program in place in your department before a suicide takes place and that the cost effectiveness of the program outweighs any wrongful death lawsuit that may be brought against you. You must be responsible for a prisoner committing suicide in your jurisdiction. This is your moral responsibility.

In the summer of 1985, Westchester County Executive Andrew O'Rourke appointed me to the Westchester County Traffic Safety Board subject to the confirmation of the Westchester County Board of Legislators. The board, consisting of various county officials, worked on various traffic safety proposals and legislation concerning Westchester County. There was no financial remuneration for this position, so there was no conflict with my position as chief of police or any of the other boards and committees I served on. I would also be appointed to the Westchester County Emergency Response Task Force and the Westchester County Suicide Prevention Committee. In November of 1985, as President of the Westchester County Chief of Police, I urged the county's Civil Service Commission to make psychological testing of police officer candidates as part of the screening process. Many of the county's police chiefs and commissioners, including myself, had their police officer candidates given a psychological test before they were hired. The tests were an investment. Many police departments have a 20-year retirement plan. If you failed to have your candidates tested, you could have a person for 20 years who should not be a police officer. During the probationary period of a recruit, you may dismiss him or her for any reason. However, after that period, you may go through one or two trials with the officer to remove him or her. You may have an officer who cannot handle the stress of law enforcement. When you receive a police officer examination test from the county personnel department, the candidate exam score will be next to his or her name. The candidate has not been given a psychological exam up to this point in the selection process. Therefore, at this time, the local department interviewing and hiring the candidates will pay for this testing out of their budgets. I do not believe that there is any reason that would justify not having the candidates tested. There is a myriad of problems that could be present in a candidate. Alcoholism, depression, paranoia, substance abuse, and persons who are reckless or make poor judgments are just a few of such problems. I use Father Joseph A. DeSanto, Ph.D., Chairman of the Criminal Justice Department at Iona College in New Rochelle, New York, for my evaluations. He does extensive testing of the candidates and will explain the results to me.

There are old timers who may say, "That young chief is wasting money on those evaluations. They could interview candidates, do a background check, and tell if a person would make a good police officer." It should be that simple. I don't think the general public realizes the stress that police officers go through. To go on a call and find a person who has committed suicide by blowing away part of his skull with a gunshot. To go on calls where babies are going through withdrawal while the parent or parents are shooting up drugs. Going on a hostage situation call or to the scene of a murder or murders. This does not make a person any less by not being able to handle these situations. There may be many professions where such a person may excel, however, the good police administrator should use every tool at his disposal to find out ahead of any of the aforementioned situations where a person possesses the needed makeup to handle them.

There may be other situations where the police officer had scored high on the evaluations and was a good police officer for a number of years before something affects him or her. He or she may benefit from an additional evaluation or counseling. A police supervisor, when doing a performance evaluation of a police officer, should note any reason that his subordinate may need such counseling.

Westchester County is fortunate to have several outstanding professionals who administer the psychological exam. Some use the Minnesota Multiphasic Personality Test, which contains over five hundred questions. Others use different tests or a combination of tests.

The police administrator must use a person he has confidence in and the evaluations should be given to every candidate.

Margaret White

In the evening of January 3, 1986, I was notified that Margaret White was getting out of a car at her residence in North Tarrytown when she suffered a fatal heart attack and died at age 51. This news about one of my closest friends and advisors was very upsetting to say the least. I don't know anyone who worked harder for her community, her neighborhood, and for anyone in need, than Margaret. I sat by myself, thinking of all the good this one person had done. She was one of the charter members of my Police Community Relations Committee going back to 1979. She never missed a meeting and most nights worked many hours to find solutions to community problems. She was one of the rare persons who not only tried to rid her residence of drug pushers, loiterers, and troublemakers, but also publicly let them know of her feelings. A brave woman when you consider that she lived alone in her apartment in the building she was complaining about.

She had been the first black person to serve on the North Tarrytown Board of Trustees having been appointed to that position by Mayor Philip Zegarelli. After serving on the board of trustees, she was elected to the Tarrytown School Board and served with distinction. I'll always remember attending work sessions of the board of trustees for budget appropriation when Margaret was on the board. I can remember long nights when I was trying to get budget items for the police department. I can remember one trustee telling me that you're not going to get more photography equipment so that you and your friends at the F.B.I. can take more pictures of me. Margaret would stand up and state that she would have no part of this nonsense. She would turn to me, say, "Goodnight, Dick," and walk out. Whenever this type of incident would happen, I would receive a telephone call early the next morning from Margaret.

She would say, "Dick, you're not down, are you? Don't let these people get you down." Even though she was on the phone I could see her bright smile. What a rare person in politics; someone with no ego who wanted nothing for herself but only wanted to have a better community and to rid her neighborhood of criminals.

On the morning of Margaret's funeral, when I entered New Hope Institutional Baptist Church, I spoke with the Reverend Sherman Nabors, Margaret's pastor and a person I had worked with in law enforcement. I told him that this was going to be hard.

He replied, "I know. I know." She had been such an important part of this church, Reverend Nabors said.

My mind drifted back to the many happy occasions that I had attended services at the church with Margaret and the Reverend Nabors. How warm and kind the members had been to me on the occasions I had been invited to speak there. I took my place with the others. I had a cold to say I was depressed on this cold winter morning would be as understatement.

Towards the end of the service, I observed Jimmy Warren with the men from the funeral home. He worked for the funeral home when he was off-duty as a police officer. I looked at Margaret's casket and nodded saying, "You sent another message to me when I was down." Yes, he was one of our accomplishments, but you're still leaving too soon. As we guided Margaret's casket out of the church, I almost had to chuckle to myself; I could visualize Jesus taking Margaret by the hand to show her the place he had for her. She would respond, "Oh, no, no, I can't be up that close. I'll stay here." But the Lord would put his humble servant where she rightfully belonged. I would have to ask his forgiveness for being upset that he had taken her and thank him for allowing us to have been with her.

On the evening of March 14, 1986, I attended the Westchester County Chiefs of Police Association Annual Dinner at the Mamaroneck Beach and Yacht Club as the outgoing President. I was completely surprised when County Legislator Diane A. Keane presented me with a proclamation from the Westchester County Board of Legislators which read: *"Whereas Chief Richard J. Spota of the North Tarrytown Police Department has served as President of the Westchester County Police Chiefs Association, for the past year and whereas, as President of the Westchester County Police Chiefs Association, Chief Richard J. Spota has demonstrated the same commitment to the highest standards of excellence in law enforcement that has earned him the respect and admiration of his fellow officers in North Tarrytown, and whereas, Chief Richard J. Spota's reputation for innovation in law enforcement is well-deserved. In addition to introducing the Canine Corps to the North Tarrytown Police Department, he was the first law enforcement official in the county to introduce Suicide Prevention Screening for jail prisoners and established Westchester's First Community Relations Board. And whereas accomplishments such as those of Chief Richard J. Spota should be properly recognized and acclaimed, therefore, be it resolved that the members of the Westchester County Board of Legislators are proud to join with the many friends who have gathered here tonight in honoring chief Richard J. Spota upon me completion of his term as President of the Westchester County Police Chiefs Association, and be it further resolved this Friday, March 14, 1986, is hereby declared Richard J. Spota Day in Westchester County and be it further resolved that the text of this Proclamation be parried throughout the County of Westchester for all people of good will be forever known."*

As I said, I didn't expect this, and this was a very humbling experience for me.

I am sure that the proclamation is for the hard work of many of the county's outstanding police chiefs and commissioners. It has been my honor and privilege to have served as their president. My mind drifted back to the man who came out of the grand jury room after having been subpoenaed to testify who said to me that we don't want police officers like you. For all of the organized crime figures in Westchester County there are many better, decent, hard-working, law-abiding citizens.

On April 2, 1986, the Policemen's Benevolent Association of Westchester County honored a total of 40 P.B.A. members for actions during incidents in 1983, 1984, and 1985. The awards, voted on by their peers, were given to the police officers at an awards dinner in Valhalla, New York. Out of the forty awards, twenty-one were given to fifteen members of the North Tarrytown Police Department. The Exceptional Merit Award was given to Officer Bernard Foley of North Tarrytown. Life Saving Awards were given to Officers John Cappello, Walter Schrank, John DiCairano, and Sergeant Lee Hayward of North Tarrytown Police Department. Detective Gordon Ferguson and I received two Meritorious Honor Awards each. Patrolman Robert Morrison of North Tarrytown received Life Saving and Meritorious Honor Awards. Officer Manuel Caixeiro of North Tarrytown received on Exceptional Merit and two Meritorious Honor Awards. Officer Ronald Biro of North Tarrytown received one Life Saving and two Meritorious Honor Awards. Needless to say, I was very proud of my police officers and the countywide recognition they received.

On May 2, 1986, at 9 a.m., it was one office area residents to be honored by the Westchester County Department of Community Mental Health. This took place at New York Hospital Cornell Medical Center, Bloomingdale Road, White Plains. The program was a celebration of Mental Health Month. The program included an address on *"The State of Mental Health"* by County Executive Andrew P. O'Rourke. Dr. Robert Sussman, Chairman of the Departments' Community Services Board presented the awards to the five of us for outstanding service to the community in promoting better mental health. Dr. Sussman stated that I was receiving the award as the chief of the police department for taking the lead in implementing the State Forensic Suicide Prevention Screening Guidelines Program in the North Tarrytown lockup and as the President of the county Police Chiefs Association for working diligently to inform and involve police chiefs in the Forensic Suicide Prevention Program. Patricia Doyle and her co-workers in the County Department of Mental Health had submitted a recommendation to the board for me to receive the award.

They truly deserve as much or more credit than anyone for their tireless work on this project. I merely had seen a system in place in the state that was not working properly. The training of our auxiliary police officers to come to police headquarters and observe a person who was classified as a high risk for committing suicide was only common sense. They were paid per diem for the number of hours they were on the suicide watch. The most rewarding fact of the program was that no one who had been classified as high risk and put under observation had committed suicide.

We were notified on May 20, 1986, that President Ronald Reagan and his wife, Nancy, would be staying at the Rockefeller family's Pocantico Hills estate during the commemoration of the Statue of Liberty Centennial. The Secret Service stated that the Rockefeller compound was selected in order to avoid the large crowds that were expected for four days of concerts, parades, and revelry between July 3 and July 6 of 1986. Details of how they would arrive were yet to be worked out. They could fly in from Manhattan by helicopter, arrive by a motorcade, or even come up the Hudson River, dock in our area, and then drive to the Rockefeller Estate. President Reagan was scheduled to preside over the torch relighting of the Statue of Liberty on July 3, 1986.

The President and Mrs. Reagan would stay in Kykuit, the largest mansion on the Rockefeller Estate. The Georgian-style, four-story house was built by John D. Rockefeller, patriarch of the family. Kykuit is an early name given to Pocantico Hills by Dutch traders. It means "lookout." The site offers a grand view of the Hudson River at its widest point. President Ford dedicated the house and 86 of its 2,700 acres as a national historic landmark in 1976.

The detectives would work with the secret service to provide security during the stay. As a detective, I worked with the Secret Service when President Nixon came to the Rockefeller Estate by motorcade during his presidency. We also had President Gerald Ford here during his presidency. Former Secretary of State Henry Kissinger would also visit the Rockefeller Estate along with many heads of state and foreign leaders. Whenever a president is scheduled to appear in an area, advanced intelligence information is critical, as many would-be assassins and mentally disturbed persons try to find a weak link in presidential protection so that they may carry out their deeds. You must take pride in the fact that this is your president and that you will allow no one to harm him.

Late in the evening of Sunday, June 29, 1986, I was notified by police headquarters of a fight between a black male and a Hispanic male over a drug deal in the area of 100 College Avenue, College Arms, a high-rise apartment building in the southern end of the village. The area has many bars and bodegas. The two police officers on duty who responded were considerably outnumbered by numerous persons on the street on that warm summer evening. The desk sergeant requested mutual aid and members of the area police departments responded. I was joined at the scene by Chief Ronald Goldfarb of the Village of Ossining Police Department. We used his vehicle during the night because he had a phone, in addition to the police radio. Before the night was over, ten persons were arrested.

The charges were possession of a controlled substance, disorderly conduct, menacing, resisting arrest, etc. While standing on the street by Cortlandt Street and College Avenue, bottles were being thrown at us from the rooftops. I put my police helmet on while on the street for the remainder of the night. The black and Hispanic persons involved were not representative of the majority of the good, hardworking minorities who live in this area. When the fracas finally quieted down, I moved the line of the police officers back approximately two blocks so as not to agitate the situation.

By eight or nine in the morning, I was surprised at the number of major TV stations with their news people who wanted to do interviews with me. It wasn't until several years later that I would find out that a person who was running an illegal establishment in the area had seen one of the detectives surveilling this person's establishment. The person then called every major news TV station on the night of June 29, reporting a race riot. The TV stations responded. I thought I had completed all interviews when Bob Trout of NBC came back for a second interview. He had gone back to the scene and had additional questions to ask me. All reporters should be as good, decent, and honest as Bob Trout.

In the following days and nights, I would be asked about the initial officer on the scene of the fight. Was he overly aggressive? The truth was that the officer was a born-again Christian minister while off-duty.

9 arrested, 4 injured in N. Tarrytown 'riot'

He would spend his off duty time taking underprivileged youngsters to ball games and other events. He was anything but overly aggressive. There were many residents in the area that I would meet with once a month at the Police Community Relations Committee meetings and others in the area that would give us information on the drug traffic in the area. I would never reveal this to the public, the press, or anyone else. Despite all of the drug arrests we were making in the area, I'm sure some of these residents were of the opinion, more should be made. I would explain to them that we would arrest a pusher and, when successful, get that pusher to introduce an undercover officer in the area to make buys of drugs. We would keep the undercover officers in the area as long as possible. This would not show up for a while and persons giving information may believe we are not doing enough, but this is the more effective way of getting indictments on pushers.

I knew I had become chief of police of a department that did not reflect the community it served at the time I started. I would continue with this as a goal.

With criticism by those arrested and their friends, I could do one of three things about the drug problem. Do nothing, do the minimal amount of action, or continue a full-scale assault on the drug trade. The latter was the only choice. All of the persons arrested would eventually plead guilty or be found guilty of the charges of June 29, 1986.

The real leaders of the minority community, especially the Hispanic leaders, wanted the drug pushers off the streets. Two of the original members of the Police Community Relations Committee were Cubans, and they had good feedback to their people, but I had to include members of all of the other Hispanic groups in the community so that we would have feedback to all of the other groups in the community. I added young black men to the committee to bridge the age gap of some of the older black committee members.

The media has a responsibility to report mistreatment of minorities. Most do this very well. However, as this incident shows, they have to be sure that their informant is not part of the problem, using them to help keep the police away from their illegal activities. The organized crime people in the area enjoyed seeing the police, who were putting their numbers and other interests out of business, getting heat. There are politicians who run for office who would try to use the arrest situations to their advantage. I think anyone who tries to make racism an issue, where there is no racism, is the lowest form of human being. There are two persons who I believe are in heaven who would ask God to strike down their son if he was involved in racism. I can hear Margaret White say to them, "Don't worry. There isn't a day in his life that he forgot, but he must get rid of the remaining drug pushers in the area where I once lived."

We continued to have extra officers and patrols in the area of the disturbance as we entered into July. Fletcher H. Graves of the U.S. Department of Justice Community Relations Service would work diligently throughout the summer to determine what problems may exist in the community and if there was any wrongdoing. He has a strong resemblance to NBC weatherman, Al Roker. He is a dedicated no-nonsense, hard-working individual.

At 6:14 a.m., Saturday, August 2, 1986, a call was received at police headquarters. The caller said, "A man was going crazy on Valley Street." He was hitting cars with a three-foot pipe. When Officers Buddy Foley and John DiCairano arrived at the scene, they checked the area and spotted Felix Jupierre, 20 years of age, of North Tarrytown, standing at the opposite end of the street near a car he had apparently struck with the pipe. DiCairano said that when Foley drove up to the suspect, Jupierre approached the vehicle with the pipe. DiCairano said, he ordered Jupierre to drop the pipe. When the suspect did not respond, the officers grabbed him. Jupierre broke free, swinging that 36 1/2 inch, 4 1/2 pound, white pipe like a baseball bat. He struck Foley on the left side of his chest. As Foley buckled over, DiCairano threw his nightstick at the suspect to attract his attention and then tackled him and brought him to the ground with Foley's help. With the assistance of Tarrytown Police Officer Dennis DeCuffa, who was passing the area, and North Tarrytown Officer Gregory Camp, the suspect was handcuffed and placed in custody. Foley would be admitted to Phelps Memorial Hospital with injuries to the left side of his chest and ribs. He was given an electrocardiogram, because of a blow that struck him near his heart. Jupierre was charged with assault in the second degree, a felony. Bail was set at $5,000.

Saturday evening, I was at the hospital to visit Officer Foley. His mother was also there. She was brave, but it was hard on her to see her son lying in the hospital bed with and IV in his arm and tubes. He was in a great deal of pain. On the way home from the hospital Mrs. Foley apologized to me for getting upset at the hospital.

Officers injured by pipe-swinging suspect

I thought she had acted very well under the circumstances. She told me that it was 20 years to the day that Officer Foley's father, her husband, had died. As I left Mrs. Foley at her house, there were several things bothering me under deadly physical force guidelines, Officer Foley had the right to use deadly physical force. Officer DiCairano, who suffered bruises to his neck and elbow, also had the right to use deadly physical force. Buddy Foley, a strong, athletic, young man, was being beaten with what is classified as a dangerous instrument. Because of the fine, decent, human being that he is, he was seriously injured but did not use deadly physical force. When I became chief of police, the first class that was taught to the department was deadly physical force, so that they could properly make a split second decision on deadly physical force. The officer was trained properly. He knew he had the right to use deadly physical force but chose not to at a time in law enforcement when others might have. Felix Jupierre was high on drugs at the time of the incident. It was believed that he purchased the drugs in our area. I made a promise to myself that every place selling drugs and every pusher would be properly investigated and charged, so help me God.

During the summer of 1986, I designed and published a booklet of common Spanish phrases with the help of my Spanish-speaking Secretary/Translator Karin Guardia. The booklet contained the most asked questions by Hispanic residents. All officers in the department were now carrying the booklet, and I had given copies of it to the leaders of the Spanish community who were very supportive and receptive of the idea. In September 1986, I recommended the appointment of Jose O. Cotarelo for the position of police officer. There would be an opening due to a retirement in a few months and the officer would enter the Westchester County Police Academy graduating on December 19, 1986. Mayor Philip Zegarelli and the board of trustees voted to approve the appointment of the bilingual Cuban native and veteran of the United States Air Force.

In late September 1986, we publicized our police department's neighborhood watch program. The program was an organized effort by concerned residents to look out for each other's safety and to help law enforcement officers protect people and their homes against criminals. If there is increasing crime in your neighborhood, car break-ins, house burglaries, if people are dealing drugs on your street or in the lobby of your apartment building, this program could help you to light back. Once a program has been established, neighborhood watch volunteers met with the police to learn how to safeguard each other's homes and reduce the risk of crime. They were taught to become more alert to unusual or suspicious circumstances, individuals, or vehicles. Neighborhood watch groups were told not to try to stop a suspicious person. They were asked to call the police immediately.

It is better to call the police when you see something suspicious, even if it turns out to be nothing, than to keep quiet and risk having a neighbor victimized by criminals. We would rather receive many unfounded complaints than miss one legitimate complaint

The police cannot fight crime they do not know about. When alert citizens keep us informed, we are far more effective against crime and citizens have better protection and safer neighborhoods. Statistics show that crime is significantly decreased in neighborhoods where neighborhood watch programs are established. But it takes residents to make it work. If you want to live in a safe neighborhood, you have to get involved. Officer William Patten, our crime prevention officer, was in charge of our neighborhood watch program. I urged all interested residents to call or come to police headquarters to discuss how they may become involved in this important program.

In the pro-dawn hours of Saturday, September 20, 1986, the African American Social Club on Cortlandt Street was raided by the State Liquor Authority and our police department. Nine persons were arrested during the Sam raid that culminated a 5-month investigation that began in May of 1986. Residents of the surrounding area, including "College Arms," had complained about illegal activities, noise, fighting, etc. at the club. An undercover officer disconnected a television monitoring system that warned if police were in the area, moments before the raid began. Police seized an undetermined amount of cocaine, crack, amphetamines, and marijuana, along with gambling records, the club's membership records, $380 in cash, approximately 60 bottles of wine and liquor, and 15 cases of beer. Two of the suspects were charged with selling alcohol to a minor. The investigation involved infiltrating with undercover police and State Liquor Authority investigators, because of the monitoring system and other problems. There were between 60 and 70 people in the club when the raid began. Many began throwing drugs onto the floor, into drinks, and out of windows, as police entered the building. A dice game was in progress in another section of the club. The club's

President was charged with running an unlicensed bottle club, operating a criminal nuisance, selling alcohol without a license, and unlicensed storage of alcoholic beverages. Another person was charged with running an unlicensed bottle club and unlawfully dealing with a child. Kevin Bonner, 20, of Elmsford, was charged with obstructing government administration. William Miller, 52, of, North Tarrytown, was charged with promotion of gambling, selling alcohol without a license, running an unlicensed bottle club, and unlicensed storage of alcoholic beverages. One person was charged with obstructing governmental administration. Michel Lacy, 30, was charged with possession of marijuana.

One person of 1 River Plaza, Tarrytown, a barmaid at the club, was charged with unlawfully dealing with a minor and selling alcoholic beverages without a license. Wayne Morris, 27, of Brannan, Texas, was charged with possession of marijuana. As we left the premises and walked out to the street, it was daylight. Residents of College Arms at the windows of their apartments cheered. There were shouts of, "Good job! Good job!" There was one of, "It's about time." The residents of College Arms deserved this. They had the right to get a good night's sleep and not be subjected to people on the street who were drunk, fighting, making noise on the street outside of where they lived. So did the residents of the adjoining streets. They made legitimate complaints, and we responded to them.

In October 1986, the U.S. Department of Justice, Community Relations Service asked me to be a consultant with them at a human rights conference to be held at the Holiday Inn, Route 9, Fishkill, N.Y. The program was to be sponsored by the Regional Advisory Council, New York State Division of Human Rights. The Community Relations Service would present a workshop on police/community relations, and I would do a workshop on my Police Community Relations Committee. The conference was well-attended. The other speakers were excellent. The lunchtime speaker was David Dinkins. My workshop began after lunch. Fletcher H. Graves of the U.S. Department of Justice Community Relations Service introduced me. He said, "If any of that garbage that was printed in the newspapers about Chief Spota was true, he wouldn't be working with us."

I was surprised that he said that publicly. I must admit it made me feel good inside. I gave out a handout of my Police Community Relations Committee: the purpose of it, the general concepts, the committee members. There were many that wanted to start such a program in their communities. I explained to them the importance of having members of all the Hispanic communities in their areas and the reasons for it: to get feedback to all Hispanic groups. Also, about having younger members of the black community, along with their elders, so as to get feedback to all age groups of the black community. There were many good questions asked during the question and answer session. I believe the workshop was beneficial to all who attended. At the wrap-up at the end of the day, when all of the various groups were assembled in a main conference room, minority leaders addressed the gathering. They were very kind to mc. I was a minority at the conference. That's a good role reversal for everyone to experience. Fletcher H. Graves and his unit of the U.S. Department of Justice did a great job. They should be commended.

In November 1986, I recommend the promotion of Police Officer Manuel Caixeiro to the rank of detective, effective December 1, 1986. Officer Caixeiro is fluent in Spanish and Portuguese. He had been with the department since November 1979, after serving 1 ½ years with the Haverstraw Police Department. He was honorably discharged in 1974 after serving in the U.S. Marine Corps. He had received 12 commendations for outstanding police work with our department. As I have mentioned before, a chief of police can transfer a patrolman to detective duty, but the fiscal appropriation must come from the board of trustees, which they moved on at their meeting.

Bobby Checchi, 26 years of age, was recommended by me to the position of police officer to fill a vacancy left by a retiring officer. A resident of the village, Checchi, graduated from Sleepy Hollow High School and majored in marketing at Westchester Community College. The appointment was approved by the mayor and board of trustees, effective December 1, 1986.

Stop-DWI Program

Our department had been very involved in the Stop-DWI program since its inception about four years ago. The state and county DWI arrest information was released to the media at the end of November 1986. For the year January through December 1985, our department ranked fifth in Westchester County for DWI arrests with I53. This was out of a total of 40 police departments in Westchester County, excluding the N.Y. State Police and the Westchester County Police, whose jurisdictions are statewide and countywide respectively. The departments in front' of ours were mostly several times ours in size and covered a much larger area. The City of New Rochelle, Town of Greenburgh, City of Yonkers, and Port Chester were those ahead of us. For the first six months of 1986, January through June 1986, we ranked sixth out of 40 departments in Westchester County with 77 DWI. arrests.

There was a lot of work involved in this operation: training and retraining of the police officers, certification and re-certification of the officers, and equipment used. I applied each month to the Westchester County Stop-DWI program for reimbursement of overtime of the police officers involved in the program. As the program continues to be more effective, the arrest figures will go down. This is through education and enforcement. We conducted Stop-DWI checkpoints with the county police from evening hours until almost dawn. I was present with the officers and other supervisors during the checkpoints. All officers greeted the motorists with a good evening or good morning, sir or madam. The motorists were asked relevant questions at times, and they usually proceeded on their way. The vast majority of the motorists expressed their support of the program. I have seen drivers get out of their vehicles intoxicated and state, "I need help."

Total traffic deaths in Westchester County rose about 27 percent from 64 in 1984 to 81 in 1985. But the number believed to be related to alcohol consumption dropped. The average number of fatalities in Westchester County dropped 23 percent from before the Stop-DWI programs were instituted. Nationwide 44, 241 people died in car accidents in 1984, a rise of four percent from the previous year. Those statistics showed that 43 percent of the drivers were drunk at the time of the accident, down from 50 percent in 1980. The public perception of the drunk driver has changed. There is now an almost zero tolerance for drunk driving. Increased use of seat belts, mandatory since 1984, have accounted for a decline in fatal accidents countywide and statewide.

There was a second, front-page article on bar business thriving in North Tarrytown in February of this year in the Gannett Westchester Newspapers. We had 27 licenses issued to bars and restaurants that year. The article mentioned General Motors and its 4,500 employees as a reason for many bars. When a community has a large number of bars, it is going to have problems in proportion to the number of bars. The more bars you have, the more DWI arrests you're going to make. That entails a lot of work and man hours. It takes a minimum of two hours to administer a Breathalyzer test and the related paperwork.

I had put police officer Ron Biro in charge of the Stop-DWI program. He and the many dedicated officers working this program have done a truly outstanding job. I could say that I don't have enough officers due to other police work and a high volume of calls for service and that my overtime budget is insufficient to run this program. However, it is my responsibility as chief of police to ensure the safety of motorists and pedestrians. Without being reimbursed for some of the overtime costs for the Stop-DWI program, I could not fund the program out of my budget.

Sing Sing Escape

It was after 6:00 p.m. on Tuesday, December 9, 1986, when I was notified of the escape of three inmates of Sing Sing Prison, which is located in Ossining, N.Y., about four miles north of North Tarrytown, N.Y. The information was that the three inmates had left the education building of Sing Sing, ran to a bathroom, bent the metal bars of a nearby window, exited through the window, and dropped to the ground, used wire cutters to cut through a fence and had lowered themselves down a 20-foot wall, using a rope made from leather shoelaces. They used smoke bombs to partially screen themselves. A guard fired a shot at them but to no avail.

The three were identified as Darius Gittens, 26 years of age, white, male of Flushing, N.Y. serving 5–10 years for burglary, Thomas Linz, 44 years of age, White, male 5'9, 160 lbs., brown hair, brown eyes of Brooklyn, sentenced to 20 years to life for murder, and Julio Giano, 24 years of age, white, male, 5' 10", 160 lbs., black hair, brown eyes of Queens, N.Y. convicted of murder, serving 48 years to life. Before trial, Giano tried to escape, shot one officer, beat another, and blinded a third with a caustic substance. I would bring in off-duty officers and the department's two K-9 officers, Walter Schrank with K-9 Mike and Richard Kiggins with K-9 Mugs. We would use the Hudson River to the west and Route 9 to the east as the perimeter of containment. Metro North was immediately notified.

Their tracks run north and south and right through Sing Sing. Ossiniug Town and Village Police, Briarcliff Manor Police, the New York State Police and State Correction Officers, and Mt. Pleasant P.D. all responded. The P.D.S to the south of us, Tarrytown, Irvington, and Greenburgh, would set up roadblocks. Metro North shut of its power, stopping trains off and on for several hours. We stationed officers along the railroad tracks in the area of North 'Tarrytown. Around 10 p.m., we gave one of the police dogs a 45-minute break, because we had been working the dog for four straight hours.

I requested Greenburgh Police Officer Sam Washington and his K-9 Bandit, because my two K-9s were being worked very hard, and we might be out most of the night with them. At 10:40 p.m., Darius Gittens was apprehended at the Scarborough train station, which is between Ossining and North Tarrytown, N.Y. He had traveled about 2/3 of a mile. But all three could be crisscrossing back and forth. We would continue our strategy of containing the area. There is a vast wooded area adjacent to the Hudson River. We believed they would use the railroad tracks and the Croton aqueduct as guideposts on their journey south. They could also use the wooded area adjacent to Rt. 9 as a guide. Temperatures were going below freezing. We would try to keep them moving, tired, and hungry. If they entered a house, they might get a taxi or steal a car. All vehicles must be checked. The roadblocks must continue. During the night and the early morning hours, we received calls from concerned residents about possible sightings, noises, and concerns for their safety. It is far better to receive numerous calls that do not turn out to be anything connected to the escape than not to receive that one important call.

In the predawn hours, our K-9 officers checked our Sleepy Hollow Cemetery, which is located east of Route 9 (Broadway). Greenburgh Police Officer Sam Washington and his K-9 Bandit searched the grounds near the old cemetery building. Bandit jumped a three-foot high wall that had a 40-foot drop on the other side. The dog was trying to get the scent of one of the escapees when he jumped the wall and fell 40 feet on the other side.

Sam heard the dog holler. He was alive but seriously injured. He tried to walk, but Sam picked him up and carried him in his arms. He realized that Bandit was in a lot of pain. When I was notified of the accident, I authorized one of our police officers to drive Sam and Bandit to the Greenburgh Animal Hospital and subsequently to the New York City Veterinary Hospital. Sam and Bandit were always there for me and my department. I couldn't have felt worse if it was one of our own canines, Mike or Mugs, or my own family Golden Retriever, Mollie. The canines are considered a part of our departments and they should be treated accordingly.

There were reports in the morning that Linz, Giano or both had been seen, but we could not confirm the information. That changed around noon on Wednesday, December 10, 1986. Scarborough, the community to the north of North Tarrytown and Phelps Memorial Hospital, had a resident that observed the escapees. A resident of Lands End Road was in his driveway peering into the engine compartment of his car when Julio Giano, outfitted like a jogger in red sweatpants and a maroon sweatshirt, approached him to ask if there was a garage nearby. The resident told him there wasn't any. He thanked the man and took off, running. A few minutes later, the man observed Linz wearing blue pants, a brown jacket, and leaving a vacant house next door and then walk north along the Croton aqueduct. Giano headed south. The man called the police.

The officers discovered the inmates' green uniforms had been left behind in the resident's 21-foot sailboat, which had been parked in his driveway and covered with a tarp. A few streets away a retired airline pilot was watching television in the living room of his home at 7 Country Club Lane, when someone knocked on his door. Country Club Lane is the last public street north of Phelps Memorial Hospital and North Tarrytown. The street is west of Route 9 (Broadway) Albany

Post Road. The man Went to his front door and observed Giano. He didn't think there was anything unusual about the man. Giano said that his car had broken down off Route 9. The man thought nothing of it until he heard a commotion and Giano suddenly returned after using the phone and bolted through the garage and into the kitchen and out the back door, breaking the latch and knocking over a stack of tables. Briarcliff Manor Police Officer Fremont Stafford had approached the escapee and asked him for identification and had followed him to the house where he offered to get his identification. Officer Stafford wasn't able to apprehend the fleeing Giano, but he was able to give us an idea of his whereabouts and what he was wearing. At approximately 2:00 p.m., we received a phone call that Linz and Giano might be inside of the abandoned Pickwick Post Restaurant on Route 9 in North Tarrytown. The building was surrounded by our officers, but to no avail. Neither of the escapees was inside of the building.

The next report was that one of the escapees had been seen near Country Club Lane. Chief Lloyd Thompkins of the Town of Ossining Police and a group of officers checked the area. The outside perimeters and roadblocks were still being maintained—still no sign of the two escapees. At approximately 6:00 p.m., a person believed to be Giano was observed near Route 9 in Briarcliff Manor. All of the areas are heavily wooded and areas of extremely rough terrain. At 7:30 p.m., Chief Thompkins's group began rechecking the area. They knocked on the door of Ivanhoe Place, which is adjacent to the property in which the escapees changed their clothes in the boat. The officers asked the owner if she had heard or seen anything unusual. She suggested they look inside her storage shed at the rear of the house. They did, but to no avail. They then decided to recheck the boat. When the officers took the tarp off, they found Linz. His hands were lacerated from the leather rope. Two of the escapees were now in custody.

The most dangerous convict was still at large. It must be remembered that Julio Giano was not only convicted of murder, but he shot an officer and beat another trying to escape at his trial. We had to contain him between the Hudson River and Route 9. South of Country Club Lane is a vastly wooded area of rough terrain. This area eventually leads to the IBM property, which also has an extensive wooded area between Route 9 and the Hudson River. He could crisscross these areas for a long period of time. All of our officers, K-9 units, and the support help we were getting were in place from the Hudson River and the important areas of the Metro-North Railroad tracks and the train station. Everyone involved knew that we could not make a mistake. If we did, and gave Giano the opportunity, he would seize it. I had no doubt that it would result in serious injury or death for residents in their homes or driving their cars. With everyone in place, I drove to a wooded area south of County Club Lane, off Route 9. I was able to open up a gate and drive down a dirt road for a while. Where the road ended, I parked my unmarked police vehicle and locked it. I had my portable police radio with me, but to keep it on in the woods would be similar to using a handheld bullhorn, so I shut it off.

I walked until I was north of the IBM property. I didn't hear or see Giano. Did he hear me? I don't know. When I walked back to the police vehicle, I entered it and drove back through the woods to Route 9. When I got on Route 9, I turned on the police radio. I learned that headquarters had been calling car 510 continuously. That was my vehicle. At 3:10 p.m. Officer Jimmy Warren was stationed near the Metro-North power station off Riverside Drive in North Tarrytown. This is next to the railroad tracks and adjacent to the Hudson River. He believed he saw Giano near the Men-o-North power station. Giano observed Officer Warren and ran. At 9 p.m., officers observed Giano fleeing into the marshland near Freemont Pond. This is in the Sleepy Hollow Manor section of North Tarrytown. The perimeter was tightened; Route 9 was sealed off. The area to the north, where Phelps Memorial Hospital is located, was sealed off. The K-9 units tracked the areas with their handlers. The helicopter used infrared lighting capable of detecting heat indicating body temperatures on the ground. Vehicles with large spotlights illuminated areas being searched. This would be continued for several hours. We were very concerned for the residents who were calling police headquarters and those who were counting on us. If Giano got to the next area south of us, he would be near where my wife and two children were located, at home alone. The officers were going house to house to look for Giano. It was now midnight and Officers John Capello and John DiCairano were assigned to cover Freemont Road, which is behind the marsh and the Freemont Pond where Giano had been observed. Officers Cappello, DiCairano, and rookie State Trooper Kimberly Adriance had just checked the residence of Cliff Barrett at 32 Freemont Road. Officer Cappello and Adriance were turning to leave when something caught their eye. The windows of the late model Lincoln Continental parked in the driveway. The windows of the automobile were foggy on the inside. The officers went to both sides of the car, and they swung open the doors. Inside the car was Julio Giano. His wet shoes were off. He was wrapped in Cliff Barrett's down vest, stretched out on the seat. As we moved in to back up the officers, Giano said, "What's the big deal? I didn't kill anyone."

An officer replied, "Not today."

Giano said, "Yeah, not today."

As elated as I was, I said to myself, "I hope you're telling the truth." I hoped that the next 24 to 48 hours would answer that, where maybe a relative or friend would find something wrong inside a house. That was my main concern at the time.

The area was now being covered with reporters from the major TV stations. They apparently had been in the area. When I returned to police headquarters, I called home and told Pat, Todd, and Melissa that it was over, everything was okay.

I didn't know when I'd be home. As calls poured into police headquarters, I kept hoping that we would not receive a call of anyone injured or killed. This was Thursday morning. He said, "I didn't kill anyone today." What about Tuesday and Wednesday? I got a phone call from Mayor Phil Zegarelli who was on a business trip to California. He said, "You caught the last one." I asked him how he knew that, and he replied that it was on television in California. He was very happy. I told him that we had incurred at least 200 hours of overtime. With all of the work before the escape, my budget had been over budget toward the end of the fiscal year. He said that we would sit down and work on the overtime when he got back. He wanted me to congratulate everyone involved in the department. All of the agencies and police departments involved in the escape deserved high praise. Everyone worked extremely well together; no ego problems, only good professional police work. I was particularly proud of my officers. They once again had given me everything they had and then some. In the next few days, there were no reports of anyone being injured by the escapees.

Some of the best news that I received concerned Bandit. He was going to be alright. There were no serious internal injuries. He would be able to return to work in 1987. That was great news.

We have a tack board in our training room that is used to put up notices, etc. The wall was being covered with cards and letters from residents, non-residents and out-of-state persons who were writing letters, season's greetings cards with notes, etc. A sample of the letters follow: *"Dear Sir, I'm sure you get many more notes of complaints than praise, so I wanted you to know what a wonderful job you and your men did to capture the escapees from Sing Sing. We are very, very grateful to you all. Sincerely, (a local resident)."*

"To all involved policemen and departments, I want to commend you for your excellent and hard work in the capture of the felons. I'm very proud of all of you and to be a part of this community. Thanks again and congratulations. You all deserve a big pat on the back. Very Truly Yours (an area resident)."

"Merry Christmas from a Grateful Philipse Manor Family (a section of North Tarrytown)."

"Dear Police of North Tarrytown, Congratulations on a fine job. We are all sleeping a lot easier now. (Local resident)."

"Thanks to you and your men for an outstanding job in capturing the Sing Sing criminals. (Local resident)."

"Dear Chief Spota, although we are residents of Bergen County, New Jersey, we have family living in North Tarrytown. We were very anxious and concerned when the convicts escaped from Ossining, as the men had to be desperate. I am writing to commend you and your officers for the fine work on the recapture. It is to your credit that with all the areas to be covered that they were recaptured so quickly. It is very comforting to know that when a job needs to be done, it gets

(lone. Very truly yours, a New Jersey resident."

"Dear Dick: Congratulations on a great job. All of us at Phelps are very proud of you and the members of your department. Please convey my appreciation for an outstanding effort. Regards, Alton W. Noyes, President Phelps Memorial Hospital Center, North Tarrytown."

"Dear Dick: You and your department did such a fine job. We wish to commend you. Sandy Galef, Minority Leader County Legislator 9th District Westchester County Board of Legislators." A nice letter from the Hudson Valley Police Canine Association attached: Letter of commendation from the Superintendent State of New York Department of Correctional Services—Sing Sing Correctional Facility James E. Sullivan attached.

The final letter of commendation was dated December 16, 1986 and received shortly thereafter.

STATE OF NEW YORK
EXECUTIVE CHAMBER
ALBANY 12224

MARIO M. CUOMO
GOVERNOR

December 16, 1986

Dear Chief Spota:

All three inmates who escaped from Sing Sing Correctional
Facility on the night of December 9th were promptly recaptured
as the result of a major operation involving more than 200
officers from various State, local, federal, and railroad law
enforcement agencies.

I have been briefed on all aspects of this operation by
Lawrence T. Kurlander, Director of Criminal Justice. It is
clear to me that all of the law enforcement agencies and
personnel involved demonstrated the highest degree of
professionalism, interagency cooperation, and personal courage.
All participating law enforcement executives, and indeed, every
officer, were motivated by an overriding concern for the
public's safety.

I know that I speak for all of the people of the State of
New York when I express my appreciation to you and your
officers for superb performance in this operation. Truly, that
performance was in the highest tradition of the profession of
law enforcement.

With best wishes for a healthy and happy holiday season, I
remain,

Sincerely,

Mario M. Cuomo

Chief Richard J. Spota
North Tarrytown Village Police Department
28 Beekman Avenue
North Tarrytown, New York 10591

STATE OF NEW YORK
DEPARTMENT OF CORRECTIONAL SERVICES
SING SING CORRECTIONAL FACILITY

THOMAS A. COUGHLIN, III
COMMISSIONER

OSSINING, NEW YORK 10562
914-941-0108

JAMES E. SULLIVAN
SUPERINTENDENT

December 17, 1986

Richard J. Spota
Police Chief
North Tarrytown Police
28 Beekman Avenue
North Tarrytown, New York 10591

Dear Chief Spota:

On behalf of the New York State Department of Correctional Services and the staff at Sing Sing, we extend our thanks to you and your staff for the cooperation we received during the capture of the three inmate escapees from Sing Sing.

At the time, what seemed like an impossible situation, ended successfully with the help of the North Tarrytown Police Department and all local police agencies without major incidents.

Special thanks to Police Officers John Cappello and John Dicairano for their alertness in noticing inmate Julio Giano inside a vehicle in North Tarrytown and for his subsequent capture.

Words cannot adequately describe our appreciation for all you did.

Best wishes for the holidays.

Very truly yours,

Jim Sullivan

James E. Sullivan
Superintendent

JES/lz

Hudson Valley Police Canine Assoc.

48 Pershing Avenue
Ossining, N.Y. 10562

J. VINCENT
President
B. MOHLENBROK
Vice-President

January 1, 1987

Chief Richard Spotta
North Tarrytown Police Department
28 Beekman Avenue
North Tarrytown, New York 10591

Dear Chief Spotta,

On behalf of the Hudson Valley Police Cainine Association, please accept my sincere appreciation and compliments for your coopera- tion and concern for Greenburgh Police Officer, Sam Washington and his K-9, Bandit, injured during the search for the escaped Sing Sing inmates on December 9 and 10, 1986.

During that search, Bandit fell into a concealed pit in the ground, and was seriously injured. Your prompt decision to dis- patch Bandit and his handler, Officer Washington and one of your Officers to the Greenburgh Animal Hospital and subsequently to the NYC Vetrinary Hospital, demonstrated your continuing support of the Police K-9 function, and your concern for the welfare of the K-9 and his handler.

In this time of emergency and high manpower demand within your village, your unselfish and immediate assistance to Bandit and Officer Washington was undoubtedly of great signifigance in Bandit's recovery. I am pleased to inform you that due to your quick response to Bandit's Vetrinary needs, he is fully recovered and working again.

You have consistently shown that you value highly the Police K-9 funtion and the benefits that the K-9 program offers to Police Agencies and the Community. Your position on this is exemplary.

As President of the Hudson Valley Police Cainine Association, I look forward to your continuing support and good relationship with you and your department. And if I can be of any assistance to you and your Department at any time, please don't hesitate to contact me.

Sincerely,

James A. Vincent
James A. Vincent
President, H.V.P.C.A.

CC: S. Washington

Breakout at Sing Sing

The last paragraph reads: *"I know that I speak for all of the people of the State of New York when I express my appreciation to you and your officers for superb performance in this operation. Truly, that performance was in the highest tradition of the profession of law enforcement. With best wishes for a healthy and happy holiday season, I remain, Sincerely, Mario M. Cuomo, Governor of the State of New York."* This was deeply appreciated by all members of the department. This would be matted, framed, and hung permanently in police headquarters.

In a year-end report (December 1986), by Gannett Newspapers, it was mentioned that we had had 13 drug raids since June as part of our crackdown on drugs and our high profile in our high crime areas. Of course, there were positive and negative comments from people living in the areas. One black woman who only gave her first name to reporters stated that we were arresting black men for drugs but what about the Hispanics and whites (Caucasians). I have chided Gannett reporters before, but I must commend their action on this complaint. They filed a freedom of information request with the department to obtain blotter reports and arrest records from June 1986 through December 1986 and they printed their findings. The records revealed that since June, we had arrested 48 Caucasians, 48 Hispanics and 33 blacks.

In March 1987, we expanded our police department youth bureau to include more programs for the youths of our community. We hope that the programs we're planning will encourage personal contact between our officers and the youth of the community. We believe that if they are exposed to the police in a positive setting, they will become more willing to approach us with their problems. If that happens, we may be able to help them before their problems become serious. We've always been there to help our youths, but many of them may only see us in the context of arresting people. We won't stop arresting people to change attitudes. However, we are seeking funds and making plans for a variety of youth programs, such as field trips, barbecues, drug awareness days, a dance and other activities. Sgt. Gordon Ferguson, the department's youth officer, will coordinate the programs and let the youths of the community know that they can meet with him if they have problems, drug-related or not. We want the whole community to be involved, the youths and their parents. A parent cannot help a youth if he or she does not know that a problem exists. Officer Don Pelligrino, who recently organized a trip to the Ice Capades for 30 children, hopes to bring groups to a Mets game, the Bronx Zoo, the Statue of Liberty and other events.

North Tarrytown P.B.A. President Greg Camp is involved in fund raising through the P.B.A. for the purpose of funding some of the previously mentioned programs and also programs for the senior citizens, He said, "It was their way of giving back to the community." The village recreation department will work with us to provide transportation, order tickets for special events, and lend whatever support they can.

One of the primary functions of the youth bureau will continue to be drug education programs in our schools.

On May 15, 1987, the North Tarrytown Police Department held its annual awards dinner at Holy Cross Parish Hall.

When I wrote and published the police department awards procedures and manual, I included the Purple Heart, knowing it had to be included, but I had hoped, I would never have to award it. But on this night, I did award it to a very deserving police officer, Bernard Foley. Officer Foley was awarded the Purple Heart and the Distinguished Service Medal. We had his mom come forward to receive a bouquet of flowers. A mother should never have to observe what Mrs. Foley observed at the hospital. Officer John D. Cariano received the Purple Heart and the Distinguished Service Medal. Greenburg Police Officer Sam Washington's police dog, Bandit, received the Purple Heart and some treats from our K-9 officers. Sam was ill with the flu, so his lovely wife accepted for him. Officer Don Pelligrino received the Distinguished Service Medal for his action on June 29, 1986. He was the first officer on the scene of the tight and disturbance. He did his job but did not use deadly physical force or excessive force. The Medal of Distinguished Service was awarded to K-9 Officer Richard Kiggins. The Medal of Commendation was awarded to Sgt. Lee Hayward, PTL. John Capello, PTL. John DiCairano, and PTL. Jimmy Warren for their roles in the capture of convicted murderer and Sing Sing escapee Julio Giano. The Life Saving Award was presented to Detective Manuel Caixiro and PTL. Richard Kiggins.

Meritorious Police Service Awards were presented to Sgts. William Booth, Gabe Hayes, Lee Hayward, William Patten, and Gordon Ferguson, to Detectives Manuel Caixeiro and James Whalen, to Lieuts. James Brophy and Michael O'Shaughnessey, to PTL. Frank Hrotko, Ron Biro, John DiCairano Gregory Camp, Nick Bizzarro, Don Pellegrino, Walter Schrank, Robert Morrison, Robert Nevelus, Bernard Foley, Jose Cotarelo, Bobby Checchi, Greenburgh Police Officer Sam Washington, and Chief Richard J. Spota.

Excellent Police Service Awards went to PTL. Robert Nevelus, Sgt. William Patten, PTL. Walter Schrank, PTL. Ron Biro, PTL. Jimmy Warren, PTL. Gregory Camp, PTL. Nick Bizzarro, PTL. Robert Morrison, PTL. Frank Hrotko, PTL. Don Pelligrino, PTL. John DiCairano, Tarrytown PTL. Dennis DiCaffa, Tarrytown PTL. Frank Giampiccolo, Sgts. William Booth, Lee Hayward, and Gabe Hayes, Lt. James Brophy, Detectives James Whalen, Manuel Caixeiro, Brian Tubbs, Carmen DeFalco, Vince Butkovich, and Chief Richard J. Spota. Civilian Awards for aid to our police department went to Asst. District Attorney Virginia Collins, to Frank and Emily Babic, to William Ashe and Otto Armstrong. The Police Department Awards Committee consisting of Chief Richard J. Spota, Lt. James Brophy, Sgt. Lee Hayward, and Det. James Whalen met twice during the past year to vote on the department awards. Any officer who was recommended for an award did not partake in the presentation or voting for that particular award. I was very proud of the work done by the officers, and I enjoyed presenting the awards. The members of the Police Community Relations Committee were present at the dinner, and we enjoyed having them with us.

New Trial for Convicted Murderer

On May 16, 1987, I was notified that Richard Winfrey would be given a new trial. Winfrey who was convicted on September 24, 1981, along with his hit-man, Merrill Willis, of the Bronx, of murder in the second degree for the August 2, 1980, murder of his father at 275 Millard Avenue, North Tarrytown. Irving Winfrey, 49 years, owned a Wall Street personnel firm, and his son stood to inherit more than $150,000. Mr. Winfrey was shot once in the head and once in the chest while he was in bed. Richard Winfrey had made an agreement with his attorney, Robert A. Hutjay, that the lawyer would receive $20,000 for defending him and an additional $25,000 if Winfrey was acquitted or found not guilty by reason of insanity. The appeals court ruled that contingency fee arrangements in criminal cases are prohibited. Winfrey hired a new attorney who filed an appeal on the grounds that the conviction should be overturned because Hutjay was more interested in trying to collect the $25,000 than presenting a defense that may have resulted in the defendant being convicted on a lesser charge.

My reaction was that the retrial was a travesty of justice. Our investigation from August 2 to October 24, 1980, showed that there was unequivocal guilt by both Winfrey and Willis. Richard Winfrey had the devious mind to plan this murder and now he was trying to get out of his conviction. This was unbelievable and totally unacceptable. The unanimous opinion was handed down this week according to presiding Justice Milton Mellon of the Appellate Division, Second Dept. in Brooklyn.

North Tarrytown man gets new trial in murder case

The Associated Press

A panel of four judges had agreed that the defendant's constitutional rights to counsel had been denied, Mellon wrote in his decision that the fee engagement may have affected the attorney's efforts.

I wholeheartedly disagreed while such a contingency fee arrangement is unethical, the attorney should have been more motivated, because more than 50% of his fee would not be received if he didn't get an acquittal for his client. If the court of appeals allows this decision to stand, defendants who are found guilty, as Winfrey was, could make the same type of arrangement that Winfrey made with his attorney—the contingency fee agreement. Defendants who were found guilty

179

of murder, if they had the foresight to make such an agreement with the attorney could, as Winfrey had done, have their convictions overturned. This is wrong. The case will be appealed.

In the latter part of May 1987, we concluded a seven-month drug investigation that started in November 1986 with the purchase of thousands of dollars in small drug buys. The Westchester County Police, Tarrytown Police, and our department were involved in the joint operation with undercover officers of the county police making the drug buys of crack, cocaine, and marijuana. Five three-member police teams arrested ten persons over a seven-hour period on Friday night with the sealed indictments obtained by a county grand jury. Five of the drug dealers were from College Avenue, "College Arms" North Tarrytown, N.Y. They were each charged with multiple counts of sale and possession of narcotics, both felonies. They were Anthony Gilles, 22 years of age, three counts, Luis Pagan, 39 years of age, nine counts, Otto Alexander, 30 years of age, six counts, Kenneth Potter, 25 years of age, six counts, and Miyddy Diaz, 21 years of age, six counts. Perez was also charged with possession of narcotics paraphernalia. Five others were charged with multiple counts of sale and possession of narcotics including Luis Herrera, 25 years of age, of North Tarrytown, charged with 12 counts.

Lieut. Michael DeVito was in charge of the county police. Dets. Manny Caixeiro James Whalen and officers in plainclothes conducted the investigation for the North Tarrytown Police Department, as did detective and plainclothes officers of the Tarrytown Police Department. The three departments were involved in the joint investigation, because the pushers would go across the borders of the two villages when making sales.

In the middle of June 1987, we would be near the culmination of a six-month investigation of a major wholesale cocaine operation. If you want to convict the heads of a major drug operation, you must have a good game plan. You must share information, make buys, turn street level dealers, and then be able to flip or turn these dealers into working for you. There is no room for big egos. We were working this investigation with the DEA (Federal Drug Administration) Task Force. This is a task force or coalition of law enforcement agencies coordinated by the DEA. Detectives from various police departments in Westchester County would form the task force. My detectives were assigned to this unit. This enables them and others to work in various areas of New York where they are not known. I was working the final part of this investigation on the street in various parts of Westchester County and New York City. At one point, in the final days of the investigation, I had an attaché case containing $50,000,00 in cash. We were in New York City where a buy-bust was to go down. A buy-bust is a drug procedure where the undercover officer meets with the pusher to purchase a large quantity of drugs. Immediately after the sale, we would move into arrest the seller or sellers and confiscate the drugs and money. On this day, I sat in a car in New York City with the regional supervisor of the DEA. We had the cash with us. The pusher wanted the two female undercover officers to meet them inside of an abandoned building to make the sale. We tried to get the sale moved to a different location because we could not surveil the transaction on the inside of the building without blowing the investigation. We felt the two undercovers could get ripped off or killed without a close backup team to watch them inside the building. We continued to try to negotiate a new location but to no avail. As much as we wanted to seize this large quantity of cocaine, it was not worth the risk of having the two undercover officers killed. At this point, we decided to put plan B into effect. We would take down (arrest) the pushers at various areas that they were operating at and then use search warrants to search those areas and other places where they were secreting the cocaine.

The surveillances would continue from North Tarrytown to New York City to Yonkers, N.Y. and back.

At approximately 5:00 p.m., on Thursday, June 18, 1987, I was with the regional supervisor of the DEA. Dets. James Whalen and Manuel Caixeiro were with the other DEA agents. We had spent the previous day and night and most of the day observing the heads of this major cocaine operation in New York City, Yonkers, and North Tarrytown. The group was selling an ounce of high-quality cocaine for $1,400 to $1,800. Throughout this investigation, the undercover officers had purchased more than $80,000 of cocaine from this group. We observed the head of the operation inside of the La Terazza Bar located on the corner of Cortlandt Street and College Avenue opposite College Arms in North Tarrytown. On a given signal, we entered the bar, guns drawn, and announced our presence. We arrested the head of the ring, Francisco Nieves, 39 years of age, of Yonkers, New York, on federal drug charges of conspiracy and distribution of cocaine. Also arrested was Antonio Lara Nieves of North Tarrytown, New York, on a charge of third degree sale of a controlled substance based on a scaled indictment from Westchester County. Another group of my officers in plainclothes with D.E.A. agents entered a bodega at 5:45 p.m. and arrested the other ringleader of the ring, Carmen Jacqueline Ramos, 25 years of age, of New York City on federal drug charges of conspiracy to distribute cocaine. The bodega is located at 111 Cortlandt Street, North Tarrytown, N.Y. Leonel Sandoval, 19 years of age, who was living in an apartment of the bodega on Cortlandt Street was arrested at the La Terazza Bar on a charge of third degree sale of a controlled substance, third degree possession of a controlled substance and seventh degree possession of a controlled substance. He sold less than a half ounce of cocaine to an undercover officer.

Ciprian Nieves, 27 years of age, of Tarrytown, N.Y., was arrested on a sealed county indictment and charged with two counts of third degree sale of a controlled substance and seventh degree possession of a controlled substance. Ciprian

Nieves, the brother of ringleader Francisco Nieves and Antonio Lara Nieves, was arrested at approximately 7:30 p.m. at Beekman Ave. and Route 9, North Tarrytown, N.Y. When we entered the La Terazzra Bar, Francisco Nieves, his brother, Antonio, and some of his people thought we were a hit squad for a rival drug operation. Fortunately, no one inside or outside of the bar was injured. As soon as the persons we had arrested were secured, I left for New York City with the group of agents I was working with. We went to an apartment on West 180th, Manhattan. Before entering the apartment, we met with a special unit of the New York City Police Dept. who would supply heavily armed officers and special equipment. We then entered the apartment of Carmen Jacqueline Ramos with a search warrant. We seized a 9mm gun and a quantity of cocaine. During the investigation, one pound of cocaine was purchased from Francisco Nieves and Ramos. They both face 36 years in federal prison. Property owned by Francisco Nieves in North Tarrytown that has been tentatively appraised at $600,000 would be seized if it can be ascertained that it was purchased with the proceeds from the drug sales.

Police say 'wholesale cocaine dealers' arrested in North Tarrytown drug bust

I cannot commend highly enough the work of the Federal Drug Enforcement Agency under Robert Strang, his regional supervisor, all of the agents of the narcotics task force, Det. James Whalen, Det. Manny Caixeiro, and all of the other officers of my department who worked on the investigation and the subsequent raids. It was very rewarding to hear the comments of residents of our community who live near the center of this drug activity. They were elated to see the top people who were supplying the street pushers arrested. But this was not time to rest on our laurels. There was still a lot of work to be done. We had already begun other drug investigations.

During the summer of 1987, I received a telephone call from Westchester County Police Officer Iris Emerson. She said that she might be interested in transferring to my department. She was attracted to our community because of its diverse population. Being Hispanic and bilingual, she felt that she could interject some understanding of the community from a cultural aspect, which other officers may not have been privileged to. I had personally worked with her in an undercover capacity on a major investigation during the past year. She had displayed as much courage and professionalism as any police officer I have ever worked with. I had an opening in the department due to an officer who transferred to another police department. I set up an interview with her.

Officer Emerson's parents had immigrated to the United States from Puerto Rico. Our community has one of the largest percentages of Hispanic residents in

Westchester County. Officer Emerson was born in the Bronx, 28 years ago. She is a graduate of James Monroe Junior High School in the Bronx and Brooklyn Technical High School. She majored in English at Lehman College in the Bronx for one year. She worked for three years with mentally and emotionally disturbed people at the Young Adults Institute in Hastings-on-Hudson. She then became assistant director of the Tibet's Health Care Center in White Plains, leaving that position to join the county police in 1985. With the county police, she was a police officer assigned to various divisions including a narcotics task force. There are many instances where it is preferable to have a female police officer respond to a crime. A sexual assault on a female is one of those situations. A battered wife is another. There are many cases where a female who is a victim of a crime will feel much more comfortable talking with another female. At the present time, we have to request female officers from the county department or other police departments. There is always the possibility of a female officer not being available. And when one is available, there is always a time lapse before the officer arrives at our department. At an August 1987 board of trustees meeting, I recommended Iris Emerson to become the first female police officer in our department. As it turned out, she would have to take a pay cut with her transfer to our department. To her credit, she agreed to that. Salaries are set by the Board of Trustees; if was up to me she would not have to take a pay cut, a police department should reflect the community it serves. In this case I unequivocally recommended an outstanding police officer who has the additional attributes of being a female and Hispanic.

In late August of 1987 I would fly up to Syracuse, New York for the New York State Association of Chiefs of Police Annual Training Conference, which was August 30 through September 3, 1987. This would be my eight training conference. The classes and workshops were always informative and educational. This year I was especially enthused because our featured speaker was the U.S. Attorney for the Southern District of New York, Rudy Giuliani. There is no one at the present time who is doing more to help attack major organized crime than Rudy Giuliani. During his presentation, he mentioned that he would often come home from work and his wife, Donna, would tell him that he should smile more during a news conference. He said, "Can you see me standing before a new conference, announcing the indictment of 14 members of the Genovese Family and then start smiling?" He was very informative and well-received.

The following morning, we were sitting next to each other's tables, both alone for breakfast at Hotel restaurant. I said, "You look like a fellow on the front page of our late chief's newspaper." He laughed, looked at my nametag and asked if I flew out of Westchester Airport, which I did. He was interested in flights from Westchester to Boston. He was a truly humble, self-effacing person. After we went to catch our flights home, I wished I had told him how much I respected him for what he had done with organized crime and yes, that he was a hero. If my dad was alive, he would have been so proud of him sending the trash to jail that had been disgracing their ethnic heritage.

One evening in the fall of 1987, Todd came home from school, Archbishop Stepinac High School in White Plains, N.Y. with one of his classmates, Jim Gordineer. They wanted to talk with me. Todd and Jim were defensemen on Archbishop Stepinac's hockey team, but they said they had a problem. The one coach of the team would not be able to be present at the start of some of the season's games for the 1987–88 season. If he wasn't there, the games would have to be forfeited. They asked me to help coach the team. My wife Pat said, "Why don't you do it?"

I answered them, "How could I? I am usually not home at dinner time, when the games would start, and I'm at work a lot of the time." I told them that I don't think I would have the time to help, but at their insistence, I said I would think about it. After a few days, I sent a letter to the board of trustees to let them know that I would be coaching the hockey team on my own time without any remuneration. There would be times when I would be running from the parking lot at Playland in Rye, N.Y., to the rink trying to avoid a forfeiture. Some of the officials would smile seeing me charging into the rink. Having coached Todd in Dad's Club baseball in North Tarrytown, this would be the last time I would be involved with him as far as coaching. It was his senior year and then he would be off to college. Archbishop Stepinac was on an austerity budget. We would practice at the Ebersole Rink in White Plains when we could pay for ice time. Ebersole Rink, at the time, did not have a roof. It was all open so when it was cold we just roughed it. The team hadn't won a game for some time before that year. There would be games when our bench would be scarce. Our first game at Playland was against Iona Prep. As I entered the rink and walked toward the bench, I saw the maroon and gold of Iona. I was waiting for one of the brothers from Iona to yell at me and ask what I was doing behind Stepinac's bench. The fine young men of Stepinac worked very hard, but we lost a few games. But their hard work paid off and we did well and won some games. I'll always remember entering the locker room before a game and then saying the Our Father together. I liked that. Our team was led by high scoring center Mike Nolan, John Morella, John Laurie, Drew Antolini, Trip Storms, and we had Jim Gordineer and Todd on defense. Todd reminded me of the hip pointer he got when I yelled at him to slide to block a hard shot. I really enjoyed being on the ice, practicing with the team. The team was able to play all of their games home and away. They deserved that. It was truly a rewarding experience for me.

The Satanic Cult

For approximately a year, our Detective Bureau had been gathering information on Satanic Cult activity. Since the investigation began, we have found more than a dozen mutilated carcasses of domestic and wild animals in various village parks. We have also found blood scattered in parks where we believe satanic rituals have been held.

The first major break in the investigation came approximately 9 p.m., Wednesday, October 14, 1987. Police Officers Bobbie Checchi observed three teens wearing jackets with "Satanic" emblems leaving Barhardt Park. He found a dead cat that had been strangled with a cable cord and mutilated in the nearby on Beekman Avenue by Officers Bernard Foley and Nick Bizzarro. They were arraigned Wednesday night 10-14-87 in Village Court accused of trespassing in the park after closing hour, which is a violation and "overdriving, torturing, and injuring an animal" which is a misdemeanor. The maximum penalty for the trespass violation is 15 days' imprisonment. The cruelty to animals charge carries a maximum penalty of one year's imprisonment, a $500 fine, or both. Two of the suspects lived in North Tarrytown and the third lived in Verplank Village. Justine Dennis Fitzgerald ordered the names of the three suspects withheld. As 16-year-olds, they could be eligible for youthful offender status which would avoid marring a person's record for their entire life. Such status, which can be granted only by judge upon conviction, could result in all court proceedings being sealed from public inspection. Two of the suspects were released after posting $250 bail and the third was released on an appearance ticket. Detectives Sgt. James Whalen and Sgt. Manny Caixeiro had been gathering evidence on one Satanic Cult known as Satan's Army. We found the carcasses of dogs, cats, skunks, raccoons, roosters, and parts of deer at Sleepy Hollow Cemetery, Barnhardt Park, Douglass Park, Patriots Park, and Rockefeller State Park. The group's logo had been painted on several buildings in the village. It is an upside-down cross signifying the Antichrist, or worship of the devil, and a goat's head in a pentagram. Several residents had reported missing pets during the time that the dead animals have been found. In November 1987, at Sleepy Hollow Cemetery in our community crosses were knocked from tombstones and inverted—a symbol of the Antichrist. We also found satanic graffiti and a dead bird that had been mutilated and placed on the head of a statue of Jesus Christ. We were very fortunate to have Maury

Terry, an award winning investigative reporter and author who is a leading expert on the satanic Cult, work with us as an unpaid consultant. His knowledge of cult activity in Westchester County and the United States is unmatched. He worked with us on the symbols and rituals of the cult that are currently being practiced. His book published that year by Dolphin-Doubleday, *"The Ultimate Evil: An Investigation of America's Most Dangerous Satanic Cull."* This book was published ten years after the arrest of David Berkowitz, the "Son of Sam."

Friday, Oct. 16, 1987
3 teens charged in animal's death
...iction could result in all court   Set. James Whalen said th»

This book by Maury Terry and his continuing investigation of the "Son of Sam" murders clearly shows that it was impossible for Berkowitz to have murdered all of the victims himself. His ongoing battle to prove what really happened during these and other murders in the United States reminded me of the struggle years ago to prove the existence of organized crime in the United States. No organized crime and no corruption to protect it. By the time organized crime was officially recognized, it was bigger than any major business in the world. Would Maury Terry's battle to expose the cult and those involved in it be successful or was it already beyond comprehension? His information about the satanic rituals at Untermeyer Park in Yonkers was very relevant. I didn't personally know Maury Terry before his book was published, but there were persons and incidents in his book that we shared a mutual knowledge of. Craig Glassman, a volunteer deputy with the Westchester County Sheriff's Department, had asked to meet with me when I was President of the Westchester County Police Chiefs Association. He asked for and received permission to address our association on behalf of the volunteer deputies. He was the person who had moved into David Berkowitz's building at 35 Pine Street in Yonkers. He then began to receive threatening letters from Berkowitz. In 1977, while I was a lieutenant, an informant called me at home in the middle of the night. The information he gave clearly indicated that the person he was describing was the Westchester Dartman. The Dartman was attacking women with a dart gun in and out of Westchester County. I gave the information to investigators of the Westchester County Sheriff's Department. They were surveilling him at the time of Berkowitz's arrest on August 10, 1977. The suspect lived within minutes by car from where Berkowitz lived. When I heard of Berkowitz' capture that night, I was wondering if they were the same person. They were not.

Maury Terry continued to advise us on the cult. I felt that education of the public was important in this case and about the cult. Not everyone shared this idea with me. In November 1987 Detectives Sgt. James Whalen, Sgt. Manny Caixeiro, Maury Terry, and myself did a cable TV show that was aired in Westchester

County. I believed that the public had a right to be informed about the satanic cult and Maury Terry was kind enough to provide valuable information. If nothing else, programs such as this would serve to enlighten parents who had children involved in the cult. Hopefully, it may help cult members before they get to a point of using humans in their rituals.

In January 1988, Maury Terry asked Sgt. Whalen, Caixeiro and myself to do a show on Channel 7's Eyewitness News program with David Navarro. David Navarro had his film crew shoot scenes in Douglas Park where there was an Altar of Sacrifice used by Satan's Army. David Navarro deserves a lot of credit for having guts to initiate this informative segment. Only through education can the public be made aware of cult activities.

Tenant Patrol Crime Grant

In October 1987, we were notified of a state grant that was approved for a tenants patrol at College Arms, 100 College Avenue. We had answered 181 calls from residents of College Arms in the previous year. Seventy-three arrests were made at the building in the past 18 months. Twenty-four of those arrests were for narcotics, seven were for assaults, seventeen were for disorderly conduct, and six were arrested on warrants. The grant applicants were a combination of local officials, the police department, and the tenant's association. The tenants association had asked for help in regulating and stopping persons entering the building who do not have a legitimate reason to be there. Samuel Gittens, President of the tenant's association, had stated that there are a lot of people, many senior citizens, who were afraid to go out because of all the intruders. The drug problem in the building accounted for a large portion of the complaints. We had requested $52,000 in the grant application, but we would receive only $11,000. But it was a step in the right direction, and it's concentrated in the right area. The tenants' patrol would be supplied with walkie-talkies and jackets for identification. A car would be used to patrol the large parking area behind the building.

We would train the members of the tenants' patrol and they would be in contact with police headquarters in case of problems. Members of the tenants' patrol would monitor persons entering the front lobby of the building. Two tenants on each floor would be designated as "floor captains." The tenants' purpose was to monitor only. If they observed a drug problem or another crime, they would contact police headquarters. There had been many good citizens in this building who had given us information on drug activity that we had either acted on or were investigating. The persons living in the building who had assisted us did not want their identities revealed, and we respected that. But with the formation of the tenants' patrol, we had a group of citizens living in the building who were coming right to the forefront and were standing tall. Their participation and our continuing drug investigations and arrests would be an extremely good combination. The residents involved in the operation should be highly commended.

On Tuesday, January 26, 1988, we would have the culmination of a four-month joint drug investigation with the Westchester County Police and our detectives. A major supplier of cocaine was the target of the investigation.

Police seize $70,000 worth of cocaine

Gustavo Marquis, 30 years of age, of North Tarrytown finally agreed to sell six ounces of uncut cocaine with a street value of $70,000 to the undercover officer. At the time of the sale, he transported the cocaine to the Hilton Inn in Tarrytown where the arrest and seizure was made with the assistance of the Tarrytown Police Department along with our detectives James Whalen, Manny Caixeiro, and the County Police Narcotics Unit under Lieutenant Michael DeVito. Shortly after the arrest, a search warrant was issued to search Marquis's apartment on Clinton Street, North Tarrytown, N.Y. Marquis's wife, Gladys, was at the apartment at the time of the search. She was charged with seventh degree criminal possession of a controlled substance, possession of drug paraphernalia, and second-degree criminal possession of gambling records. She had a small amount of cocaine, scales, and grinders that are used in the processing of cocaine and about 120 numbers used in illegal gambling. Gustavo Marquis was charged with first degree sale of a controlled substance. He was transported to the county jail where he was held without bail. It is unusual to get a large amount of uncut cocaine. The cocaine would have been cut, diluted several times before being sold on the street. With the large amount of profits in cocaine, investigations and surveillances must be continued.

In March 1988, I was notified by the campaign committee for the Rev. Jesse L. Jackson that they would like to meet with me concerning a campaign appearance near the General Motors Plant in North Tarrytown. The Rev. Jesse L. Jackson was an active candidate for the Democratic Presidential Nomination. Bill Scott of Rockland County, one of the organizers of the campaign, met with me to go over the plans. He wanted to arrange the campaign stop to coordinate with the changing of the shifts, day-night, at the General Motors Plant. He realized that very serious safety precautions were necessary. His original plans called for the appearance to take pace in front of the UAW (United Auto Workers) Building that was located next to the GM Plant on Beekman Avenue. I went over the site with my supervisors and detectives. We were troubled by numerous rooftops and buildings before the arrival of the motorcade, that someone with a high-powered rifle could get in position after the check. The rear entrance-exit area of the GM Plant appeared to be a much safer choice. We could close off the road leading into the plant and put police on the periphery of the wooded area and adjacent streets. The front of the UAW Hall building on Beekman Avenue has approximately 4,500 employees and their cars pass that area at the change of the shifts. That would leave too much to chance. A platform could be set up by the rear gate, and we could provide a much more secure area. Bill Scott and his people worked well with us, and I believe they knew that we were trying to provide the safest location. The campaign appearance was set for April 1988. There are always crackpots and other deranged persons following the appearance of presidents and presidential candidates. Some are trying to get their name linked to history in connection with a possible assassination attempt. In the case of Rev. Jackson, there were additional hate mongers to be on the lookout for. Just days before the campaign stop, New York City Mayor Koch would come out with some racially charged remarks in reference to Rev. Jackson. The remarks will not be repeated here because I believe saying them once is too much. In addition to hate mongers, realizing that Rev. Jackson was a viable candidate for the Democratic Presidential Nomination our task would be much more difficult. We continued to work with the advance team to ensure a safe appearance. The motorcade must be surveilled from the time it enters our community until the time it leaves. On the day of the campaign, we had all of our police officers and detectives in position. As the motorcade entered the community and headed toward the GM Plant, everything appeared to be going well. They finally arrived near the site. A young man wearing a dark-colored suit approached me and put out his hand.

He said, "Chief, I am Jesse, Jr." I believe you can get a feeling for a person by meeting his children. After talking with Jesse Jr., I thought to myself, what a fine young man. He was there, of course, to help look after his dad. Local and county dignitaries were already on the platform waiting for the candidate. He then emerged from his limo and was escorted to the platform. The large crowd that was gathered was very enthusiastic when they observed him. Once on the platform, he greeted everyone. He would then lead a chorus of his campaign themes. "Up with hope. Down with dope."

I couldn't agree more. After the well-received program was over, he came down from the platform and started walking back to his limo. He walked over to me and said, "Chief, I need your help."

I responded, "You have it." He then broke out with a wide smile and gave me a warm handshake. I found him to be a very positive, outgoing, warm person. There are persons who may differ with his view of politics, but there isn't anything not to like about this man. He then entered his limo, and we would continue to escort it and surveil the area. Everything had gone very well. All of the police officers and detectives deserve credit for a job well done.

Arrested and Charged with Drug Sales

On Thursday night, April 21, 1988, we concluded that a joint operation with the Westchester County Narcotics Unit arresting twelve drug pushers on separate drug sale charges. We used more than a dozen county indictments and three village arrest warrants to arrest the twelve persons who had sold cocaine to undercover police officers. Of the twelve arrested, six were charged with two counts each of third degree criminal sale of:1 controlled substance, third degree, criminal possession of a controlled substance, and seventh degree criminal possession of a controlled substance. Two others were charged with three counts of each charge and one with a count of each charge and additional charges of third degree attempted criminal sale, seventh degree attempted criminal possession and petty larceny. Four teams of three officers each arrested the suspects. They were then brought to our courtroom which was used as a temporary processing center for fingerprinting and to gather arrest information from the suspects. Our detectives Sgt. Manuel Caixeiro and Sgt. James Whalen, in addition to our officer in plainclothes, made the arrests with the county officers. Sgts. Caixeiro and Whalen had coordinated the investigation. Those who had local charges were arraigned before North Tarrytown Village Justice Dennis Fitzgerald and held in lieu of $5,000 bail. Those arrested on Westchester County indictments would be arraigned in County court.

A total of 21 officers were involved in the operation. This operation part of our campaign to halt drug activity in the village. We have made 62 narcotics arrests since December 1986. Many have been with the help of the County Narcotics Unit. For almost two years, it has been a war with the pushers. You have to keep at it. You can't back off. With our combined operations with the County Narcotics Unit, we have been more effective in charging the pushers with drug sales rather than just possession charges. The twelve arrested and the charges were: Rosemary DePhillips, 43 years of age, of College Arms. She was arrested outside of College Avenue and charged with one count of fifth degree criminal sale of a controlled substance. Rigobeno Lee, 33 years of age of North Tarrytown, N.Y. He was arrested at the General Motors Corp Plant in North Tarrytown and charged with one count of criminal sale fifth degree. Kenneth Runker, 26 years of age, of North Tarrytown, arrested at College Arms and charged with one count of criminal sale, fifth degree. Arrested on Westchester County indictments were Otto Alexander, arrested at Valley Street and College Avenue and charged with one count each of third degree criminal sale, third degree criminal possession, and seventh degree criminal possession. He was also charged with third degree attempted criminal sale, seventh degree, attempted criminal possession, and petit larceny. Norris Lee Atkins, 50 years of age, charged with two counts each of third degree criminal sale and third and seventh degree criminal possession. Eric Caldwell was arrested at the county jail where he was serving an eight-month sentence on a second degree robbery charge. He was charged with two counts each of third degree criminal sale, and third and seventh degree criminal possession. Robert Val Carney, 34 years of age of One River Plaza, Tarrytown, arrested at One River Plaza and charged with three counts each of third degree criminal sale and third and seventh degree criminal possession. Julian Delesus Donovan, 41 years of age of, North Tarrytown, N.Y., arrested at La Terraza, North Tarrytown, N.Y., and charged with two counts each of third degree criminal sale and third and seventh degree criminal possession. Luis Rosas, 25 years of age of, North Tarrytown, N.Y., arrested outside of North Tarrytown and charged with two counts each of third degree criminal sale and third and seventh degree criminal possession. Luis Hilario, 27 years of age of North Tarrytown, N.Y., and arrested there. He was charged with two counts each of third degree criminal sale, and third degree and seventh degree criminal possession. Terence Hopper, 28 years of age of North Tarrytown, N.Y., and arrested there. He was charged with two counts each of third degree criminal sale and third and seventh degree criminal possession and Miyuddy Diaz of North Tarrytown, N.Y. She was arrest and charge d with three counts each of third degree criminal sale and third and seventh degree criminal possession.

All of the officers involved in the investigation and arrests did an outstanding job.

*****

Top State Court Rules Against New Trial for Murderer article

I was notified that the court of appeals overturned a decision by the lower appeals court in May 1987 that would have granted convicted murderer Richard Winfrey a new trial. The Court of Appeals acted on an appeal from the Westchester County District Attorney's Office. After Winfrey was convicted of murder, he appealed the verdict, citing among other issues the fee arrangement he had made with his lawyer, Robert Hufiay of Mount Vernon, N.Y. The agreement called for Winfrey to pay an additional $25,000 if Winfrey was acquitted of the charges.

Winfrey's appeals lawyers had contended that the agreement was inherently prejudicial to Winfrey. The high court took note of the longstanding condemnation of lawyers taking criminal cases on a contingency fee basis. But it said that while the practice created a potential conflict of interest between attorney and client, it did not necessarily result in an inadequate defense. The court explained that if it were to rule otherwise, lawyers and clients would be able to strike contingency-fee deals that, in the event of a conviction, would form the basis of a retrial order. *"Such a ruling,"* the court wrote, *"would give sophisticated defendants and unscrupulous attorneys a delayed trigger weapon to be sprung at some later, strategic phase of the proceeding if events developed very badly for a defendant and the stakes made it worthwhile to assert even an illegal bargain."* This was a correct appeal by the Westchester County District Attorney's Office. I applaud the court of appeals for their sound decision. Richard Winfrey will continue to serve his prison term of 25 years to life.

Police Awards Dinner

On Thursday, May 19, 1988, we held our annual Police Awards Dinner at Holy Cross Parish Hall. The highest awards that I had the pleasure of presenting were Distinguished Service Medals. They were awarded to Detectives Sergeant James Whalen and Sergeant Manuel Caixiero for their outstanding work in major drug investigations in the past year. Lt. Michael DeVito of the Westchester County Police Narcotics Unit received the Distinguished Service Medal for his work on the many drug investigations with our department in the past year.

Commendation Medals were awarded to Sgt. Gabe Hayes, Patrolmen John DiCairiano and Jose Cotarelo.

Life Saving Awards presented to those officers who helped to save lives were presented to Sgt. Lee Hayward, Patrolmen John DiCairiano, Frank Hrotko, Robert Nevelus, Jose Cotarelo, and Robert Morrison.

Meritorious Police Service Awards were presented to: Patrolmen Jose Cotarelo, Walter Schrank, Robert Morrison and Jimmy Warren, Sergeants James Whalen, Manuel Caixiero, Lee Hayward, and Chief Richard J. Spota.

Police Recognition Awards were presented to Patrolmen John DiCairiano and Robert Checchi.

The Civilian Awards were presented to those civilians who rendered invaluable service to our police department. Receiving the Civilian Awards were David Emma, Joseph Emma, Antonio Soares Sr., Antonio Soares Jr., Paul Cappello, Sam Gittens, Anita Babski, Tina Lewis, Maury Terry and Nancy Guren.

The Best Dressed Award was presented to Officer Jose Cotarelo.

All of the members of the Police Community Relations Committee were at the dinner. They work hard with us to solve problems.

Members of our Auxiliary Police Department who aid us year-round were present. The members of the department awards committee, Lieutenants, Sergeants, Detectives, and myself met twice during the year to review and vote on the awards. Anyone who is being considered for an award does not vote or participate in the discussion of that award. The Rev. Msgr. Cyril J. Potocek, pastor of Holy Cross Church, gave the invocation at the start of the program. Why am I so proud of the officers receiving the awards? Because in a department that is understaffed and overworked, they gave me everything that they had.

In May 1988, one of my patrolmen told me that a police officer with the White

Plains Police Department was interested in transferring to our department. The background information on the officer was impressive so I agreed to grant the officer an interview. The officer had been on the White Plains Police Department for a year and a half. Prior to that he had been a football player who had tryouts with the New England Patriots, the New York Giants, and a Canadian professional football team. The rugged, well-built officer had a good background, and I felt that he would be an asset to our police department and the community. After a thorough background check, I recommended him for appointment to the department at the June 7, 1988, board of trustees meeting. Barry Campbell was appointed to the position of patrolman. At the appointment I stated that Barry Campbell, 24 years of age of White Plains, N.Y., was an outstanding police officer who would be a role model for the youths of the community, particularly the black youths. At the same meeting Officer Walter Schrank, the department's canine officer, was promoted to the rank of sergeant. Sgt. Gordon Ferguson was promoted from uniformed sergeant to the full-time youth officer's position.

Motorcycle Patrol

I was able to get fiscal approval in the June 1988 through May 1989 budget for a motorcycle patrol. After bids were received at the June 7, 1988, board meeting a Police Package Harley-Davidson Motorcycle was purchased. There were many reasons that I felt a motorcycle patrol would be advantageous for our police department and the community. Almost everyone would like to have an officer on foot patrol in certain areas of the community. But if you have three patrols to cover five or six different areas on a particular shift you will substantially weaken your coverage by replacing one patrol car with a walking beat. It does not take long for a particular area to size up the situation. The foot patrol is the least cost effective form of patrol. If the officer is needed to back up another officer in another area he or she may at best get to that crime scene too late. By utilizing a motorcycle patrol you can cover the area that would be covered by foot patrol and still be mobile enough to respond to other areas. The motorcycle officer can patrol our high crime areas, drive through their parking lots, stop and check out possible problems. He can park the motorcycle and talk with residents and store owners. A person about to commit a crime can time an officer on foot patrol and know that he has that 5–10 minutes to pull off his deed. However, if he observes the motorcycle drive up one block, he knows that it can return in a very short period of time. The motorcycle officer will give an omnipresence. WE have numerous parks and the historic Sleepy Hollow Cemetery that are being frequented by satanic cult members and others for drug use. The motorcycle will be an invaluable aid in these areas, as well as the huge General Motors parking lots.

I have assigned Police Officers Robert Morrison and Jose Cotarelo to the motorcycle squad. They will both have to complete and graduate from a special New York City Police Motorcycle training school. This is a two-week course that is one of the better schools in New York State. Upon Successful completion of the course they will be able to patrol in the first week of July 1988.

You need creative solutions to policing problems to do more with less. There are some who will not venture outside of routine policing for fear of criticism if something goes wrong. This is the wrong profession to be in if you fear criticism. Chief Ronald Goldfarb of the Ossining Police Department has used the motorcycle patrol very effectively and I thank him for his help on this project and his friendship.

On Tuesday, August 3, 1988, at approximately 7:50 p.m., a call was received about trespassers at Sleepy Hollow Cemetery. Officer Jose Cotarelo rode into the cemetery, shut off the motorcycle's engine, and coasted to where he observed three men. They were charged with seventh degree criminal possession of a controlled substance believed to be cocaine and two counts each of criminal possession of a hypodermic instrument. Sgt. James Whalen and Officer Gregg Camp assisted in the arrest and took the prisoners to police headquarters. Arrested were Coral Bolden, 28 years of age and Cecil Bolde, 27 years of age, both of Meadowbrook Drive in Ossining, N.Y., and Arthur Thomas, 27 years of age of Kings Ferry Road, Verplanck, N.Y. This is a good example of arrests that could not have been made without the motorcycle. If you have good qualified police officers who want to do a good job, give them the proper tools to enable them to do the job.

The Citadel

In the latter part of August 1988 Todd would enter The Citadel in Charleston, South Carolina as a freshman cadet. Pat and I would load up the family station Wagon and drive Todd to The Citadel. This would be the first August since becoming chief of police that I would miss the N.Y. State Chiefs of Police Training Conference. On the way to South Carolina we would stay overnight in Virginia. The following morning, we would drive until reaching Charleston, South Carolina that evening. We would stay overnight at a hotel and then bring Todd to The Citadel the next morning. It was very apparent that the people of Charleston greatly admired the school and its cadets. Early the next morning we drove Todd to The Citadel. I went up to Todd's barracks with him while Pat stayed outside of the barracks with the other mothers. Later that morning, the cadets in uniform marched by where we were standing. They had their haircuts (or head shaved). Todd marched by Pat without her recognizing him. We would spend the better part of a week staying at a hotel and observing the operation of this historic school. I was very satisfied with the diversified mix of the cadets and how everyone was treated equally.

The hot, extremely humid weather would be difficult for any cadet that came in out of shape. One evening I went over to the citadel's football stadium to watch the team practice. I sat in the end zone area that was full of spectators. I enjoyed the company and friendliness of the people in that seating area. I was the only Caucasian in the group, and I believe everyone appreciated how hard the team practiced after having spent the day completing all of their cadet duties. Pat, being a teacher, was impressed by the quality of the instructors and the curriculum. Every afternoon there would be large groups of spectators to watch the cadets on the main parade field; a very impressive display of dedication, intelligence and discipline. It was time to leave and drive home. It was a strange feeling to leave one of your children almost permanently for four years. However, we knew that if Todd worked hard, he would be graduating from one of the truly great military schools in the United States in four years. About the time we would be arriving home, Melissa would begin her sophomore year in high school at Good Counsel Academy in White Plains, N.Y.

Unsolved Mysteries Television Program

Maury Terry contacted me about a movie on David Berkowitz and the Satanic Cult that he was producing for the Unsolved Mysteries television show. He asked me if some of my police officers, detectives, and myself would play the parts of some of the key law enforcement personnel who had done the initial investigation and arrest in the Son of Sam case. I said I would ask some of the officers and mention it to the Board of Trustees, because some of the shoots would be in police headquarters. After it was decided that there was no conflict of interest I told Maury that we would proceed with it. He had continued up until the present time to be an unpaid advisor to the department on the Satanic Cult. His reason for doing the movie was to ask for help in apprehending the other members of the Satanic Cult who he believed to be involved in the "Son of Sam" murders. Some of my officers would be used in scenes at Untermeyer Park in Yonkers, N.Y. This is where David Berkowitz and other members of the cult conducted their devil worship and sacrifices of animals. Some of the other officers were in the scenes as Berkowitz left his apartment in Yonkers, walked to his vehicle, entered same, and was apprehended. My office at police headquarters was used for a scene where noted attorney Harry Lipsig played himself as the attorney representing two of the victims. New York City detectives playing themselves also used my office for a shoot to reenact their parts in the investigation. I played the part of Assistant District Attorney Ron Aiello, head of the Brooklyn D.A.'s Homicide Bureau. Aiello Was the first D.A. to question Berkowitz after his arrest, because the arrest had been made by detectives from Brooklyn. He questioned Berkowitz from 3:30 a.m. until 4:34 a.m. on August 11, 1977. The questioning was in part about the murder of Stacy Moskowitz and the shooting and blinding of Robert Violante in Bensonhurst, N.Y., on July 31, 1977. The scene was shot in our booking room at police headquarters. The actor playing David Berkowitz, that I was questioning, had a strong resemblance to David Berkowitz. He had all of his lines to the questioning memorized. I had put mine on index cards so that I could look at them between shoots. I have a lot more respect for actors after observing him answer all of the questions in the interrogation without looking at the script. While I was questioning him with the exact questions that had been asked of Berkowitz, my mind kept wandering back to the scenes of the actual crime. I kept saying to myself, "Berkowitz could not have carried out all of the murders by himself." This interrogation of Berkowitz had originally been done in a conference room of the Chief of Detectives at One Police Plaza in New York City. In October 1988, the movie on the "Son of Sam" was shown in two parts on consecutive weeks on the Unsolved Mysteries program hosted by Robert Stack. Why would I ask some of my officers if they wanted to be in this movie? First of all, I've gotten to know, trust, and respect Maury Terry for his extensive knowledge and expertise of the Satanic Cult and for his crusade to expose the other persons he believes are responsible for their involvement in the Son of Sam murders. I also know that you cannot always reward police officers for outstanding police work with promotions and assignments to the Detective Bureau in small to medium sized police departments. But there are times such as this when you may be able to give them some perks. I would donate the residual that I received for my part in this film to our local C.O.C. (Community Opportunity Center).

Injury

On November 28, 1988, I was parking my unmarked police vehicle in the rear of police headquarters when Alarm 114 was sounded. Sgt. Lee Hayward was coming out of the rear of headquarters. He told me that a student was having a seizure at Sleepy Hollow High School, which is located diagonally opposite the rear lot of police headquarters. I told Sgt. Hayward that I would follow him up to the school in case he needed any help.

When we arrived on the scene, a 17-year-old boy with Down's syndrome was on the floor, having a severe seizure. Sgt. Hayward checked his mouth to make sure he had not choked on his tongue. He was banging the floor with his body, particularly with his legs. I held his legs close to me to avoid him injuring himself. He finally stopped the seizure. Sgt. Hayward continued to check his mouth while the student rested his legs against my chest. All of a sudden, the student went into a strong seizure and thrust me backward into the air and falling back to the floor. As I lay there, he stopped the seizure and said, "I'm sorry I hurt you, Chief."

The ambulance took the student to the hospital and Sgt. Hayward drove me to the Medical Center up Route 9 (Broadway). As both vehicles sped up Route 9, I heard Sgt. Hayward call headquarters to report a two-vehicle accident that struck a Con Ed pole. As we traveled up Route 9, I was experiencing severe pain and back spasms. The doctor worked on me for about an hour to an hour and a half. The doctor told Sgt. Hayward to drive me home for complete bed rest. On the way home, I asked him (Sgt. Hayward) if the boy knew what happened to me. He said, "No."

I said, "Good. Don't let him find out. He's got enough to go through in life with." Instead of getting better in the following days, I was getting worse. The pain shooting down my leg was excruciating. The doctors set up an MRI examination for me and then an S.S.E.P. (Somatosensory Evoked Potential) study that would reveal extensive nerve damage. The MRI revealed that I had another herniated disc to go with the first one I had before. In the months that followed, my condition got worse. A low point was a day when I was lying on my back (my most comfortable position), and I had to go to the bathroom. The seconds that it would normally take me to get to the bathroom from the room I was in took me over two hours, trying to crawl to the bathroom. When I discussed the medical options with my doctors, they told me it was their intention to get me well not to just get me to a point where

I would return to my office and put in the long hours they knew I would work. That, in their opinion, would make my condition worse and would hamper their efforts to get me well.

On December 17, 1988, I received an award (a beautiful plaque) for my contribution to the Hispanic community. Because I was physically unable to attend because of the injury, Pat accepted the award for me at the Rock of Salvation Church in North Tarrytown. One of the leaders of the Hispanic community telephoned me after he learned of my injury. He told me not to worry about medical bills for an operation or any other treatment that I may need. He said that members of the Hispanic community would take up a collection for me. Of course, I could not accept this money, but what a nice sincere gesture from people who were far from being wealthy. I really appreciated their warm gesture.

In June 1990, I would retire after completing 29 years on the police force. My medical team, consisting of Dr. A. Cocchiarella, who was Director of Physical Medicine of Phelps Memorial Hospital, Dr. Richard Sperdini DC, and Dr. Richard Peress, an orthopedic surgeon, were all outstanding in their treatment of me. Dr. Cocchiarella directed medical treatments that I would receive and was always there to help me. Dr. Sperdini would work countless hours on my back and right leg. He devised a Tens (Transcutaneous electric nerve stimulation) program that had my right leg jumping up and down while I was on the medical table. At one point while doing rehabilitation, he told me that he wanted me to stop using my cane. There were times when I would try to walk upstairs without the cane, and I'd fall flat on my face because I could not feel the steps with my right leg. When I explained this to Dr. Sperdini, he said, "I expected that to happen."

At first, I thought that this was cruel, but then I realized that he knew I would get mad when I would fall, and that would make me work even harder during rehab. He was right. I would develop a hernia on my right side, possibly because of doing roll-ups to strengthen my abdominal muscles. Strong abdominal muscles are key to a healthy back. Dr. Robert Raniolo would operate to repair the hernia in November 1990. I thank all of the previously mentioned doctors for their time and efforts on my behalf.

I hope the police department is a little better than when I first became chief of police. When I became chief, there were no minorities on the force. As I leave, 25 percent of the department is represented by minorities, all of whom are quality productive police officers.

*****

I am a proud member of the following organizations:
A member or former member of the following organizations
The International Association of Chiefs of Police.

The New York State Association of Chiefs of Police, Life member (served on the communications committee).

The Westchester County Police Chiefs Association, (President-1985) The Westchester County Detectives Association, (President 1972 & 1973)

N.Y.S.L.E.T.C. (New York Statewide Law Enforcement Telecommunications Committee), one of four Police Chiefs who represented the State of New York

The Governor's Task Force on Emergency Communications.

The Westchester County Policemen's Benevolent Association.

The Police Columbia Association of Westchester County

The New York State Federation of Police. The Sleepy Hollow P0licemen's Benevolent Association.

The North Tarrytown Dad's club (Coach). The Board of Directors of the YMCA of the Tarrytown.

The Westchester County Traffic Safety Board appointed by County Executive Andrew O'Rourke and confirmed by the Westchester County Board of Legislators in 1985.

Deputy Director of the Westchester County Office of Disaster and Emergency Services. Westchester County Emergency Response Task Force.

The Westchester County Suicide Prevention Committee

The United States Navy. Served on active duty for three years and four months. Remainder of commitment on reserve duty.

The Dating Game Serial Killer Case

Before Christmas 2010, I was told that New York City P.D. detectives and an Assistant D.A. in Manhattan District Attorney Cyrus R Vance's office wanted to speak with me about the Rodney Alcala-Ellen Hover and Cornelia Crilley Cases.

One of the detectives on the N.Y.P.D's Cold Case Squad told me that Police had seized approximately 230 photos that Alcala had in a locker in Seattle Washington. He had taken the photos of women/girls before being in prison. Police are now trying to identify the women and girls. My only thought was not if but how many of these women/girls he had killed!

In January 2011, I discussed the cases with Assistant D.A. Melissa Mourges of Manhattan D.A. Cyrus R Vance's Office and detectives of the Cold Case Squad. They had all of the extensive reports and documents of my investigation of Rodney Alcala and victims Ellen Jane Hover and T.W.A. flight attendant Cornelia Crilley. They had new DNA and bite mark evidence.

Dating Game Serial Killer Indicted

I was notified on January 28th, 2011, that Rodney Alcala was indicted for the murders of Ellen Hover and Cornelia Crilley. He was charged with several Class A felonies that reflect the laws at the time of the murders. He was charged with intentional murder, felony murder, and second degree murder. Each charge is punishable by 25 years to life in prison. Manhattan District Attorney Cyrus R. Vance stated that the process to bring Alcala back to New York is underway.

When the media contacted me for a response, I told them that I was pleased to know that the man known as the Dating Game Serial Killer would face justice in New York. This is someone that we definitely want to be held accountable for what he did in New York.

June 2012, Rodney Alcala would be extradited to New York from California where he was on death row at San Quentin prison following his February 2010 conviction. Alcala has twice had murder convictions overturned, those reversals came in the 1980s when Alcala was twice found by the California Supreme Court to have received an unfair trial in the 1979 murder of his 12-year-old victim, Robin Samsoe. Alcala was eventually convicted of the Samsoe murder a third time when California Jurors found him guilty of all five of the LA-area slayings and put him on death row. It should be noted that no one has been executed in California for many years.

Rodney Alcala would plead not guilty to the murder charges in New York.

I was in Florida in December 2012. I flew home to New York in case I was needed to testify at the trial of Rodney Alcala.

On December 14th, 2012, at New York Supreme Court, Rodney Alcala pleaded guilty to the 1971 murder of Cornelia Crilley and the 1977 murder of Ellen Hover, both in New York.

On January 8th, 2013, New York Supreme Court Judge Bonnie Wittner handed down a sentence of 25 years to life in prison for Rodney Alcala. Judge Wittner said, "This kind of case is something I've never experienced." Judge Wittner then dissolved into tears, as I said, "In 30 years, I've never had a case like this." Many in attendance at Monday's sentencing wore stickers bearing the black and white photographs that appeared in stories about Crilley's death *"Cornelia Always in Our Hearts"* the stickers read. Crilley's sister, Katie Stigell, spoke to the court using more of her time talking about her sister, who was in her prime and wouldn't hurt anybody, but she also had words for Alcala. "Mr. Alcala, I want you to know you broke my parents' hearts. They never really recovered." Hover's stepsisters declined to appear in court. Prosecutor Alex Spero read a letter on their behalf "Ellen was a sweet, kind, generous, compassionate, loving, and beautiful young woman. She chose to see the good in everyone she met because she had a huge and open heart, her senseless murder irreparably damaged our family."

Manhattan District Attorney Cyrus Vance said Alcala would be returned to California where he is appealing his death penalty conviction. "Should that conviction be overturned," Vance said, "Alcala would return to New York for his sentence."

D.A. Cyrus Vance defended questions of the fiscal propriety of extraditing, prosecuting, housing, and trying a man who is already on California's death row for five slayings

D.A. Cyrus Vance, Asst. D.A. Melissa Mourges, Detectives of the N.Y.P.D. Cold Case Squad, Detectives of the D.A.'s Cold Case Squad should receive nothing but high praise for bringing these two cases to a conclusion. Every victim of a crime, their families and close friends deserve to have the person responsible for their death brought to a conclusion.

I was in my second year as a young lieutenant when I started this investigation. I know that the deaths of these two fine young women can never be reversed, but I finally have some peace that their murderer has been convicted.

****

SLAYING: Serial killer, in Calif. prison, indicted in 1970s N.Y. death

CONTINUED FROM 1A   When prosecutors   say the murder of a 23-year-old girl with dark hair

JUSTICE WEEPS
Crying judge gives 'Dating Game killer' life

Acknowledgments

For my wife, Pat; my son, Todd; and my daughter, Melissa, for having tolerated my career in law enforcement. I know that I always put my profession first. Whether it was investigations or surveillances on holidays and vacations, studying for examinations, or being on call for crimes that had been committed, you and everything else would come second to my profession. Todd and Melissa, your mother would teach elementary school and then take care of you while I was working. She deserves most of the credit for the fine persons you have become. Todd graduated from The Citadel in 1992. He joined the Virginia State Police in 1993 as a state trooper. He was promoted to special agent with the Virginia State Police in 1997. There was only one agency that he would leave the Virginia State for. He graduated from the F.B.I. Academy in Quantico, Virginia, on January 8, 1999. He was assigned to the New York office. On May 24, 1998, Todd married Laura Brown. Laura, an elementary school teacher like Todd's mother, has been a great addition to our family. We were very happy that they decided to move to our community. Our lovely, highly intelligent daughter-in-law is a joy to be around. This book would not have been possible without her perseverance in this project.

For my years as chief of police, I thank all of my supervisors for carrying out our goals. For the difficult job of scheduling when short on manpower, because of injuries, mandated schools, etc., for the continuous job of training our officers and recertification for the maintenance of our vehicles and equipment, for assistance with our never-ending grant applications, for the setting up and training on our computers, the supervision of major crime scenes, accidents, and other emergencies. A job well done to all of you.

To our Detective Division and Youth Bureau, there was no major crime committed in our jurisdiction that wasn't solved and successfully prosecuted no matter how difficult the case. For all of the times that I would put myself in the Detective Division because of a particularly heinous crime or because we were short on manpower or I'd be on your backs until a particularly upsetting crime was solved, I apologize. I'm sure you realized my love for working in the Detective Division and put up with me. Again, a thank you to all of the previously mentioned agencies for their continuing support. A special acknowledgment to the Federal Drug Enforcement Agency (DEA), some of us would become members of their task force, for their outstanding joint efforts in the war with the drug pushers. Only through such joint efforts can major drug networks be successfully prosecuted. I don't think there was a major pusher who was targeted that wasn't apprehended. A great job by all of you.

To the police officers of my department, when I became chief, many changes were made. You were not allowed some of the perks other police may have been allowed to receive. It took a while to get good police vehicles and equipment and a good functional police headquarters. But you responded well. You continuously performed outstanding police work and earned the respect of all in law enforcement. The number of commendations from outside of the department and within the department that you earned every year was truly outstanding. The more difficult and almost impossible the task, the better you performed. The continuous amount of letters I received from persons whose lives you affected were always very moving. You always gave me everything you had and then some. And for that I'll always be grateful. You were simply the best!

To all of the civilian employees, you all performed a valuable service that enabled our police officers to respond to crimes and emergency calls. In the bitter cold and continuous rain, you helped cross schoolchildren and seniors at dangerous crossings. You helped move traffic on our congested streets by issuing parking summonses and calling in infractions of the law to police headquarters. I thank the many minority persons who came to work for an all-Caucasian police department. This enabled us to attract more qualified minorities to the department and eventually have a department that reflected the community it serves. You were a critical part of this process. I've enjoyed working with all of you.

To the members of the Police Community Relations Committee, from the charter members to those who came on board at a later date, you all provided a valuable service to the community and the police department. Almost all of you would work late into the evening to try to find solutions to the problem affecting the community. Many of us had to get up early the next morning, but no one would leave the meeting until we felt we had some answers to the problems that were discussed that evening. All of you who served on this committee are to be congratulated. The community is a better place because of you.

To the members of the Auxiliary Police, you provided a valuable service to our police department and the community. You assisted me and my officers continuously on a regular basis without remuneration. I always enjoyed attending your meetings and your fund drives for the Rosary Hill Home for cancer patients. I sincerely thank each and every one of you.

To the volunteer members of our Fire Department and Ambulance Corps, you have continuously performed above and beyond the call of duty for our community. For all of the help and assistance you have given to my department and myself, I sincerely thank you.

To all the citizens of our community, the surrounding communities, and

Westchester County, for all of the information you have given to us concerning crimes, suggestions, constructive criticism, letters of appreciation for the jobs well done by our officers, I thank you. It was a pleasure to have served you. You have all given far more to me than I could have given in return.

I was a member of the following organizations, boards, and committees: the International Association of Chiefs of Police (they have outstanding training programs, seminars, and educational aids for law enforcement), the New York State Association of Chiefs of Police, a member of Communications Committee (Executive Director Chief [ReL], Joseph S. Dominelli, and former Counsel Francis B. Looney were always available for advice and counseling, as were many dedicated police chiefs throughout the state), the Westchester County Police Chiefs Association, President 1985, (I owe a debt of gratitude for the advice, counsel, and friendship of the dedicated police chiefs and commissioners of Westchester county), the Westchester County Detectives Association, President 1972–73, N.Y.S.L.E.T.C. (New York Statewide Law Enforcement Telecommunication Committee), the Governor's Task Force on Emergency Communications, the Westchester County Traffic Safety Board, the Office of Disaster and Emergency Services (Westchester County Deputy Director), the Westchester County Policemen's Benevolent Association, the New York State Federation of Police Inc. (President Ralph Purdy, always there for me and all others in law enforcement, as was Counsel Edward L. Ford and the other members of the staff), the Police Columbia Association of Westchester County and the North Tarrytown (now Sleepy Hollow) Policemen's Benevolent Association.

To the members of the F.B.I. Organized Crime Strike Force, it was an honor to have worked with you.

You took down and convicted the leaders of all five major organized crime families; the Genovese, Gambino, Luchese, Colombo, and Bonanno crime families. They have made cases against the Commission, the ruling Board of Directors of Organized Crime and convicted all members. Every decent person in the United States owes a debt of gratitude to this outstanding group of F.B.I. Agents.

To the victims of certain crimes and their families, I'll never forget you. To those who were addicted to hard drugs and came all the way back through rehabilitation to become productive citizens, some of whom would do drug education seminars with us, I admire and respect you. Don't ever go back.

To the citizens who provided me with information to help solve crimes, I thank those of you who were acknowledged publicly for your efforts and those who, for obvious reasons, could not be. Law enforcement cannot function at a high level without input and information from citizens like yourselves.

In the 1990s, North Tarrytown, New York, had a name change and became Sleepy Hollow N.Y.

There were some serious problems in Sleepy Hollow. Former Mayor Phillip Zegarelli decided to return and run for Mayor in the March 1999 election. After all the campaigning and debates, Phillip Zegarelli was elected Mayor of Sleepy Hollow, N.Y.

In May 1999, Mayor Zegarelli appointed me Chairman of the Sleepy Hollow Public Safety Committee. The committee meets with Police, Fire Dept., Ambulance Corp Officials, and residents who are members of the committee.

In May 1999, Mayor Zegarelli appointed me Chairman of the Ethics Board of Sleepy Hollow, N.Y.

On Monday June 10th, 2002, our daughter in law, Laura Spota, gave birth to twin girls, Abigail Frances and Grace Margaret. They have brought a great deal of happiness to our family.

In November 2002, Mayor Zegarelli appointed me to the Sleepy Hollow Board of Trustees. I would fill the seat of a person who was resigning from the Board. I would have to run for election for a two-year term in March 2003.

March 2003, I would run as an independent on the Republican line with Mayor Zegarelli who would run for re-election. There were two candidates for Mayor and six candidates for the three Trustee positions.

Mayor Zegarelli would win the Mayoral position, and I would win one of the Trustee positions.

I served as Chairman of the Police Committee (Police Commissioner) the Fire Dept. Committee, the Ambulance Corp, the Administration Committee, and the Governmental Relations Committee.

I served as Board Liaison to the Public Safety Committee. I served on the P.F.A.C. Committee. The Committee meets regularly with the mayor, Police, Fire, and Ambulance Corp Officials. The purpose of the Committee is to plan for personnel equipment and building structures that will be needed because of the current development that is underway, Ichabod's Landing, Kendal, and the future development of the General Motors property.

On the March 15, 2005, I would run again for a two-year term on the board of trustees as an independent on the Republican line. There were six candidates for three seats. The residents and voters were kind enough to vote me in 1st place. The term would run to April 2007.

On September 3, 2005, our daughter Melissa would marry Emanuel at St Patrick's Cathedral in New York City. Emanuel is an outstanding son-in-law. Melissa had graduated from the University of Rhode Island. She would work to become photo editor of Parent's Magazine. On July 17, 2007 Melissa gave birth to Carolina, our beautiful intelligent granddaughter. On April 29, 2010, Melissa gave birth to Olivia Kate, our fourth beautiful intelligent granddaughter.

I would like to thank the senior editor and the Board of Editors for the time and care you have put into refining the narrative. Your support and enthusiasm have been invaluable. The production executive and team, thank you for guiding me through the editorial process. You have worked with me every step of the way. Your attention to detail in every area is truly outstanding.

CPSIA information can be obtained
at www.ICGtesting.com
Printed in the USA
BVHW041924130120
569406BV00005B/178/P